WILDFLOWERS

of the
EASTERN SIERRA
and adjoining
MOJAVE DESERT
and GREAT BASIN

Laird R. Blackwell

LONE PINE 🌲 PUBLISHING

The Publisher: Lone Pine Publishing

10145 – 81 Avenue	1808 B Street NW, Suite 140
Edmonton, AB T6E 1W9	Auburn, WA 98001
Canada	USA

Website: http://www.lonepinepublishing.com

National Library of Canada Cataloguing in Publication Data

Blackwell, Laird R. (Laird Richard), 1945–
  Wildflowers of the Eastern Sierra and adjoining Mojave Desert and Great Basin

Includes bibliographical references and index.
  ISBN 13: 978-1-55105-281-6
  ISBN 10: 1-55105-281-4

  1. Wild flowers—California—Identification. 2. Wild flowers—Nevada—Identification. I. Title.
QK149.B616 2002   582.13'09794   C2001-911467-2

Editorial Director: Nancy Foulds
Project Editor: Dawn Loewen
Editorial: Dawn Loewen, Shelagh Kubish
Technical Review: Stephen Ingram
Illustrations Coordinator: Carol Woo
Production Coordinator: Jennifer Fafard
Book Design, Layout & Production: Heather Markham
Cover Design: Rod Michalchuk
Maps: Elliot Engley, Colin Laroque
Photographs: Laird R. Blackwell
Illustration, p. 238: Linda Kershaw
Scanning, Separations & Digital film: Elite Lithographers Co.

Cover photo: blue flax

We acknowledge the financial support of the Government of Canada through the Book Publishing Industry Development Program (BPIDP) for our publishing activities.

PC: P13

Contents

Dedication

Angelica, Iris, Rose, Violet, and Rue,
Veronica, Lily, and sweet Mary too.
From goddess to saint to the lady next Dora,
We're lucky to live in this world of wild Flora.

To Melinda: my wife, my love, my wild flora

Acknowledgments

Thanks to all the joyful people I've met on the trails and at wildflower celebrations. A delight shared is a delight delighted!

Special thanks to Nancy Foulds, Heather Markham, and the other wonderful people at Lone Pine Publishing, whose skill and warm humor have made my partnership with Lone Pine such a professional and personal joy. It has been a special pleasure working with my new editor, Dawn Loewen. Her knowledge and talent have greatly improved this book, and I look forward to future collaboration with her.

Thanks to David Tibor, rare plant botanist of the California Native Plant Society in Sacramento, and to Dr. Barbara Ertter, curator of western North America flora at the University and Jepson Herbaria, University of California at Berkeley, for their help with the derivations of some of the more obscure Latin names.

And gratitude to Stephen Ingram, botanist in the Bristlecone Chapter of the California Native Plant Society, for his expert and enthusiastic professional review. His love for the eastern Sierra is deep and his knowledge of its flora is profound.

California buckwheat
p. 47

Wright's buckwheat
p. 84

Nude buckwheat
p. 139

Spurry buckwheat
p. 139

Prickly poppy
p. 81

WHITE

Inyo onion
p. 81

Death camas
p. 82

Sand corm
p. 82

False Solomon's seal
p. 83

Sego lily
p. 83

WHITE

Leichtlin's mariposa
lily, p. 137

Corn lily
p. 137

Western tofieldia
p. 138

Sierra rein-orchid
p. 138

Brown-eyed evening-
primrose, p. 47

WHITE

Desert evening-
primrose, p. 84

Diffuse gayophytum
p. 141

Bush peppergrass
p. 48

Hairy caulanthus
p. 85

Cut-leaf thelypodium
p. 86

WHITE

Brewer's bittercress
p. 140

Lyall's bittercress
p. 140

Shieldleaf
p. 140

American dogwood
p. 85

Deer's tongue
p. 141

WHITE

Steer's head
p. 142

Alkali heliotrope
p. 48

Sierra forget-me-not
p. 219

Evening snow
p. 49

Bushy linanthus
p. 148

WHITE

Grand collomia
p. 86

Spreading phlox
p. 148

Slender phlox
p. 149

Coville's phlox
p. 217

Prickly phlox
p. 217

WHITE

Ballhead gilia
p. 218

Wishbone bush
p. 49

Wild licorice
p. 50

Black locust
p. 90

Spurred lupine
p. 90

WHITE

Pine lupine
p. 146

Carpet clover
p. 147

Richardson's geranium
p. 147

Wire lettuce
p. 50

Desert sandwort
p. 87

WHITE

Maguire's catchfly
p. 154

Sargent's campion
p. 220

Mountain chickweed
p. 155

Nuttall's sandwort
p. 221

Desert ceanothus
p. 87

WHITE

Tobacco brush
p. 155

Whitethorn
p. 156

Varied-leaf phacelia
p. 88

Timberline phacelia
p. 218

Spreading dogbane
p. 88

WHITE

Indian hemp
p. 88

Field bindweed
p. 89

Piute morning glory
p. 89

Hot-rock penstemon
p. 91

Buckskin keckiella
p. 91

WHITE

Alpine paintbrush
p. 222

Horehound
p. 92

Common mallow
p. 92

Coyote tobacco
p. 93

Dwarf chamaesaracha
p. 158

WHITE

Parish's yampah
p. 93

Poison hemlock
p. 94

Soda straw
p. 159

Cow-parsnip
p. 160

Ranger's buttons
p. 160

WHITE

Thimbleberry
p. 142

Mountain strawberry
p. 143

Sticky cinquefoil
p. 143

Dusky horkelia
p. 144

Mousetail ivesia
p. 144

WHITE

Bitter cherry
p. 145

Western chokecherry
p. 145

Desert sweet
p. 145

Serviceberry
p. 146

Creambush
p. 221

WHITE

White heather
p. 149

Labrador tea
p. 150

Green-leaf manzanita
p. 150

Pinemat manzanita
p. 150

Pine drops
p. 151

WHITE

Rock star
p. 151

Smooth grass-of-
Parnassus, p. 152

Alumroot
p. 152

Brook saxifrage
p. 153

Bog saxifrage
p. 153

WHITE

Alpine saxifrage
p. 220

Toad-lily
p. 154

Macloskey's violet
p. 156

Buckbean
p. 157

Red elderberry
p. 157

WHITE

Blue elderberry
p. 158

California valerian
p. 159

Dirty socks
p. 161

Alpine gentian
p. 219

Alpine columbine
p. 222

WHITE

Parry's rock pink	Desert pincushion	Blepharipappus	White layia	Ox-eye daisy
p. 51	p. 52	p. 94	p. 52	p. 95

WHITE

Eaton's daisy	Coulter's daisy	Cut-leaf daisy	Mugwort	Yarrow
p. 162	p. 162	p. 223	p. 95	p. 163

WHITE

Pearly everlasting	Drummond's thistle	Yerba mansa	Nevada lewisia	Three-leaf lewisia
p. 163	p. 164	p. 51	p. 161	p. 161

WHITE

Dwarf lewisia	Marsh marigold	Curl-leaf mountain	Desert trumpet	Yellow nude
p. 223	p. 162	mahogany, p. 164	p. 53	buckwheat, p. 53

WHITE   **YELLOW**

Bear buckwheat	Lobb's buckwheat	Sulfur flower	Butterballs	Yellow ladies' tresses
p. 165	p. 166	p. 166	p. 224	p. 165

YELLOW

| Kelley's tiger lily p. 167 | Pretty face p. 167 | Bush chinquapin p. 168 | Yellow peppergrass p. 54 | Desert plume p. 54 |

YELLOW

| Wallflower p. 96 | Tumble mustard p. 96 | Lemmon's draba p. 224 | Yellow bee plant p. 55 | Little gold-poppy p. 55 |

YELLOW

| Tall evening-primrose p. 97 | Woody-fruited evening-primrose, p. 168 | Northern sun-cup p. 97 | Little wiry evening-primrose, p. 98 | Tansyleaf sun-cup p. 169 |

YELLOW

| Golden linanthus p. 56 | Yellow navarretia p. 170 | Fiddleneck p. 56 | Venus blazing star p. 57 | Giant blazing star p. 101 |

YELLOW

| White-stemmed stickleaf, p. 101 | Nevada stickleaf p. 101 | Flower baskets p. 102 | Creosote bush p. 57 | Bitterbrush p. 98 |

YELLOW

Five-finger cinquefoil
p. 171

Drummond's
cinquefoil, p. 171

Bush cinquefoil
p. 225

Alpine Drummond's
cinquefoil, p. 226

Large-leaf avens
p. 171

YELLOW

Gordon's ivesia
p. 226

Club-moss ivesia
p. 226

Sibbaldia
p. 227

Bird's-foot lotus
p. 99

Yellow sweet-clover
p. 99

YELLOW

Woolly mullein
p. 100

Moth mullein
p. 100

Primrose monkey-
flower, p. 169

Common monkey-
flower, p. 169

Large monkeyflower
p. 170

YELLOW

Western sweet-cicely
p. 102

Terebinth pteryxia
p. 174

Fern-leaf lomatium
p. 174

Sierra podistera
p. 227

Tinker's penny
p. 172

YELLOW

Narrow-leaf
stonecrop, p. 172

Stream violet
p. 173

Pine violet
p. 173

Mountain violet
p. 173

Alpine buttercup
p. 225

YELLOW

Silver cholla
p. 58

Mojave prickly pear
p. 103

Cottontop
p. 58

Desert dandelion
p. 59

Scale bud
p. 59

YELLOW

Common dandelion
p. 178

Woolly daisy
p. 60

Pringle's woolly
sunflower, p. 60

Woolly sunflower
p. 175

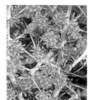
Cotton-thorn
p. 61

YELLOW

Spineless horsebrush
p. 110

Balsamroot
p. 104

Mule ears
p. 104

Kansas sunflower
p. 105

Common tarweed
p. 105

YELLOW

Single-stemmed
groundsel, p. 106

Arrow-leaf senecio
p. 177

Rayless daisy
p. 106

Rayless cut-leaf daisy
p. 223

Curly gumweed
p. 107

YELLOW

Big sagebrush
p. 107

Budsage
p. 108

Dusty maidens
p. 108

Yellow salsify
p. 109

Rabbitbrush
p. 109

YELLOW

| Soft arnica p. 176 | Streambank arnica p. 176 | Whitestem goldenbush, p. 177 | Brittlebush p. 61 | Shaggy hawkweed p. 178 |

YELLOW

| Alpine gold p. 228 | Golden-aster p. 228 | Silky raillardella p. 229 | Green-leaf raillardella p. 229 | Alpine goldenrod p. 229 |

YELLOW

| Alpine gold p. 228 | Golden-aster p. 228 | Silky raillardella p. 229 | Green-leaf raillardella p. 229 | Alpine goldenrod p. 229 |

| Yellow pond-lily p. 103 | Green ephedra p. 110 | Water-plantain buttercup, p. 175 | Stream orchid p. 62 | Aspen onion p. 111 |

YELLOW   **PINK OR RED**

| Lemmon's onion p. 179 | Sierra onion p. 179 | Swamp onion p. 179 | Blue dicks p. 111 | Tiger lily p. 180 |

PINK OR RED

| Prince's rock-cress p. 62 | Holboell's rock-cress p. 112 | Dagger pod p. 112 | Fireweed p. 181 | Smoothstem willow-herb, p. 181 |

PINK OR RED

California fuchsia
p. 182

Rock fringe
p. 231

Mountain sorrel
p. 230

Rosy sedum
p. 230

Pussypaws
p. 231

PINK OR RED

Showy gilia
p. 63

Great Basin gilia
p. 63

Bridge's gilia
p. 190

Scarlet gilia
p. 190

Desert calico
p. 64

PINK OR RED

Stansbury's phlox
p. 113

Tiny trumpet
p. 191

Apricot mallow
p. 64

Desert five-spot
p. 65

Checkermallow
p. 191

PINK OR RED

Bog mallow
p. 192

Storksbill
p. 65

Scarlet locoweed
p. 66

Paper locoweed
p. 66

Whitney's locoweed
p. 232

PINK OR RED

Humboldt River
milkvetch, p. 114

Case's milkvetch
p. 115

Pursh's milkvetch
p. 192

Dedecker's clover
p. 113

Red clover
p. 114

PINK OR RED

Nevada pea
p. 193

Bigelow's
monkeyflower, p. 67

Dwarf monkeyflower
p. 119

Lewis' monkeyflower
p. 188

Scarlet monkey-
flower, p. 189

PINK OR RED

Torrey's monkey-
flower, p. 189

Rosy penstemon
p. 116

Owens Valley
penstemon, p. 117

Bridge's penstemon
p. 187

Mountain pride
p. 186

PINK OR RED

Desert paintbrush
p. 67

Applegate's
paintbrush, p. 117

Long-leaved
paintbrush, p. 118

Lemmon's paintbrush
p. 187

Great red paintbrush
p. 188

PINK OR RED

Copeland's
owl's-clover, p. 118

Bull elephant's head
p. 185

Little elephant's head
p. 186

Purple mat
p. 68

Sticky yellow throats
p. 119

PINK OR RED

Salt cedar
p. 68

Wild rose
p. 115

Desert peach
p. 116

Mountain spiraea
p. 195

Old man's whiskers
p. 196

PINK OR RED

Purple cinquefoil
p. 196

Flax-leaved
monardella, p. 120

Horse-mint
p. 193

Showy milkweed
p. 120

Narrow-leaf
milkweed, p. 120

PINK OR RED

Jeffrey's shooting star
p. 182

Bog shooting star
p. 183

Snowplant
p. 183

Alpine laurel
p. 184

Bog wintergreen
p. 184

PINK OR RED

Red heather
p. 185

Crimson columbine
p. 194

Alpine pink
columbine, p. 194

Wax currant
p. 195

Corymb broomrape
p. 197

PINK OR RED

Sierra primrose
p. 232

Beavertail cactus
p. 69

Hedgehog cactus
p. 70

Spiny hopsage
p. 69

Mojave thistle
p. 70

PINK OR RED

Cobweb thistle
p. 121

Bull thistle
p. 121

Yellowspine thistle
p. 122

Anderson's thistle
p. 198

Wandering daisy
p. 197

PINK OR RED

Western eupatorium
p. 198

Alpine Douglas'
pincushion, p. 233

Wild iris
p. 122

Blue-eyed grass
p. 199

Camas lily
p. 123

PINK OR RED

BLUE OR PURPLE

Alpine veronica
p. 199

American brooklime
p. 199

Hiker's gentian
p. 200

Sierra gentian
p. 200

Desert larkspur
p. 71

BLUE OR PURPLE

Glaucous larkspur
p. 204

Mountain marsh
larkspur, p. 204

Anderson's larkspur
p. 205

Monkshood
p. 205

Western desert
penstemon, p. 71

BLUE OR PURPLE

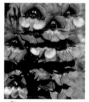
Showy penstemon
p. 203

Slender penstemon
p. 204

Davidson's
penstemon, p. 234

Whorled penstemon
p. 235

Yellow throats
p. 72

BLUE OR PURPLE

Wild heliotrope
p. 72

Low phacelia
p. 126

Notch-leaf phacelia
p. 127

Desert dwarf
phacelia, p. 127

Star lavender
p. 128

BLUE OR PURPLE

Rothrock's nama
p. 207

Sand blossoms
p. 73

Heavenly blue
p. 128

Low polemonium
p. 206

Great polemonium
p. 206

BLUE OR PURPLE

Showy polemonium
p. 233

Sky pilot
p. 234

Indigo bush
p. 73

Yellow eyes
p. 74

Silver lupine
p. 123

BLUE OR PURPLE

Inyo bush lupine
p. 124

Broad-leaf lupine
p. 202

Brewer's lupine
p. 202

Torrey's lupine
p. 203

Winter vetch
p. 124

BLUE OR PURPLE

Chia
p. 74

Purple sage
p. 125

Self-heal
p. 126

Pennyroyal
p. 208

Beckwith's violet
p. 125

BLUE OR PURPLE

Western dog violet
p. 209

Blue flax
p. 129

Squaw carpet
p. 129

Felwort
p. 200

Star felwort
p. 201

BLUE OR PURPLE

| Explorer's gentian p. 201 | Mountain bluebells p. 207 | Velvety stickseed p. 208 | Mojave aster p. 75 | Rocky mountain aster, p. 130 |

BLUE OR PURPLE

| Bachelor's button p. 130 | Blue sailors p. 130 | Hoary aster p. 209 | Dwarf alpine daisy p. 235 |

BLUE OR PURPLE

| Davidson's fritillary p. 131 | Broad-leaved twayblade, p. 210 | Stinging nettle p. 210 | Mojave desert-parsley, p. 75 |

OTHER COLOR

| Fendler's meadow rue, p. 211 | Brewer's mitrewort p. 211 | Brown's peony p. 131 |

OTHER COLOR

Introduction

Imagine a solid, rectangular block of granite 400 miles long, 50–100 miles wide, and over 2 miles deep into the earth, a block running northwest–southeast along the eastern half of California. Now imagine a hulking giant, whose head pierces the clouds, bending down and working his fingers way down into the earth under the eastern edge of this block. He slowly, agonizingly heaves it up and up until the entire block is tilted rakishly toward the west. This is the great Sierra Nevada mountain range of California, which runs from the Mojave Desert in the south to Lassen Peak and the Cascade Range in the north.

From its upper eastern edge, jutting 2 miles into the air, the range slopes gradually to the west, but to the east it drops in a breathtaking precipice to the high desert floor below. This eastern escarpment of the Sierra Nevada is one of the most dramatic landscapes on earth and is home to one of the most interesting and diverse floras anywhere on the planet.

In a previous book, *Wildflowers of the Sierra Nevada and the Central Valley,* we followed the wildflower blooming of the western slope of the Sierra Nevada as it progressed from the Central Valley (at about sea level) in late February and March up through the foothills to culminate on the crest of the Sierra (at 10,000–14,000') in August and early September. In *Wildflowers of the Eastern Sierra,* we will explore the wildflower blooming of the eastern escarpment of the Sierra Nevada from the high desert at the base of the escarpment (4000–4500') in March to May, to the summits of the highest peaks (10,000–14,496') in July to September, and everything in between. Although some of the wildflowers we will encounter in the eastern Sierra will be old friends to those of you familiar with the flowers of the western Sierra, many will be new to you—desert or mountain plants specially suited to the much drier conditions of the east side.

blue flax (above); eastern escarpment at Lone Pine (opposite)

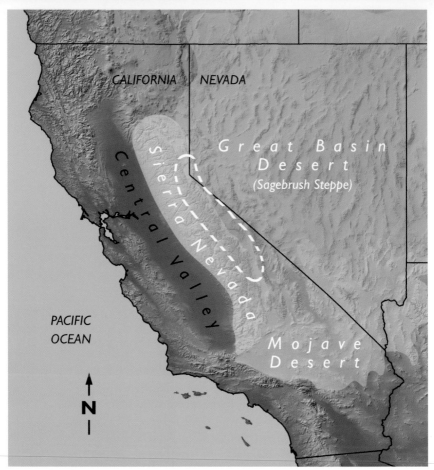

CALIFORNIA | NEVADA

Great Basin Desert
(Sagebrush Steppe)

Central Valley

Sierra Nevada

PACIFIC
OCEAN

Mojave Desert

N

Map of bioregions with broken line indicating area covered by this book

This book covers the most spectacular stretch of the eastern Sierra—the 250 miles from Mt. Whitney in the south to Mt. Rose, at the north end of Lake Tahoe, in the north. More specifically, the road to Horseshoe Meadow just south of Mt. Whitney marks the southern end of the book's coverage, and the Thomas Creek trail just north of Mt. Rose marks the northern end of the coverage. Within the southernmost 60 miles of this stretch (Owens Valley, from Bishop south to Mt. Whitney) more than a dozen peaks exceed 14,000' (culminating with Mt. Whitney, the highest peak in the lower 48 states, at 14,496'), and scores of peaks reach 13,000'; all rise nearly straight up almost 2 miles above the desert floor, which is at about 4,000'. To add to the drama, the White Mountains and the Inyo Mountains (in some places nearly as high as the Sierra) parallel the Sierra only a few miles to the east. Owens Valley, then, is an enormous trough 60 miles long and 15–20 miles wide that sinks an astonishing 1–2 miles below the mountains that border it on *both* sides!

In the 190 miles of the stretch north of Bishop, the peaks gradually become lower and the valley rises, so the escarpment reaches 'only' about a mile above the adjoining valley floor—modest compared to the southern stretch but still awesome and majestic. Mt. Rose is the northernmost Sierra peak over 10,000'; north of it the mountains taper off significantly.

Our wildflower journey through the amazing terrain of the Sierra's eastern escarpment and adjoining deserts takes us from massive, bristling cactus to dwarfed, delicate, alpine 'belly flowers'; from searing, sandy desert flats to lush, grassy meadows and rushing mountain streams; from deep coniferous forests to precarious granite cliffs and exhilarating, windswept mountain summits. In a number of places along this 250-mile escarpment, a mere 10 miles or so of climbing (by driving and/or hiking) takes you from desert to alpine, from the equivalent of Mexico to northern Canada, from summer back to winter.

Come with me now and be prepared to be dazzled by the landscape and delighted by the flowers. The eastern Sierra will astound you, charm you, and haunt you. Once you get it in your blood, you will never be the same again.

scarlet locoweed in the Mojave Desert

Elevation Zones

In the eastern Sierra, 3 very distinctive bioregions with vastly different temperature and moisture conditions intersect—the Mojave Desert, the Great Basin Sagebrush Steppe, and the Sierra Nevada. Two factors play important roles in creating these different bioregions and contribute tremendously to the area's remarkable floral diversity: the range of latitude covered by the 400 north–south miles of the Sierra and the incredible range of elevation (3700–14,496') in such a limited east–west

Mixed Conifer Forest (Hope Valley)

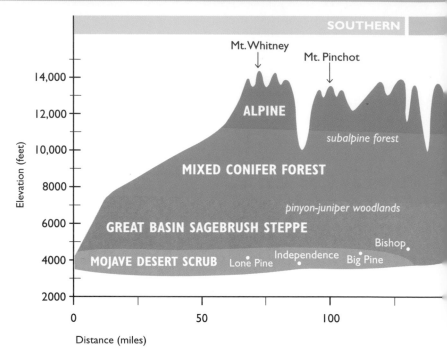

SOUTHERN

Mt. Whitney

Mt. Pinchot

Elevation (feet)

14,000

12,000

ALPINE

subalpine forest

10,000

MIXED CONIFER FOREST

8000

pinyon-juniper woodlands

6000

GREAT BASIN SAGEBRUSH STEPPE

Bishop

4000

MOJAVE DESERT SCRUB Lone Pine Independence Big Pine

2000

0   50   100

Distance (miles)

distance. Both these factors influence temperature and moisture, which in turn have profound effects on growing seasons and species distributions.

There are many ways to differentiate and label the different areas in the eastern Sierra where you will find different associations of plants. I have chosen a simple way that I believe will be most helpful to wildflower enthusiasts who may use this book to identify a flower they have found or to find a flower they seek. The eastern Sierra area can be divided into 4 zones, which some might call 'life zones' or 'elevation zones' or perhaps 'plant communities':

eastern escarpment south of Yosemite

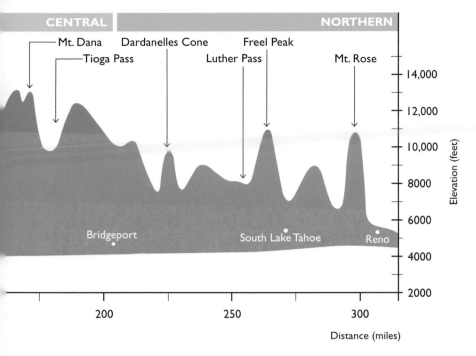

1 the Mojave Desert Scrub (to about 4500')

2 the Great Basin Sagebrush Steppe (about 4500–7500'), including at its upper elevations the pinyon-juniper woodlands

3 the Mixed Conifer Forest (about 7500–11,500'), including at its upper elevations the subalpine forest

4 the Alpine (above about 11,500').

Of course, these zones are influenced not only by elevation, but by latitude as well. The elevation ranges indicated for the zones apply best to the Mt. Whitney area, while at Mt. Rose at the northern end of our region there are several differences, as shown in the illustration above.

First, in the north there is no Mojave Desert Scrub—it reaches very little north of Big Pine, though you may find a few traces of it as far north as Bishop (the 60 miles from Lone Pine to Bishop stay at about 4000' elevation). Second, there are only a few peaks that extend into the Alpine zone at the north end. Third, the elevation ranges of the Sagebrush Steppe, Mixed Conifer Forest, and Alpine zones are about 1000' lower at the north end than they are at the south end. In the 250-mile stretch of the Sierra covered by this book, each 50 miles you travel north is roughly equivalent to climbing 200'. The approximate elevation ranges of the zones at Mt. Whitney (at the southern end) and at Mt. Rose (at the northern end) are given in the table at the top of p. 27.

Alabama Hills

Although many flowers occur in more than one zone, the zones are still helpful in distinguishing quite different environmental conditions and, in most cases, quite different floras. Of course, within zones you will find different habitats (e.g., dry flats, creekbanks, rock ledges, forests) that tend to support different plants. In many cases these habitats are at least as influential as the zones in determining plant distribution, but you'll still find the zones a very useful general guide to different associations of plants. If you have trouble finding a plant in the book in the zone you're in, check the sections corresponding to the surrounding zones as well.

Read the introductions to the 4 zones (beginning on pp. 42, 76, 132, and 212) for more information on the characteristics of each zone, where you can find it in the eastern Sierra, and some places you can go in the zone to find particularly wonderful wildflowers.

Mono Lake and tufa towers

	South End (Mt. Whitney)	North End (Mt. Rose)
Mojave Desert Scrub	3700–4500' *	not present
Great Basin Sagebrush Steppe	4500–7500'	4500–6500' **
Mixed Conifer Forest	7500–11,500'	6500–10,500'
Alpine	over 11,500'	over 10,500'

*3700' is the lowest elevation at the base of Mt. Whitney (Lone Pine)
**4500' is the lowest elevation at the base of Mt. Rose

Where to See the Flowers: Roads and Trails

One of the great delights of the Sierra's eastern edge is its accessibility. Highway 395 runs north–south along the eastern base of the Sierra for practically its entire length; several major east–west routes cross over passes that range from 8000' to 10,000'; a number of paved and dirt roads snake up from Highway 395 to reach lakes, resorts, and trailheads as high as 10,230'; and several trails climb as much as 7000' to reach passes or summits above timberline.

Paradoxically, another of the great appeals of this eastern Sierra region is its inaccessibility. There are no trans-Sierra routes south of Tioga Pass (the gateway into Yosemite), so the southern 100 miles of the stretch of the Sierra covered by this book is uncrossed by roads. And in the entire 250-mile stretch between Mt. Whitney and Mt. Rose, only a few roads and a couple of dozen trails ascend the eastern escarpment to or toward high passes or summits. Most of this 250 miles, then, is devoid of roads and trails, leaving a tremendous expanse of mountain country to wander in solitary splendor.

Such wandering will take you to incredible mountain scenery and to glorious wildflower displays. Although I hope you will get out and hike the eastern Sierra and find your own special wildflower spots, almost all of the flowers in this book (except those of the Alpine zone) can be found in places easily accessible by car or by a little easy walking. Even most of the alpine flowers can be found on relatively short hikes from the ends of high-elevation roads. For the most part, the flower locations I have indicated in the flower descriptions and in the zone introductions are easily accessible without extensive hiking.

eastern escarpment

Mosquito Flat

Look in the list of places mentioned (p. 241) for descriptions of how to find any of the locations indicated in the text.

Highway 395

In the 250 miles between Mt. Whitney and Mt. Rose, Highway 395 runs through 3 of the 4 elevation zones, from the Mojave Desert Scrub at Lone Pine (about 3700') through the Great Basin Sagebrush Steppe for most of its length, and into the lower parts of the Mixed Conifer Forest in several places. The road peaks at Conway Summit (8138'), just north of Mono Lake.

Quite a few of the flowers in this book can be found along this north–south highway or very close to it on short side roads or hikes. The Alabama Hills just west of Lone Pine, only about a mile or so from Highway 395, is one of the finest places anywhere to see the flowers of the Mojave Desert Scrub.

Trans-Sierra Routes

Take any of the trans-Sierra routes and you will penetrate high into the Mixed Conifer Forest. On Route 120 over Tioga Pass (9941') into Yosemite, on Route 108 over Sonora Pass (9624'), and on Route 431 over Mt. Rose Summit (8900'), you will climb well into the high mountains and you will see wonderful varieties of flowers along the way.

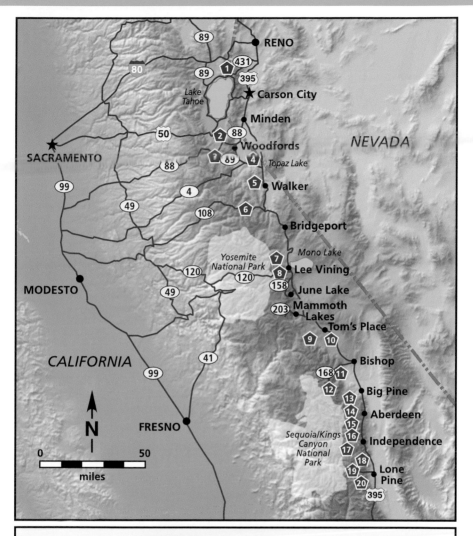

POINTS OF INTEREST

1. Mt. Rose, Thomas Creek
2. Luther Pass
3. Carson Pass
4. Monitor Pass
5. Mill Canyon
6. Sonora Pass
7. Saddlebag Lake
8. Tioga Pass
9. Mosquito Flat, Mono Pass
10. Sherwin Summit
11. Bishop Creek
12. South Lake
13. Big Pine Creek
14. Taboose Pass trailhead
15. Sawmill Pass trailhead
16. Baxter Pass trailhead
17. Onion Valley
18. Alabama Hills
19. Whitney Portal
20. Horseshoe Meadow

riparian garden

Paved Spur Roads from Highway 395

Of the many paved roads that climb from Highway 395 to end high in the mountains, the roads to Horseshoe Meadow (at 10,040'), to Onion Valley (at 9200'), and to Mosquito Flat (at 10,230') will take you through and to some of the best wildflower displays of the High Sierra.

Walking Trails and Wanderings

If you'd like to take some fairly leisurely wildflower hikes or walks, many easy trails or trail-less wanderings from roads will take you to gorgeous wildflower displays. Most of these are in the Mixed Conifer Forest, but some reach up into the Alpine zone above timberline. Some of the best are the 1–2 mile trail from Carson Pass at 8500' to Frog Lake and Winnemucca Lake at about 9000'; the mile or so wander from Saddlebag Lake at 10,100' up onto the Tioga Crest at almost 12,000'; the wander above Grant Lake on June Lake Loop Road (about 7700'); and the first mile or two on the trails to Morgan Pass and Mono Pass from Mosquito Flat (10,230').

Serious Hiking Trails

Of course, if you want to move *slowly* with the flowers through the elevation zones, and if you really want to feel every inch of the journey up the Sierra's eastern escarpment, gather your strength and courage and hike one of the strenuous trails reaching up the east side all the way to the crest of the Sierra.

Some of these trails are moderately strenuous, climbing 1500–4000'. Some examples are the 12-mile roundtrip on the Thomas Creek trail and scramble from about 7000' to the summit of Mt. Rose at 10,778'; the 6-mile roundtrip from Tioga Pass at 9945' to the summit of Mt. Dana at 13,033'; and the 10-mile roundtrip from Onion Valley at 9200' to Kearsarge Pass at 11,823'.

Other trails, those in the southern stretches of the eastern Sierra, are very demanding, climbing 6000–7000'. Among these trails are the 16-mile roundtrip from Taboose Creek at 5400' to Taboose Pass at 11,400'; the

desert five-spot

16-mile roundtrip from Oak Creek at 6000' to Baxter Pass at 12,320'; and the 21-mile roundtrip from Division Creek at 4640' to Sawmill Pass at 11,347'.

And, of course, if you want to reach the summit of the highest peak in the Sierra—and the highest in the lower 48 states—you can climb the 10.7 miles from Whitney Portal at 8365' to the summit of Mt. Whitney at 14,496'. This is a very popular hike and you will need tolerance for crowds and, if you plan to overnight, a permit, which can be difficult to get.

About This Book

When many people think of wildflowers, they think only of flowering herbaceous plants, so it's not uncommon to find separate books for an area's wildflowers and for its woody plants. I wanted *Wildflowers of the Eastern Sierra*, however, to include most of the flowering plants you would be likely to notice in the wild in the eastern Sierra. Because many of the shrubs in this area have showy blooms and are widespread (in some cases, dominant), I chose to include about 30 flowering shrubs in the book. For similar reasons I included a couple of flowering trees and even one shrubby plant (green ephedra) without actual flowers but with showy, flower-like cones.

summit of Mount Whitney

paintbrush

sand blossoms

There are at least 4 ways you might use this book to find a flower you've come across in the eastern Sierra region:

1 Turn to the section of the book corresponding to the elevation zone you are in and look through the photos. Within each elevation zone the flowers are sequenced by color—white, yellow, pink/red, blue/purple, and other—and then by petal number—3/6, 4, 5, and none or variable. The header bar at the top of each page lists the zone as well as color and petal category of the species on that page.

2 Use the quick key at the beginning of the book. This easy-to-use pictorial index presents all flowers organized by color, for quick reference if you're not sure what zone you're in.

3 If you know the flower's name or the name of the family it belongs to, turn to the back of the book and use one of the indexes: to family and genus (p. 244), scientific name (p. 247), or common name (p. 251).

4 What the heck—read through the entire book and look at all the photos before you go out looking for flowers.

If you take the time to read about each flower and, more importantly, to really look at it, you will be richly rewarded. I believe that plants have much to offer us, both in scientific understanding of our world and in aesthetic and emotional connection to it. The more we come to know and respect our flora, the more we come to know and respect our world, each other, and ourselves.

Plant Descriptions and Photos

However you use the book to identify flowers, I hope you will also read the descriptions. They might help you go beyond just identifying the flower to truly *knowing* it as a unique individual with its own life and personality.

Desert (Mojave Desert Scrub)

For the most part, the descriptions use easy-to-understand language, but you may come across some unfamiliar terms. See 'The Parts of a Flower' (p. 38) and the glossary (p. 236) for clear explanations of these terms. Bold font in the flower descriptions indicates particularly important features for quick identification.

I took the photos to show the plants and flowers as you are likely to see them in the field—I used no color filters, artificial light, or artificial backgrounds and did not pick any of the photographed specimens. For many of the flowers, two photos are included to show you the plant in its environment and the flower close up.

Steppe (Great Basin Sagebrush Steppe)

Names Each entry includes the meaning or origin of the scientific (Latin or Latinized) name, and often of the common name as well. Though you may not think you are interested in learning the scientific names, they can be quite fascinating and can tell you a lot about the plant or about its discovery. They can tell you where the plant is typically found, its growth form, its lore, medicinal uses, special features of the flowers, stems, leaves, or fruits, or even who discovered it and what they thought of it!

The system of scientific naming is hierarchical, so a genus name (e.g., *Artemisia* in *Artemisia tridentata*) will apply to many species. For this reason, the second part of the Latin name (the specific epithet,

Forest (Mixed Conifer Forest)

Alpine

view east toward White Mountains, from near Independence

e.g., *tridentata*) is usually more revealing about a particular plant. Still, many genus names are interesting and helpful. Some intriguing examples from this book include *Eremalche* ('lonely mallow'), *Eriogonum* ('woolly knees'), *Senecio* ('old man'), *Erodium* ('heron'), *Astragalus* ('dice'), *Echinocereus* ('hedgehog candle'), *Delphinium* ('dolphin'), *Oenothera* ('wine-scented'), *Thelypodium* ('woman foot'), *Lupinus* ('wolf'), *Mimulus* ('mime'), and *Iris* ('rainbow').

Some interesting, vivid, or melodious specific epithets of flowers in this book include *curassavicum* ('of Curacoa'), *aureus* ('golden'), *nitens* ('shining'), *coccineus* ('scarlet'), *demissum* ('humble'), *basilaris* ('regal'), *flavoculatus* ('yellow-eyed'), *tortifolia* ('twisted leaves'), *munita* ('armed'), *venenosus* ('deadly poisonous'), *nauseosus* ('nauseating'), *quamash* ('sweet'), *nudum* ('naked'), *margaritacea* ('pearly'), *sanguinea* ('blood red'), *odoratissima* ('fragrant'), and *pulcherrimum* ('pulchritudinous,' i.e., 'beautiful'). Take a few minutes and let these names roll off your tongue!

Still other scientific names, at both genus and species levels, honor explorers, scientists, plant collectors, even gods and goddesses, e.g., *Cassiope, Eschscholzia, Grayia, fremontii, lemmonii, douglasiana, whitneyi, andromedea.*

Alternate common names are also given in the 'Names' section. Common names may be easier to learn, but they have the disadvantage of varying widely from region to region. As well, the same common name is sometimes used for many different plants. Scientific names, by contrast, are not only colorful and exotic, they are the same all over the world and over long periods of time. Occasionally a name changes if scientists come up with new information on the plant's relationship to other plants. In this book, if the scientific name has been changed recently, the previous name (synonym) is also indicated.

Varieties and subspecies are generally not indicated except when more than one variety or subspecies of a given species is included in the book.

Where Found Unless otherwise specified, a plant occurs throughout the zone indicated at the top of the page: **Desert** (Mojave Desert Scrub), **Steppe** (Great Basin Sagebrush Steppe), **Forest** (Mixed Conifer Forest), or **Alpine**. Sometimes, though, a plant may not be found along the entire length of the Sierra. In the 'Where found' section, if a zone is qualified with the word **southern,** the plant will be found in the eastern Sierra only from Bishop south. If **central** is indicated, it will be found in the eastern Sierra only between Bishop and Yosemite. If **northern** is indicated, it will be found in the eastern Sierra only north of Yosemite. If no such specification is given, the plant can be found throughout the length of the Sierra covered by this book. The Mojave Desert Scrub zone never receives a designation because this zone occurs only from Bishop south.

Similarly, if a plant does not occur all the way through the elevation range of a zone, its elevation limitations are indicated, e.g., Sagebrush Steppe to 6000'. A plant's distribution outside the eastern Sierra is not indicated.

Each plant also occurs *only* in the zone noted at the top of the page unless otherwise indicated. A number of plants, particularly those which occur in the Great Basin Sagebrush Steppe or in the Mixed Conifer Forest, can be found in at least one other zone. The plant is placed in the section corresponding to the zone in which it is most common; any additional zone(s) are listed in the 'Where found' section.

hedgehog cactus in April

subalpine rock garden

In this section you will also find the type of habitat the plant prefers, e.g., sandy flats, creekbanks, forests, or rock ledges.

As well, a location where you are likely to find the plant is indicated (see p. 241 for more information on these sites). For most plants, many locations could have been chosen, but usually only one (often an easily accessible one) is given here as an example. In a few cases, two very different locations have been indicated. For each location, the month when the plant is likely to be found in full bloom is also given. Depending on the weather in any given year, the plant may or may not be found in bloom in other months. Even in the specified month, the flowers may be blooming profusely or sparsely depending on the amount of winter and spring rain.

Finally, you may see the word 'alien' at the end of the 'Where found' section. It indicates that the plant has been introduced to the eastern Sierra, often from Europe or Asia, and is now growing wild here. Such non-native plants often present a real problem in disrupting the ecology of an area. Whereas the native species have evolved together and with the local wildlife in a complex balance for millennia, introduced species often have no predators or other constraints on their growth and may outcompete their native counterparts.

Related Plant In some cases, a plant that is closely related to the featured plant is briefly described and a photo of it may be included.

Color To help with quick identification, flower color is indicated both in the header bar at the top of the page and at the bottom of each entry in bold type.

It is also indicated by the color of the title bar for each species. The following 5 color categories are used: **white, yellow, pink/red, blue/purple,** and **other color** (the last often includes inconspicuous green flowers as well as brown and other unusual flower colors).

| WHITE |
| YELLOW |
| PINK/RED |
| BLUE/PURPLE |
| OTHER COLOR |

At the bottom of each entry, the most common and conspicuous color for the flower is indicated first. Be aware that the flower color of some species can vary. In such cases, the other common colors are indicated in parentheses, and the full range of color variability will be noted in the plant description paragraph.

Number of Petals Also in the header bar and at the bottom of each entry is the number of petals the flower has—a number that is not always obvious. (See 'The Parts of a Flower,' p. 38) If the number of petals indicated doesn't seem right to you, look at the photo and read the plant description for clarification.

The following petal number categories are used in the header bars: **3/6, 4, 5,** and **no/many**. Three and 6 petals are lumped together because many plants have flower parts in groups of 3. 'No' and 'many' petals are lumped together to include all species that do not have a set number of petals.

At the bottom of each entry, the bolded petal specification gives a bit more detail than the header about the true nature of the petals (e.g., whether they are really sepals or are ray flowers that resemble petals), and the plant description explains the situation more fully if necessary.

Mojave Desert Scrub in the Alabama Hills

Blooming Season Finally, the range of months specified in bold type at the bottom of each entry indicates the blooming season of the species throughout the eastern Sierra area. You will be likely to find it in bloom in the earlier part of its blooming season in the south and/or in the lower elevations; you will be likely to find it in bloom in the later parts of the indicated blooming season in the north and/or in the upper elevations.

The blooming season is highly variable, especially in the desert areas, depending on the type of year it has been. In general, look for blooming in the 4 zones as follows:

Mojave Desert Scrub	March–May
Great Basin Sagebrush Steppe	May–July
Mixed Conifer Forest	June–August
Alpine	July–September

The Parts of a Flower

It has been my experience in more than 25 years of teaching wildflower field courses that the easiest way to identify flowers is to learn about plant families and their characteristics. Many beginners, however, are uncomfortable with a taxonomic approach and find it easier to use flower color as a guide to identification. This book presents a compromise in its organization.

One characteristic that helps define plant families is the number and arrangement of petals, so this book is organized, within elevation zones and flower color, by the number of petals or petal-like parts. Although no special botanical knowledge is required to use this approach, I believe it is still helpful (and, I hope, interesting) to understand a little about the parts of a flower. This section describes these parts in plain language. See also the diagram on p. 238 of the glossary, and the glossary entries, for quick reference. You will find a magnifying glass or a hand lens with 10x magnification handy for examining flowers with small parts.

5 tiny petals; many flowers in clusters

Flowers consist of a concentric series of some or all of the following parts, from the outside in: sepals, petals, male parts (stamens), and female parts (pistils). We will consider the petals first, because petals are what people generally notice first when they see a wildflower in bloom.

varying number of petals

Petals

The showiest parts of most flowers are the **petals,** collectively called the **corolla.** The petals tend to be relatively large and dramatic because their job is to attract pollinators, which they can do by means of color, markings, fragrance, and nectar (nectar comes from glands called **nectaries** at the base of the petals). Sometimes we can't appreciate the insect-attracting features; for example, some flowers emit a rotting stench, and some have markings visible only to insects and other creatures that can see reflected ultraviolet light.

5 divided petals

After their color, the most noticeable feature of petals is usually their number. Most species have 5 petals, some have 4, some have many (often a varying number; e.g., Nevada lewisia may have 6–10 petals), and a few have none. Some of the showiest species—e.g., many in the lily and iris families—appear to have 6 identical or similar petals. Technically, only 3 of these are true petals, while the other 3 are actually sepals. In these cases where the sepals look like the petals, all the petal-like parts are called **tepals.**

regular flower with 6 tepals

In many plants of the composite family, such as daisies, the blossom seems to consist of many ray-like petals and a central 'button' of narrow tubes. This apparently multipetaled flower is actually a **flowerhead**—a 'composite' of many individual **ray flowers** (rays) surrounding a central cluster of many tubular **disk flowers.** Some composite species have only ray flowers or only disk flowers. Each tiny ray or disk flower has its own reproductive parts.

flowerhead with ray and disk flowers

In other species, such as larkspurs, the showiest petal-like parts are actually sepals (5 in larkspurs), while the true petals (4 in larkspurs) are much smaller and are hidden within the sepals. In still other species, such as the paintbrushes, some of the petals have atrophied because other plant parts, such as sepals or **bracts** (modified leaves) have taken over the petals' job.

In this book, the flowers are organized by the *number of petal-like parts* on the flower or flowerhead, so, for example, larkspurs are included in

flowerhead with disk flowers and spiny phyllaries

5 showy sepals around 4 true petals

5 spurred petals and 5 showy sepals

showy bracts

irregular flower with 5 petals

'5-petaled flowers' rather than in 4-petaled ones. Similarly, composites are included in 'no/many petals' even though each tiny flower has only 1 petal.

In figuring out the number of petals, you may need to study the structure of the corolla. In some species, such as diffuse gayophytum, the petals are separate to the base, so you could imagine pulling an individual petal off the corolla. In such cases the number of petals is readily apparent. In other species, such as the Piute morning glory, the petals are connected partly or completely to form a tube, funnel, bowl, star, or other structure, so you would have great difficulty pulling off 1 petal and leaving the others. Usually such fused corollas are divided at the outer ends, so you can count the number of petals making up the structure, but in some cases the petals are so united you might think there is only 1 petal. The quick key at the front of the book, organized by color, will be helpful for picking out such tricky flowers.

One more feature of the corolla that may be important to note is whether it is **regular** (all petals are identical and the flower is symmetrical in many planes) or **irregular** (at least 1 petal is quite different than the others and the flower is symmetrical along only 1 plane).

Sepals

Around the outside of the flower, you will usually find the **sepals,** collectively called the **calyx**. The sepals protect the developing flower in bud and so are often thick and green. After the flowers open, the sepals usually remain on the flower directly under the petals, but in some species, such as many poppies, the sepals fall off when the flowers open. Showy sepals serve the double function of protecting the developing flower and later of attracting pollinators.

In the composite family, the green **phyllaries** that protect the flowerhead in bud serve an analogous purpose to the sepals, but the phyllaries are technically bracts. Each tiny flower has either no sepals or a modified bristly or scaly calyx called a **pappus**.

Stamens

Inside the petals are the male sexual parts of the flower, called **stamens**. A stamen is made up of 2 parts: the pollen-producing, knob-like or cylindrical structure at the tip, called the **anther,** and the column or thread supporting it, called the **filament.** Often a flower has the same number of stamens as petals, though flowers of some species have twice or three times as many stamens as petals. In still other species, such as members of the rose family, there are clusters of many stamens (a variable number).

petals united in bell; red sepals

Pistils

At the inside of the flower is the female sexual part, called the **pistil**. A pistil has three parts: the pollen-receiving tip, called the **stigma;** the column or thread supporting it, called the **style;** and the enlarged, seed-producing base, called the **ovary,** which becomes the fruit. Typically a flower has only 1 pistil, though the stigma may be branched or split into 2 or more parts. Some species, such as members of the rose and buttercup families, have flowers with clusters of many pistils. In those species of the composite family that have both ray and disk flowers, the ray flowers have only pistils, and the disk flowers have both pistils and stamens. In composites with only ray flowers or disk flowers, the flowers have both male and female parts.

5 petals, many stamens; green sepals enclosing buds

Every flower is based on the blueprint described above. That underlying simplicity is comforting, while the countless variations on the basic plan are fascinating. On your wildflower outings, take some time to examine flowers up close. Not only will you more easily identify species and find them in this book, but you will better understand and appreciate each lovely blossom.

5 petals fused in 2-lipped tube

regular flower with 4 petals and globe-shaped stigma

Mojave Desert Scrub

to 4500'

eastern escarpment at Owens Lake

sand blossoms & woolly daisy

'A desert is a region of deficient and uncertain rainfall' (SHREVE AND WIGGINS, 1964). In other words, deserts are dry, and sometimes they are really dry!

Most of the precipitation in the Sierra comes from moisture-laden air masses that sweep in from the Pacific Ocean. When they hit the Sierra, they are forced upward and drop most of their water (as rain or snow) on the western slope, which receives an average of 20–80 inches of precipitation annually. By the time these clouds reach the eastern Sierra, their moisture is pretty well gone. Owens Valley, which extends along the 60 miles from Lone Pine (the southern limit of the eastern Sierra covered in this book) to Bishop, receives only about 5 inches of precipitation a year. The average high temperature in July is 97 degrees, the average low temperature in January is 25 degrees.

scarlet locoweed & Mt. Whitney
opposite: cottontop cactus, Alabama Hills

beavertail cactus

western desert penstemon, a drought resister

The Mojave Desert, which lies in the rainshadow of the Sierra Nevada, San Bernardino, and San Gabriel mountains to its west, is the driest desert in North America. Most of it extends south and east of the area covered by this book into southern California, southern Nevada, and small parts of western Arizona and western Utah, but it does reach up into Owens Valley along the eastern edge of the Sierra.

Over its full area, the Mojave Desert ranges from about 500' elevation to over 4000', so Owens Valley (at 3700' in Lone Pine to 4140' in Bishop) is not only its northernmost limit but also its upper elevational limit as well. Most authorities consider Big Pine to be the northern limit of the Mojave Desert, though you can find some Mojave Desert plants as far north as Bishop, 16 miles north of Big Pine. If you go only 5 miles west of Highway 395 and above 4500' anywhere between Lone Pine and Bishop, or if you go north of Bishop, the Mojave Desert will be replaced by the Great Basin Desert (which I am calling the Great Basin Sagebrush Steppe).

Plant Adaptations

When you think of deserts, you may think of cacti and hard-leaved shrubs, but these are not the only plants that can tolerate the drought and heat of the desert. The desert flora is remarkably rich and varied. Some authorities place desert plants into 3 categories depending on how they cope with drought: *drought escapers, drought evaders,* and *drought resisters.*

Drought escapers are annuals whose seeds can remain dormant for years until there is enough rain for germination. Then they sprout, grow, and bloom quickly, often completing their entire life cycle (including pollination and setting seed) in only a few weeks. These plants create spectacular spring flower displays in years of unusually high winter and spring precipitation. We were lucky enough to experience such a year in 1996, when instead of hosting a few scattered flowers, the desert flats and washes were carpeted with wildflower color. Such springs in the desert are glorious sights that I hope everyone is fortunate enough to experience at least once.

riparian areas in Alabama Hills (above & below)

Drought evaders are perennials that reduce their 'bodily' processes to a bare minimum during the drought season, going dormant or at least dropping their leaves during the hottest and driest times.

Drought resisters are perennials that have evolved various means of reducing evaporation and/or storing moisture. Some of these 'resisters' have tiny, scale-like leaves (e.g., wire lettuce) or needle-like leaves (e.g., western desert penstemon); some have leaves that are covered with hair (e.g., scarlet locoweed) or coated with wax or varnish (e.g., creosote bush). And, of course, the cacti with their spectacular flowers resist drought by storing moisture and by eliminating leaves altogether. Their inflated stems take over the functions of the leaves.

There are many other less visible strategies plants use to cope with drought, involving root structures, metabolic rates, and the like. And, of course, one effective way to avoid drought is to live in one of the few wet areas of the desert!

Alabama Hills & Mt. Whitney

desert paintbrush

Where and When to Find the Flowers

You can find Mojave Desert flowers in many places along Highway 395 in the 42 miles between Lone Pine and Big Pine. Just look along the highway or along the first few miles of any of the many dirt roads that branch west toward the Sierra Nevada. The Goodale Creek road west of Aberdeen and the Division Creek Powerhouse road to the Sawmill Pass trailhead (just a couple of miles south of Aberdeen; see map on p. 29) have wonderful displays in good years. However, the place where you will usually find the most spectacular display of Mojave Desert flowers is the Alabama Hills. From Lone Pine, drive west on Whitney Portal Road for a couple of miles, then turn right on Movie Road or left on Horseshoe Meadow Road, or explore any of the numerous unmarked dirt roads that wander through this area. Within a couple of miles of Highway 395 (up to about 4500' elevation) are acres of desert flats, washes, and rock formations that are home to almost all the flowers included in this Mojave Desert Scrub section of the book.

Some of the desert wildflowers will begin blooming in late March, but the Alabama Hills show won't reach its peak until April or May. Even in June you can find some flowers blooming there, though the peak will definitely have passed by then.

In April or May, as you stand among the sensational flowers of the Alabama Hills, the eastern escarpment of the Sierra will tower almost 2 miles above you, reminding you of all the flowers and adventures awaiting you higher up after the desert's blooming is past.

CALIFORNIA BUCKWHEAT
Eriogonum fasciculatum • Buckwheat Family

At least 13 species of *Eriogonum* grow in the Alabama Hills alone, and at least 30 species grow in the eastern Sierra. They all have tiny flowers with papery, petal-like sepals (no true petals), and the flowers usually form dense clusters (heads or umbels). Most species have basal leaves and lemon yellow, creamy white, or dirty white flowers. • California buckwheat is a **1–7' shrub with large, dense heads of white flowers.** The sepals boast pink midveins, giving the flowers an off-white appearance. Under the heads are leaf-like bracts. The gray-green, **oblanceolate or linear leaves are somewhat unusual** for an *Eriogonum*, for they are **not basal but occur in clusters** up the stem.

Names: *Eriogonum* means 'woolly knees,' in reference to the hairy nodes of some species. *Fasciculatum* means 'clustered.' **Where found:** also in southern Sagebrush Steppe to 7000'. Washes, sandy slopes; e.g., Alabama Hills (4000') in May.

white (pinkish) • 6 tiny, petal-like sepals • May–June

BROWN-EYED EVENING-PRIMROSE
Camissonia claviformis • Evening-Primrose Family

Amazingly, evening-primrose flowers open for only one night, then wilt the next day. Perhaps because their blossoming is so brief, the flowers hold nothing back, filling the night air with a rich fragrance that lures pollinators and nocturnal flower-lovers alike. • Although the flowers of most *Camissonia* species are not true evening-primroses, because they open at dawn and wilt later that day, *C. claviformis* is true to its common name and opens at dusk. • In bud, the 20–40 flowers nod in a tight cluster off the upper part of the 4–20" reddish stem. In bloom, the white or pale yellow flowers branch off the stem horizontally or vertically. The 4 wedge-shaped petals form a shallow bowl ¹/₂" wide, out of which project the narrow anthers and the large, **greenish, creamy white or yellow, globe-like stigma.** The **petals fade purple.** There is a **distinctive brown-purple 'eye' in the center.** The ³/₄" club-like fruits are at the tips of short, erect pedicels. The toothed leaves are mostly basal.

Names: L.A. von Chamisso was a French-born German botanist of the early 19th century. *Claviformis* means 'shaped like a club,' in reference to the fruits. **Where found:** sandy slopes and washes; e.g., along Whitney Portal Road in the Alabama Hills (4000') in April.

white (pale yellow) • 4 separate petals • March–May

BUSH PEPPERGRASS
Lepidium fremontii • Mustard Family

The bright white flowers of bush peppergrass are small (¹/₄"), but they grow in great profusion on the **short (to 2') shrub, almost completely covering the needle-like leaves**. The **round, silvery buds resemble lustrous pearls**. In spring these plants can sparkle and shine in the sun like the finest jewels. They also emit a delicate fragrance that can sweeten the air for quite some distance. The 4 petals are spoon shaped and widely separated. The reproductive parts are short but stick up noticeably above the petals. The fruits are flattened and heart shaped (silicles). Often you will find old, dead, gray stems still on the plant in among the new, green stems. The various tones of greens, grays, and silvery whites on this shrub give it a gentle appearance that seems a perfect match for its subtle fragrance.

Names: *Lepidium* means 'small scale,' in reference to the seed-pods. Cpt. John C. Fremont was a 19th-century explorer of the American West who led the 1844 expedition across the Mojave Desert. Also called Fremont's peppergrass and desert alyssum. *Alyssum* is another genus in the mustard family whose fragrant flowers bear some resemblance to those of bush peppergrass. **Where found:** rocky or sandy flats, slopes, washes, canyons; e.g., Alabama Hills (4000') in May.

white • 4 separate petals • April–May

ALKALI HELIOTROPE
Heliotropium curassavicum • Borage Family

With its **sinuous, braided-looking coils of blossoms,** alkali heliotrope may make you think of snakes or exotic octopus tentacles more than of flowers. Scores of the ¹/₄" white to bluish flowers with yellow throats are **crammed together on 4–24" prostrate or erect stems, which uncoil as the flowers open.** The ¹/₂–2" tongue-like leaves are gray-green and fleshy and are often well hidden by the coils of flowers. The flowers have a slightly unpleasant smell. The anthers are inside the narrow flower tube, so they are not usually visible without very close inspection.

Names: *Heliotropium* means 'sun-loving,' in reference to the reputed blooming of some species at the time of the summer solstice. *Curassavicum* means 'of Curacoa,' the island in the West Indies where one of the first collections of this plant was made. **Where found:** also in southern Sagebrush Steppe to 6500'. Saline and alkaline soils; e.g., along Whitney Portal Road above the Alabama Hills (5000') in June.

white • 5 petals united in bowl • May–June

EVENING SNOW
Linanthus dichotomus • Phlox Family

Evening snow has large (to 1"), **snowy white flowers**, creating the impression of a delicate white blanket of blossoms in the dim dusk or pre-dawn light. But if you go to a field of evening snow just before dawn hoping to see them 'ignite' when the morning sun strikes them, you're in for a big surprise. As the name suggests, these glorious, fragrant **flowers open at dusk and close again in the light of morning**. It is amazing how quickly and tightly they close when struck by sunlight and even more amazing how they seem to disappear when they close, for the **brownish-pink splotches and streaks on the backs of the petals** and the brown 2–8" stems blend perfectly with the plant's gravelly habitat. There are only a few short (to 1"), needle-like leaves scattered along the stem. Just before the sun strikes, you are surrounded by blossoms; a few minutes after the sun strikes, you appear to be standing on bare ground!

Names: *Linanthus* means 'flax flower.' *Dichotomus* means 'split in 2,' in reference to the branching growth form. **Where found:** sandy or gravelly flats; e.g., Alabama Hills (4000') in April.

white • 5 petals united in funnel • March–June

WISHBONE BUSH
Mirabilis bigelovii • Four-o'clock Family

Wishbone bush is a wonderful name for this low (to 2½') shrub, because its **slender, forking stems (especially when aged white)** closely resemble wishbones. The stems of new growth are yellowish green and sticky to the touch. The shrub is thick with pairs of stiff, fleshy, heart-shaped or kidney-shaped leaves that are often somewhat cupped. Rising from the leaf axils are short pedicels bearing clusters of ½" funnel-shaped flowers. The **5 white, petal-like sepals are 2-lobed and usually have at least tinges of pink**. Sticking out of the greenish flower tube are 5 stamens with bright yellow anthers. The flowers open in late afternoon and close again by mid-morning.

Names: *Mirabilis* means 'wonderful.' J.M. Bigelow was a 19th-century physician who collected plants in the American West. The common name refers to the forked stems. Also called four-o'clock, which refers to the late-afternoon opening of the flowers. **Where found:** rocky places; e.g., along Whitney Portal Road in the Alabama Hills (1000') in April.

white (pink) • 5 petal-like sepals in funnel • March–May

WILD LICORICE
Glycyrrhiza lepidota • Pea Family

You can easily recognize wild licorice as a member of the pea family, with its distinctive flowers and its pinnately compound leaves with many pairs of opposite leaflets. Flowers of pea family species usually have 5 unequal petals: the *banner* is the large, more or less upright petal forming the flower's upper lip; the *wings* are the 2 side petals cupped like the 'hands of Allstate'; and the *keel* consists of 2 partly joined petals inside the wings, also cupped like 2 hands, cradling the reproductive parts. • Wild licorice has $1/2$–1" **tubular flowers tightly packed in brush-like spikes**. The horizontal wings and reflexed banner are narrow and **white or pale yellow** with a red-purple tinge. The 1–2" leaflets are narrow and pointed with 9–19 leaflets per leaf (there is 1 terminal leaflet in addition to the opposite pairs). The leaves and flowers are slightly sticky to the touch. • These plants spread by rhizomes, so they can become aggressive invaders.

Names: *Glycyrrhiza* means 'sweet root,' in reference to the licorice extracted by boiling the roots of another species in the genus. *Lepidota* means 'scaly,' referring to the covering on the leaves. **Where found:** disturbed places, wet areas such as streambanks; e.g., along Whitney Portal Road in the Alabama Hills (4000') in June.

white (yellowish) • 5 irregular petals • May–July

WIRE LETTUCE
Stephanomeria pauciflora • Composite Family

At first glance, you may think that wire lettuce is just a **mass of slender, rigid, green stems,** perhaps pausing briefly before resuming a windblown tumble across the desert scrublands. A closer look will reveal, however, that this 1–2' subshrub *is* attached to the ground and that there *are* leaves, though they are often no more than small scales. Clearly this is a plant that has gone to extremes to minimize evaporation! You may notice that scattered across this network of branches are a **few (3–10) delicate white or pink 'flowers,'** looking as if they had blown there and become snagged. Each $1/4$–$1/2$" blossom has 5 petals with blunt, finely toothed tips and 5 slender, projecting, pink stamens. When you notice the 2 series of phyllaries under the flower, you will probably realize that wire lettuce is in the composite family, and therefore each '5-petaled flower' is actually a flowerhead consisting of 5 ray flowers.

Names: *Stephanomeria* translates as 'wreath division,' the relevance of which is unknown. *Pauciflora* means 'few-flowered,' an apt name for this 1–2' subshrub with only 3–10 flowerheads. **Where found:** sandy flats; e.g., along Whitney Portal Road in the Alabama Hills (4000') in June.

white (pink or lavender) • 5 ray flowers • June–August

PARRY'S ROCK PINK
Stephanomeria parryi • Composite Family

The dandelion-like flowerheads of Parry's rock pink are deliciously delicate, both in structure and in color. The 10–14 (sometimes as many as 21) strap-like ray flowers gently overlap and are shallowly fringed at the tips. They are usually **pink or white with a subtle pink tinge**. The reproductive parts are soft pink and stick up well above the rays. Each 8–16" plant can be much branched, bearing quite a few of the ¹/₂–³/₄" flower-heads. Complementing the touch of pink in the flowers is the soft blue-green of the leaves, stems, and phyllaries. The inner phyllaries are erect and form a neat, tight cylinder under the flowerhead, but the **outer phyllaries are usually reflexed, creating a rather messy, spiky appearance.** The **1–3" leaves are thick and asymmetrically lobed.**

Names: *Stephanomeria:* see p. 50. C.C. Parry was a 19th-century American botanist who made collecting trips to the California deserts. **Where found:** also in Sagebrush Steppe to 6500'. Sandy or gravelly flats; e.g., Alabama Hills (4000') in April, and along lower part of the Sawmill Pass trail (5000') in May.

white (pink) • many ray flowers • May–June

YERBA MANSA
Anemopsis californica • Lizard-Tail Family

Yerba mansa spreads by creeping rhizomes, so you will usually find it in large **masses in its wet environment** along creeks or in marshy fields. It puts on quite a show, for the 'flowers' are large and showy— **5–8 flaring 'petals' under a 1–2" white and yellow cone.** But yerba mansa is deceptive. The showy white 'petals' are actually bracts; the true flowers are tiny and crammed into the cone that sits atop these petal-like bracts. And even then there is some deception, because the white 'tongues' that stick out of the cone are also bracts, and the yellow thread-like structures are reproductive parts. There are no true petals. The leaves are long (2–8"), broad, and fleshy and clasp the stem, which is hollow.

Names: *Anemopsis* means 'anemone-like.' *Californica* means 'of California.' Yerba mansa is Spanish for 'gentle herb,' in reference to this plant's extensive medicinal uses ranging from healing skin sores and stomach ulcers to treating blood diseases. **Where found:** wet areas along creeks, marshes; e.g., Alabama Hills (4000') in June.

white • no petals (5–8 petal-like bracts) • May–June

DESERT PINCUSHION
Chaenactis fremontii · Composite Family

Even without the flamboyant rays that are such a striking feature of so many composites (e.g., daisies, sunflowers, dandelions), desert pincushion still brings an exuberant dash of color to dry, rocky desert flats. The 4–16", reddish, much-branched stems bear at their tips ¹/₂" **flowerheads that are crowded with many elegant, showy, creamy white disk flowers**. Each of these flowers has a long tube ending in a flaring, 5-pointed or sometimes 6-pointed star. The yellowish-white reproductive parts stick slightly out of the tube. Early in the blooming you can compare the open flowers around the periphery of the flowerhead with those still tight in bud at the center; the latter look like tiny cotton balls. The leaves are mostly near the base of the plant, and they are deeply divided into needle-like segments.

Names: *Chaenactis* means 'gaping ray,' in reference to the almost ray-like, enlarged outer flowers of some species. Fremont: see p. 48. **Where found:** gravelly or rocky flats, among sagebrush; e.g., Alabama Hills (4000') in April.

white • many disk flowers • April–June

WHITE LAYIA
Layia glandulosa · Composite Family

White can be every bit as dramatic as the wildest, boldest colors. White layia illustrates this point well, for its 1–2", bright white, daisy-like blossoms light up its sandy habitat as few flowers of the high desert can. As with all members of the composite family, the 'flowers' of white layia are actually heads of many flowers, in this case **3–14 radiating, white ray flowers and a central button of up to 100 yellow disk flowers**. The rays are distinctively broad and 3-toothed. The phyllaries under the flowerhead are somewhat cobwebby. The 1–2' reddish-brown stems and the narrow leaves are covered with sticky hairs. White layia leaves have no petioles; the blades attach directly to (and sometimes clasp) the stems.

Names: George T. Lay was a 19th-century English plant collector. *Glandulosa* means 'glandular,' in reference to the sticky stems and leaves. Also called white tidy tips. **Where found:** also in southern Sagebrush Steppe to 7500'. Sandy or gravelly flats, pinyon-juniper woodlands; e.g., Alabama Hills (4000') in April.

white • many ray and disk flowers • April–May

DESERT TRUMPET
Eriogonum inflatum • Buckwheat Family

Though the flowers of desert trumpet are tiny ($^1/_8$–$^1/_4$")
and inconspicuous and don't appear until late in the
desert season (late April, May, or even June), desert trumpet is nonetheless a noticeable and interesting plant. Its
height (up to 4') and much-branched form make it easy to
identify even well before and well after its blooming. The
**new stems are a beautiful blue-green and wonderfully
smooth to the touch.** Older stems often become ribbed
and rough. The **conspicuous swellings of the leafless
stems at the branching points** (nodes) are sometimes
used by wasps as nests for their eggs. The roundish leaves
are dark green with a silvery sheen and lie flat on the
ground. The tiny flowers are yellow with hairy, reddish-
brown midribs on the petal-like sepals. The flowers grow
in small clusters at the ends of long, slender pedicels.

Names: *Eriogonum:* see p. 47. *Inflatum,* as you would expect,
means 'inflated,' referring to the swollen, hollow nodes of the
stems. A variety of this plant with stems that lack swellings is
called *E. inflatum deflatum.* Who says botanists don't have a sense
of humor! **Where found:** roadsides, sandy flats, washes; e.g.,
along Whitney Portal Road in the Alabama Hills (4000') in April.

yellow • 6 petal-like sepals • April–June

YELLOW NUDE BUCKWHEAT
Eriogonum nudum var. *westonii* • Buckwheat Family

Yellow nude buckwheat is a striking plant, both for its **tall
(to 3'), blue-green, leafless stems and for its heads of bright
yellow flowers**. It is somewhat similar to desert trumpet
(above), which has smooth, blue-green stems and yellow
flowers, but yellow nude buckwheat stems are not swollen
at the nodes and its clusters of flowers are much larger. It is,
of course, very similar to nude buckwheat (p. 139), another
variety of the same species, but var. *westonii* has yellow
rather than white flowers and it occurs at lower elevations.
The basal leaves have roundish, 1–3" blades with long
petioles and are usually gray-green with matted, white hairs.
• Unlike many *Eriogonum* species, this variety has **no conspicuous leaf-like bracts under the flowerheads**. Instead,
the bracts are scale-like and barely discernible.

Names: *Eriogonum:* see p. 47. *Nudum* means 'naked,' which
refers to the long, leafless stems. Also called long trumpet.
Where found: also in southern Sagebrush Steppe. Sandy
slopes; e.g., Alabama Hills (4200') in April, and along Horseshoe
Meadow Road (5000') in May.

yellow • 6 separate petal-like sepals • April–June

YELLOW PEPPERGRASS
Lepidium flavum • Mustard Family

Though the flowers of yellow peppergrass are tiny ($^1/_8$–$^1/_4$"), they can bring lovely color to the sandy flats where they grow. The smooth, yellow-green stems of this plant form **dense mats, often several feet across, which are thick with clumps of sulfur yellow flowers**. In a good flower year you may find large areas in the high desert where more ground is covered by these yellow mats than is not! • As in all mustards, the flowers have 4 petals; in this peppergrass the petals are spoon-shaped, forming a Maltese cross. The 6 protruding stamens are the same lemon yellow as the petals and stick out about as far. The narrow leaves have irregular lobes (somewhat dandelion-like but without the spines) and form showy, basal rosettes often mostly hidden under the clusters of flowers.

Names: *Lepidium:* see p. 48. *Flavum* means 'yellow.' **Where found:** alkaline or sandy flats; e.g., along Whitney Portal Road in and above the Alabama Hills (4000–4500') in April.

yellow • 4 petals in cross • March–May

DESERT PLUME
Stanleya pinnata • Mustard Family

Desert plume is a wonderful name for this striking plant whose 2–5' stem terminates in a **showy, densely flowered 'plume' up to 1$^1/_2$' long**. Each $^1/_2$" flower has **4 lemon yellow petals** that are narrow and widely spaced and have delicate hairs at their bases. These petals and the long, slender stamens sticking out give the flowers an airy look and give the dense flower spikes a bottle-brush appearance. Even without blooms, desert plume is a dramatic plant, for the yellowish buds are up to 1" long, thick, and cylindrical, and the nearly horizontal seedpods can be up to 3" long. If you visit the plant at the right time, you can find all 3 stages represented on the plumes—buds at the top, blossoms in the middle, and seedpods at the bottom. The thick bottom part of the stem bears 2–8", deeply pinnately lobed leaves.

Names: Edward Stanley was a 19th-century English ornithologist who was once president of the Linnean Society. *Pinnata* means 'plumed.' Also called prince's plume. **Where found:** also in Sagebrush Steppe to 6000'. Sandy flats and slopes, washes; e.g., northern end of the Alabama Hills (4500') in May.

yellow • 4 petals • April–June

YELLOW BEE PLANT
Cleome lutea • Caper Family

Despite growing on roadsides and in other disturbed places, yellow bee plant is elegant and attractive, both in its appearance and in its bee-beguiling fragrance. The 1–3' stem bears **many palmately compound leaves on long petioles,** each leaf blade consisting of 3–7 graceful, finger-like leaflets. The stem is topped by a **showy cluster of** $1/2$**", lemon yellow, 4-petaled flowers.** The yellow stamens stick way out of the blooms, giving the flower cluster a gentle, fuzzy look. Adding to the grace of the plant are the **1–3", green, banana-shaped pods that curve down off the stem.** There is a wonderfully pleasing symmetry to this plant late in the blooming season when it bears both blossoms and seedpods.

Names: *Cleome* means 'shut,' an unclear reference. *Lutea* means 'yellow.' When you hear all that buzzing around the plant, the derivation of its common name will be obvious. **Where found:** also in Sagebrush Steppe to 8000'. Dry flats, roadsides; e.g., along Highway 395 just north of Bishop (4000') in June.

yellow • 4 separate petals • May–July

LITTLE GOLD-POPPY
Eschscholzia minutiflora • Poppy Family

With their 4 separate, wedge-shaped petals, their numerous stamens, and their long, narrow, cylindrical seedpods, the flowers of little gold-poppy really do look like poppies. Although the **yellow flowers are often smaller than most poppies** (sometimes only $1/2$" across), they can reach more poppy-like dimensions (1–1$1/2$" across). If you had any doubt that this plant was in the poppy family, the leaves would probably dispel it, for they are the typical blue-green and characteristically dissected into many short, finger-like segments. The **flowers are scattered on the ends of nearly leafless, smooth, blue-green, 2–18" stems.**

Names: J.F. Eschscholtz, the doctor on the Russian ship *Rurik,* botanized in California in the early 19th century. *Minutiflora* means 'small-flowered.' **Where found:** also in southern Sagebrush Steppe to 6500'. Sandy flats and washes; e.g., Alabama Hills (4000') in April, and lower part of the Sawmill Pass trail (5000') in May.

yellow (orange) • 4 separate petals • April–June

GOLDEN LINANTHUS
Linanthus aureus • Phlox Family

Of all the bright yellow flowers of the high desert, golden linanthus may be the showiest, for both its color and its profusion. The **petal lobes are a dazzling golden yellow surrounding an intensely yellow-orange throat.** Though the flower is relatively small ($^1/_4$–$^1/_2$") and the plant short (2–6"), the plants generally grow in extensive colonies, **carpeting large patches of sandy desert flats** with their golden hue. Often you will find them interspersed with the deep blue of sand blossoms, the color contrast seeming to intensify the hues of both. • The slender, wiry stems of golden linanthus are much branched, bearing several flowers and a few tiny, 3–7-cleft, needle-like leaves that appear to be in whorls around the stem. The orange anthers stick up slightly above the petals; the pale yellow or white stigma is 3-lobed and protrudes much farther than the stamens. As with many flowers, you will find the stigma lobes closed up early in the blooming, unfolding to readiness only after the anthers begin to shrivel.

Names: *Linanthus:* see p. 49. *Aureus* means 'golden.' **Where found:** sandy flats; e.g., Alabama Hills (4500') in April.

golden yellow • 5 petals united in bowl • April–June

FIDDLENECK
Amsinckia tessellata • Borage Family

Although fiddleneck is a very common and widespread plant—often dismissed as a weed—it is really very striking, with an interesting inflorescence and delicate, colorful flowers. Its erect 1–2' stems, its bright green 1–4" leaves, and its urn-shaped calyces all **bristle with stiff, silvery hairs** that can give you a rash if you touch them. A field of fiddleneck can be very dramatic early or late in the day, because the bristly hairs seem to glow silver when backlit by a low sun. The **yellow, tubular flowers are in long spikes that terminate in curling, caterpillar-like cymes.** The flower throats are often tinged with orange.

Names: Wilhelm Amsinck was a 19th-century patron of the Hamburg Botanic Garden. *Tessellata* means 'checkered,' in reference to the rough-speckled backs of the nutlets. Also known as devil's lettuce, which refers to the rash-producing hairs. **Where found:** also in Sagebrush Steppe to 7000'. Dry flats and disturbed places; e.g., along Whitney Portal Road in the Alabama Hills (4000') in March.

yellow • 5 petals united in tube • March–April

VENUS BLAZING STAR
Mentzelia nitens • Loasa Family

There seem to be countless species of 5-petaled, bright yellow flowers in the high desert along the eastern base of the Sierra Nevada, making identification somewhat challenging. If the **petals are glossy** and there are many protruding stamens, it is probably a member of the genus *Mentzelia*. If there is also a **swollen, green cylinder (an inferior ovary) under the petals,** you can be certain of this. • Venus blazing star has ¹/₂" flowers with rather square-tipped petals and a clump of many yellow stamens. The 4–12" stems are whitish and much branched. The basal leaves and the smaller clasping leaves in the axils of the stem branches are deeply pinnately lobed.

Names: Christian Mentzel was a 17th-century German botanist. *Nitens* means 'shining,' probably in reference to the whitish stems, though it could apply as well to the bright yellow flowers. **Where found:** also in southern Sagebrush Steppe to 6000'. Sandy or gravelly flats and slopes; e.g., Alabama Hills (4500') in April.

yellow • 5 separate petals • April–June

CREOSOTE BUSH
Larrea tridentata • Caltrop Family

Creosote bush is probably the **most common and widespread plant of the arid regions of North America**. In our area it is the primary indicator plant of the Mojave Desert; just a few miles south of Mt. Whitney you can find acres of sandy, gravelly desert flats covered almost solidly with creosote shrubs (top photo). In the Whitney area, near the northern edge of the Mojave Desert, it is less common, found occasionally on the sandy flats in the Alabama Hills. • The shrub can reach 10' tall, though 3–5' is more common. The **gray branches are covered with a resinous incrustation, and the small leaflets are covered with a sticky coating** that helps reduce evaporation. The 1" yellow flowers have long-protruding reproductive parts. When the flowers go to seed, the **plant is thick with fuzzy, white, cottony balls**.

Names: J. Anthony de Larrea was a Spanish clergyman and advocate of science. *Tridentata* means '3-toothed,' in reference to the leaves. The 'creosote' in the common name refers to the strong, resinous odor exuded by the leaves, especially after rain. **Where found:** dry desert flats; e.g., Alabama Hills (4000') in May.

yellow • 5 separate petals • April–May

SILVER CHOLLA
Opuntia echinocarpa • Cactus Family

Silver cholla looks distinctly unfriendly. Its cylindrical stems are so **thickly covered with 1–2" spines** that you can scarcely make them out. These straight spines occur in clusters of 8–20 and point in all directions, so there's no sneaking up on this plant. Often the spines are silver; sometimes they are straw-colored—the particular version of the common name used reflects their color. The plant is 2–5' tall and intricately branched. The large (to 2" wide) flowers are **greenish yellow inside, frequently with a reddish-brown tinge on the backs of the many petals**. The many anthers are yellow; the large stigma is white or greenish yellow. The buds look like reddish-bronze torpedos.

Names: *Opuntia* may be derived from the Papago Indian name *opun*. *Echinocarpa* means 'hedgehog fruit,' in reference to the densely spiny fruits. Also known as gold cholla. **Where found:** dry flats and slopes; e.g., Alabama Hills (4000') in May.

greenish-yellow • many petals • April–May

COTTONTOP
Echinocactus polycephalus • Cactus Family

All the cacti along the eastern edge of the Sierra are imposing plants with big, showy flowers. Though the flowers of cottontop are not quite as large or showy as those of some of its relatives, the plant stands out nonetheless for at least 2 reasons. First, cottontop **blooms late in the summer** after the flowers of most other cacti are long gone; second, even without flowers it can appear to be in spectacular bloom because its **long spines are often intense scarlet**. Cottontop usually grows in clumps of several to as many as 40 or so watermelon-size stems (heads). Each stem can be up to a foot thick and has 13–21 vertical ribs, each of which is covered with dense clusters of long (to 3") spines. Nestled in the spines at the tops of the stems are 1–2", yellow, fragrant flowers. **Tufts of cottony hairs** surround the bases of the flowers and, later, the bases of the edible fruits.

Names: *Echinocactus* means 'hedgehog cactus,' in reference to the many spines. *Polycephalus* means 'many heads,' in reference to the rounded clumps of numerous stems. The common name refers to the white-woolly hairs at the tips of the stems. Also called clustered barrel cactus. **Where found:** rocky or sandy flats; e.g., Alabama Hills (4000') in July.

yellow • many petals • July–August

DESERT DANDELION
Malacothrix glabrata • Composite Family

With its large (to 1¹/₂" wide), **canary yellow flowerheads** and its tendency in wet years to **grow in great masses,** desert dandelion can turn a barren desert expanse into a sunny garden full of cheer and light. Because each 4–16" tall plant may have a dozen or more flowerheads open at once, large stretches of ground may appear nearly covered by these startlingly bright blooms. • As with other dandelions, the flowerheads of desert dandelion consist of only rays with no central button of disk flowers, though sometimes early in the blooming season the unopened flowers in the center of the head form a red sphere that may resemble disk flowers. When the ray flowers open, they become a bright, flashy yellow that, with age, fades to a pale, creamy yellowish white. At night the flowerheads close, resembling drooping bells, but with the caress of the sun, the heads open again. The leaves are very narrow, pinnately lobed, and hairless. The reflexed phyllaries are red-tipped.

Names: *Malacothrix* means 'soft hair,' in reference to the hairy leaves of many species. *Glabrata* means 'glabrous' (smooth), in reference to the hairless leaves of this species. **Where found:** sandy flats, among shrubs; e.g., Alabama Hills (4000') in April.

yellow • many ray flowers • March–June

SCALE BUD
Anisocoma acaulis • Composite Family

You might confuse scale bud with desert dandelion (above), for both plants have large (to 1¹/₂" across), **dandelion-like, pale yellow flowers** that brighten up the sandy desert floor. There are, however, some easily noticeable differences. Scale bud is a shorter plant (2–8" tall) whose flowerheads rise above **basal, pinnately compound leaves that are wide, crinkly, and hairy** (the leaves of desert dandelion are narrow and hairless). The flowerheads of scale bud are the same pale yellow throughout, though sometimes there is a small patch of darker yellow or orange at the center, while the flowerheads of desert dandelion are often 2-toned—pale yellow at the periphery and darker yellow toward the center. Look under the flowerheads of scale bud and you will see that the phyllaries are often striped black-purple or red-purple.

Names: *Anisocoma* means 'unequal tufts of hair,' in reference to the 2 sets of pappus bristles. *Acaulis* means 'stemless'; what seem to be stems are technically peduncles. **Where found:** also in Sagebrush Steppe to 7000'. Sandy flats and slopes; e.g., along the Goodale Creek road west of Aberdeen (4100') in April, and along Horseshoe Meadow Road (5000') in June.

yellow • many ray flowers • April–June

WOOLLY DAISY
Eriophyllum wallacei • Composite Family

Though woolly daisy is a **miniature plant with stems only 1–4" tall and flowers only ¹/₂" or less across,** it can still bring great color and cheer to desert washes and flats. Its bright yellow flowerheads often seem to carpet large areas. Each flowerhead consists of a central cluster of **yellow-orange disk flowers surrounded by 5–10 yellow rays, which are broad and have 3 distinct teeth at the tip.** It often appears that the flowers burst directly from the ground, for the short, branching stems and the tiny rectangular or spoon-shaped leaves are usually almost completely hidden under the flowerheads. The stems, leaves, and phyllaries are covered with white, cobwebby hairs.

Names: *Eriophyllum* means 'woolly-leaved.' William Wallace was a 19th-century plant collector in southern California. **Where found:** sandy or gravelly flats and washes; e.g., Alabama Hills (4000') in April.

yellow • 5–10 rays and many disks • March–May

PRINGLE'S WOOLLY SUNFLOWER
Eriophyllum pringlei • Composite Family

Now this is a *woolly* sunflower! In most species of *Eriophyllum* (e.g., above and p. 175), the plant is covered with hairs, but in Pringle's woolly sunflower the **white, cobwebby hair is so dense that it's difficult even to find the leaves and stems.** You might overlook the entire plant, for it hugs the ground (only ¹/₂–3" tall) and its flowerheads are only ¹/₄" across. Unlike its close relative and frequent neighbor woolly daisy (above), Pringle's woolly sunflower does not have showy ray flowers. Instead, each flowerhead consists of only **10–25 disk flowers that seem to emerge directly from the dense pile of wool beneath them.** • Despite its small size and lack of ray flowers, Pringle's woolly sunflower can still be quite conspicuous, for its 'wool' is startling and its flowerheads are bright yellow.

Names: *Eriophyllum:* see above. Cyrus Pringle was a Vermont botanist of the late 19th and early 20th centuries who collected extensively in the American Southwest. Also called golden tuft. **Where found:** also in southern Sagebrush Steppe to 7000'. Sandy flats often with sagebrush; e.g., Alabama Hills (4000') in May, and lower part of the Sawmill Pass trail (4700') in May.

yellow • many disk flowers • May–June

BRITTLEBUSH
Encelia actoni • Composite Family

Of all the 'sunflowers' of the high desert (with yellow rays and yellow, brown, or black disks), brittlebush is probably the showiest. **Rising 1' or even 2' above the rounded clump of leaves of this 2–5' shrub are near-leafless, unbranched stems. At the end of each stem is one of the large (up to 2" across) flowerheads.** Each flowerhead consists of 15–25 bright yellow rays contrasting dramatically with the orangish central button of disk flowers. The soft green of the flowerheads still in bud and of the 1–1¹/₂" ovate leaves adds to the aesthetic appeal of this plant. Usually several dead, white stems from previous years are mixed in with the fresh, green stems to complete the picture. With its large size—the shrub is usually quite broad as well as tall—and flashy flowers, brittlebush makes itself known even from a considerable distance.

Names: Christopher Encel was a 16th-century expert on oak galls. Acton is a small town in the western Mojave Desert. Also called bush sunflower. **Where found:** sandy or gravelly flats and slopes; e.g., Alabama Hills (4000') in April.

yellow • many ray and disk flowers • April–June

COTTON-THORN
Tetradymia axillaris • Composite Family

It can be difficult to figure out which of the many species of yellow composites you are looking at. Several sunflower-like species have ray and disk flowers, and several other species have brush-like flowerheads of only disk flowers. Cotton-thorn is one of the few species of the latter type that can be easily identified. The common name and species name point to the distinguishing characteristics: the **stems of this 2–5' shrub are white and are armed with long (¹/₂–1¹/₂"), sharp spines; the fruits are densely covered with long, white hairs;** and the yellow, brush-like flowerheads are in the axils of the previous year's growth (so the twigs usually extend beyond the clusters of flowerheads). The spines are actually modified leaves, but there are also clusters of short, narrow, green leaves along the stem.

Names: *Tetradymia* means '4 together,' in reference to the 4-flowered heads of some species. *Axillaris* means 'in the axils.' **Where found:** also in southern Sagebrush Steppe. Dry flats with sagebrush; e.g., Alabama Hills (4000') in April.

yellow • 5–7 disk flowers • April–June

STREAM ORCHID
Epipactis gigantea • Orchid Family

Stream orchid is an imposing plant with large (to 1¹/₂"), intricate, showy flowers. Like all orchids, it has 6 perianth parts (3 petals and 3 sepals), one of which (the lower petal) is significantly different than the others. In most orchids the other 5 parts are nearly identical, but in stream orchid the petals and the sepals are quite different: the **upper 2 petals are pinkish while the 3 sepals are longer and yellowish green**. The third (lower) petal is large and colorful—yellow-green with red-purple veins and mottling. Protruding well out of the flower tube is a bright yellow, oblong pistil. The 2–8" leaves are narrow and pointed with conspicuous veins. They clasp the stout stem most of its 1–3' height. The 3–9 flowers tend to arch off the same side of the stem. • Despite this plant's size and showiness, it can be difficult to find because it frequently hides under the trees and shrubs growing with it along streambanks.

Names: *Epipactis* is an ancient Greek name derived from a word meaning 'to coagulate.' *Gigantea* means 'giant,' in reference to the flowers. Also called giant helleborine. **Where found:** also in Sagebrush Steppe to 7500'. Wet areas such as seeps, creekbanks; e.g., Alabama Hills (4000') in May.

red-purple and green-yellow • 3 petals and 3 petal-like sepals • May–July

PRINCE'S ROCK-CRESS
Arabis pulchra • Mustard Family

Although prince's rock-cress has beautiful **rose-purple blossoms,** the plant—like many members of the mustard family—is probably more noticed for its seedpods than for its flowers. Though the flowers are a striking color, they are **small (¹/₄–¹/₂") and tend to be spread out rather loosely through the inflorescence on long (to 1") pedicels.** When the blossoms go to seed, the narrow seedpods (siliques) are quite conspicuous, growing to 2¹/₂" long and spreading downward on their pedicels. The horizontal or downward orientation of the pedicels when bearing flowers or seedpods is one of the distinguishing characteristics of this species. The 1–2¹/₂' reddish stems are somewhat hairy or felty, as are the stemless, 1–4" leaves, which sometimes clasp the stem.

Names: *Arabis* means 'of Arabia.' *Pulchra* means 'beautiful.' **Where found:** also in southern Sagebrush Steppe to 7000'. Gravelly or rocky slopes, washes, canyons; e.g., Alabama Hills (4000') in March.

red-purple • 4 petals in cross • March–May

SHOWY GILIA
Gilia cana • Phlox Family

Showy gilia is a dazzling flower, both for its size (to 1" across) and for its spectacular colors. Each 4–12" plant is much branched and can bear several flowers in bloom at once, and often these plants grow in large masses, sometimes covering entire slopes. Even all by itself, a showy gilia flower puts on quite a show. The **long flower tube is dark purple at the base with a yellow band above leading to blue-purple or violet at the**  **throat. The flaring petal lobes are violet to pink with splotches of white.** To top off the multicolored display, the long, slender stamens, which stick out of the flower tube, are tipped with blue-purple anthers. Just imagine a hillside thick with these floral rainbows! • The leaves, pinnately lobed and mostly basal, are usually gray-green and somewhat cobwebby. There are a few narrow leaves on the stem.

Names: Felipe Gil was an 18th-century Spanish botanist. *Cana* means 'ash-colored,' in reference to the gray-cobwebby basal leaves. **Where found:** sandy or gravelly flats, washes, rocky slopes; e.g., along Whitney Portal Road in the Alabama Hills (4200') in April, and along the lower part of the Sawmill Pass trail (4600') in April.

**pink-purple (violet) • 5 petals united in tube
• March–May**

GREAT BASIN GILIA
Gilia brecciarum • Phlox Family

Although the flowers of Great Basin gilia have much the same spectacular coloring as those of showy gilia (above), they are less showy because of their **small size** (¹⁄₃"). You may have to examine a flower closely to see the array of colors—the narrow, **yellow flower tube with purple splotches at its base and the pink or lavender, flaring petals.** An interesting addition to the coloration of these flowers is the **black, ribbed calyx with its minute, stalked glands.** The 3–12" plant has a basal rosette of leaves, which are thick and toothed. There are usually a few lobed stem leaves as well.

Names: *Gilia:* see above. *Brecciarum* means 'of breccia,' in reference to the plant's sandy or gravelly habitat (breccia is rock consisting of sharp fragments embedded in sand or clay). **Where found:** also in Sagebrush Steppe. Sandy or gravelly flats; e.g., Alabama Hills (4500') in April, and the lower part of the Sawmill Pass trail (4600') in April.

**pink-purple (lavender) • 5 petals united in tube
• March–May**

DESERT CALICO
Loeseliastrum matthewsii • Phlox Family

Though desert calico has the narrow leaves, pro-truding reproductive parts, and 5 united petals typical of the phlox family, it is nonetheless a very peculiar and distinctive member of the family. **Three of the petals are broad, erect, and close together, while the other 2 (sometimes 3) are narrower, bent out or down, and splayed apart. In addition, the lower petals are usually a solid color (pink or white), while the upper 3 are pink with a large white splotch bordered above by maroon arches** and marked with maroon spots or lines. The tips of the petals are squarish and/or notched. The delicate, white style and the cluster of stamens are about as long as the petals. The stems are only 1–6" tall, so the flowers bloom practically right on the ground. Narrow, spiny leaves cover the stems.

Names: *Loeseliastrum* means 'resembling *Loeselia*,' a genus in the phlox family named for John Loesel, author of *Flora Prussica* (1703). W. Matthews, of the U.S. Army, was stationed in Owens Valley in 1875. The 'calico' in the common name refers to the multicolored blossoms. **Where found:** sandy flats, washes; e.g., Alabama Hills (4000') in May.

pink with white and maroon markings • 5 irregular petals • March–May

APRICOT MALLOW
Sphaeralcea ambigua • Mallow Family

Of the many plants of the high desert with colorful, showy flowers, apricot mallow is a frequent favorite. This tall (to 3'), soft-looking plant bears many 1$^1/_2$–2" **flowers, which are as striking for their wide-open bowl shape as for their deep, rich apricot or red-orange color.** The delicate veins on the petals and the central column of deep purple stamens with yellow pollen on the anthers add even more drama to the beauty and intrigue of this remarkable flower. Fortunately we get to appreciate its beauty for quite some time each year, because the flowers often bloom for 2 months or more. The stem and 3-lobed, maple-like leaves are covered with gray, felty, star-shaped hairs. Though they give a soft look to the plant, beware of touching them, for they can irritate skin and eyes. The plant is somewhat shrubby at the base.

Names: *Sphaeralcea* means 'globe mallow,' in reference to the globe-like fruit. *Ambigua* means 'uncertain,' in reference to some taxonomic difficulties with this species. Sometimes members of this genus are called 'sore-eye poppies' because of the hairs on the stem and leaves. **Where found:** also in southern Sagebrush Steppe to 7500'. Dry slopes, washes, canyons, pinyon-juniper woodlands; e.g., along Whitney Portal Road in the Alabama Hills (4000') in April.

red-orange • 5 separate petals • March–May

DESERT FIVE-SPOT
Eremalche rotundifolia • Mallow Family

Desert five-spot has spectacular and highly unusual flowers—the petals curl up to form a **nearly closed globe**. The outside of the globe (formed by the undersides of the curled petals) is a **soft, pale pink**; the inside is a stunning kaleidoscope of colors: yellow-white petals with **bright red splotches** at their bases, and at the center of the flower a dark red, frothy-looking stigma from which radiate scores of yellow anthers on white spokes (filaments). The 3–24" stem is reddish brown and hairy and bears several 1–2" wide, round, scalloped leaves. A few to several of the 1–1¹/₂" spherical flowers cluster at the tips of the stem branches. Directly under each flower is a pointed, hairy bract. The flowers close at night, opening only slightly in the mid-morning.

Names: *Eremalche* means 'lonely mallow,' in poignant reference to the plant's desert habitat. *Rotundifolia* means 'round leaves.' **Where found:** sandy or gravelly flats, washes; e.g., Alabama Hills (4000') in April.

pink with dark red splotches • 5 separate petals • March–May

STORKSBILL
Erodium cicutarium • Geranium Family

Storksbill is a low plant (4–20") whose reddish stems often spread out in prostrate rosettes. At the tip of each stem is a cluster of 2 or more delicate, ¹/₄", **pink flowers whose 5 narrow petals form a graceful star. Purplish streaks mark the base of each petal**. The narrow, greenish sepals show through the spaces between the petals. The hairy leaves are deeply pinnately lobed into tiny, sharply pointed segments. • The amazing seedpods become **spiraled spears up to 2"** long that can be as dangerous as they look. They keep twisting as they develop, building up considerable torque. When the seeds are ripe, the outside membrane of the pod splits and peels up in segments, which act like helicopter blades to propel the seeds through the air and plant them forcefully in the ground (or in anything else that intervenes).

Names: *Erodium* means 'heron,' in reference to the long, bill-like fruits. *Cicutarium* means 'like *Cicuta*,' the water hemlock genus, though the similarities aren't obvious. **Where found:** also in Sagebrush Steppe to 6500'. Gravelly flats and slopes, disturbed places; e.g., along Whitney Portal Road in the Alabama Hills (4000') in March. Alien—and one of the most invasive weeds in the Mojave Desert.

pink • 5 separate petals • March–May

SCARLET LOCOWEED
Astragalus coccineus • Pea Family

Scarlet locoweed is the only desert plant of the eastern Sierra that rivals desert paintbrush (p. 67) for intensity of red. Scarlet locoweed often grows by itself on open, sunny flats or banks, so its **brilliant crimson** flames can be seen from quite a distance even though the plant grows low to the ground. It usually forms nearly stemless clumps 1' or so across, dense with small, white-woolly, pinnately compound leaves and scores of slender, bright red flowers. The 2–4" leaves consist of 7–15 tiny, oval leaflets. When the plant is in full bloom, however, you may not even see the leaves, the 1–1¹/₂" flowers can be so thick. The **wings and the banner are the same rich red; the banner flares up vertically and is streaked with white at its base.** The 1–1¹/₂" **seedpods are plump and white-furry** and have an up-curving, pointed tip.

Names: *Astragalus* means 'ankle bone' or 'dice,' probably referring to the rattling sound the dried seeds can make inside the pods. *Coccineus* means 'scarlet.' Also called scarlet milkvetch. **Where found:** also in Sagebrush Steppe to 6500'. Sandy or gravelly banks, flats, and outwash fans, especially between rocks; e.g., along Whitney Portal Road in the Alabama Hills (4000') in April.

scarlet • 5 irregular petals • March–May

PAPER LOCOWEED
Astragalus lentiginosus • Pea Family

The eastern Sierra and adjoining desert flats are home to many locoweeds, all with pinnately compound leaves, inflated seedpods, and the banner-wings-keel flowers typical of the pea family. The flowers of some species are spectacular for their showy displays of intense colors. Though scarlet locoweed (above) is probably the showiest of these locoweeds, paper locoweed is not far behind. Its ¹/₂" flowers are a **stunning rose-purple with white, rose-striped patches on the banner and white tips on the wings.** The plant can be sprawling or bushy with stems as long as 1¹/₂', but usually shorter. Each stem bears 9–19 silvery green, oval leaflets that rarely exceed ¹/₂" in length. Unlike some locoweeds, the flower stems of paper locoweed hold the clusters of flowers well above the leaves. The **seedpods are papery and strongly inflated with a distinct central groove and a pointed beak.** They are usually mottled red or purplish. • This species of *Astragalus* is highly variable, with over 20 recognized varieties.

Names: *Astragalus:* see above. *Lentiginosus* means 'freckled,' in reference to the purplish or reddish mottling on the seedpods. Also called freckled milkvetch and dapple-pod. **Where found:** also in southern Sagebrush Steppe to 8000'. Open slopes, sandy or gravelly flats, pinyon-juniper woodlands; e.g., Alabama Hills (4000') in April.

red-purple (blue-purple) • 5 irregular petals • March–April

DESERT PAINTBRUSH
Castilleja chromosa • Snapdragon Family

Sometimes desert paintbrush grows in washes or on sandy banks out in the open, but more often it **grows up through sagebrush or other shrubs**. Even when it's part of a tangle of shrubs, however, its **flaming scarlet color** is so bright that it is easily visible from hundreds of feet away. As with all paintbrush species, most of the color is located on the tips of the modified upper leaves (bracts) and on the sepals. The true flowers are yellowish-green tubes mostly hidden by the bracts and calyx. Each bract has several (usually 5) rounded, lateral segments whose tips are scarlet and bases are usually dark red-brown. The lower leaves are green and have 3 or 5 narrow lobes; both the leaves and the $1/2$–$1^1/2'$ stems are covered with stiff gray or white hairs.

Names: Domingo Castillejo was a Spanish botanist. *Chromosa* means 'color.' Sometimes called *C. angustifolia*, though many botanists consider this to be a separate species. **Where found:** also in Sagebrush Steppe to 7000'. Dry sagebrush slopes, sandy canyon bottoms, pinyon-juniper woodlands; e.g., Alabama Hills (4000') in April, and along lower part of the Sawmill Pass trail (4800') in April.

scarlet (pink-purple, yellow-orange) bracts • 5 petals in 2-lipped tube • March–May

BIGELOW'S MONKEYFLOWER
Mimulus bigelovii • Snapdragon Family

Many *Mimulus* species grow in the high desert, and many more thrive in the high Sierra. Whatever their color or size, there is something delightful about monkeyflowers: their broad flower 'faces' seem to have such personality. Many species have flowers that are yellow and many more are some shade of red, ranging from pale pink to scarlet. • Bigelow's monkeyflower has an especially showy flower, both for its color and for its size. The 2–5" stem (reaching 10" in a particularly favorable year) bears several of the **1" rose-purple flowers**. The **flower tubes are so long and the faces are so broad in relation to the short plant that it appears almost overwhelmed with blossoms**. The flowers have bright yellow marks in their throats; the anthers are deep inside the tube, making the throats look empty. The petals persist long after withering. The opposite leaves are hairy and often red edged.

Names: *Mimulus* means 'mime,' in reference to the somewhat face-like flowers. Bigelow: see p. 49. **Where found:** also in southern Sagebrush Steppe to 7000'. Sandy washes and canyons, rocky flats and hillsides; e.g., Alabama Hills (4000') in April.

rose-purple • 5 petals united in 2-lipped tube • April–May

PURPLE MAT
Nama demissum • Waterleaf Family

In a favorable year, purple mat can be stunning, covering large areas of gravelly flats in the high desert with **mats of dazzling, rose or red-purple (sometimes blue-purple) flowers**. Although the plant hugs the ground—it is rarely more than 6" tall—the stems can spread 1–2' and the flowers can form dense clusters. The ¹/₂" tubular flowers are an amazingly intense color, **almost neon against the pale, sandy or gravelly desert floor**. The flower tubes are bright yellow, and there is a narrow ring of white between the tube and the rosy petal lobes. The anthers and stigma are also bright yellow. The small, slender, tongue-shaped leaves and the narrow-lobed calyx are sticky-hairy. • Like many desert plants, purple mat is extremely sensitive to the amount of moisture available, especially in winter and spring. In dry years, it may form just a tiny tuft with only 1 flower.

Names: *Nama* means 'spring' or 'stream,' probably referring to the many desert species of this genus that depend on local moisture. *Demissum* means 'humble,' in reference to the ground-hugging growth form. **Where found:** sandy or gravelly flats and slopes; e.g., west of Aberdeen (4000') in April, and along lower part of the Sawmill Pass trail (4800') in April.

rose or red-purple (blue-purple) • 5 petals united in a tube • March–May

SALT CEDAR
Tamarix ramosissima • Tamarisk Family

Salt cedar is a **shrub or small tree (to 25') with scale-like leaves overlapping along its branches**. The resulting lacy but rough appearance of the twigs may remind you of a cedar tree. Contributing to the lacy look of the plant are the **1–3" spikes of tiny, pink flowers**. Scattered among the leaves are salt glands from which the plant can excrete excess salt. This adaptation allows salt cedar to tolerate highly alkaline soil. • Despite its graceful, plumy appearance, salt cedar can be a troublesome invasive weed in the desert, and its deep roots and its heavy water uptake can significantly lower the water table.

Names: *Tamarix* refers to the area along the Tamaris River in Spain where the plant was first described. *Ramosissima* means 'much branched.' **Where found:** wet areas such as washes, ditches, streambanks; e.g., Alabama Hills (4000') in May. Alien.

pink • 5 tiny petals • May–June

SPINY HOPSAGE
Grayia spinosa • Goosefoot Family

Although spiny hopsage is a common shrub of the high desert, it is nonetheless an unusual plant. It is covered with colorful, showy flowers, yet its flowers lack petals. The 1–3', much-branched shrub is thick with small, fleshy, green leaves and either male or female flowers or both. (If both, the male and female flowers grow on different branches.) Neither the pistillate (female) flowers or the staminate (male) flowers have petals, just reproductive parts and bracts. In the female flowers, the 2 bracts fuse to form a ¹/₂", sac-like, winged structure that surrounds the ripening seeds. It is these **bracts that appear to be petals, for they turn a beautiful rosy or creamy yellowish white**. They are so colorful and showy that this shrub will catch your eye from quite a distance. In the spring the **leaves are gray-tipped,** as if they had been dipped in white chocolate. The stems end in whitish, spine-tipped twigs.

Names: Asa Gray was an eminent 19th-century American botanist. *Spinosa* means 'spiny.' **Where found:** also in Sagebrush Steppe to 7500'. Grows among other shrubs on sandy or gravelly flats and in pinyon-juniper woodlands; e.g., Alabama Hills (4000') in May, and along Highway 395 near Big Pine (4000') in May.

rose bracts • no petals • March–June

BEAVERTAIL CACTUS
Opuntia basilaris • Cactus Family

Beavertail cactus is one of the most inviting-looking cacti, for not only does it have large (to 3"), gorgeous flowers, but it appears to be spineless. Technically it *is* spineless, although the little eyespots on the fleshy stems have nasty, ¹/₈–¹/₄", red-brown bristles that can be irritating if you touch them. The broad, flat stems are usually called pads. • This cactus is a low plant rarely reaching more than 1¹/₂' tall. The **intense magenta of the flowers makes a stunning contrast to the blue-green (sometimes slightly purple-tinged) pads**. The **many crinkly, satiny petals overlap,** forming a beautiful and delicate cradle for the dense cluster of almost crimson, white-tipped or yellow-tipped reproductive parts. In the dim light of dusk the petal color seems to deepen to a rich purple, and the pads seem to become a bluer blue-green. • Beavertail cactus is usually the first cactus to bloom in the eastern Sierra.

Names: *Opuntia;* see p. 58. *Basilaris* means 'regal.' Also called beavertails. **Where found:** also in southern Sagebrush Steppe to 6500'. Grows with shrubs on dry flats, washes and rocky slopes; e.g., Alabama Hills (4000') in May.

magenta to rose • many petals • March–June

HEDGEHOG CACTUS
Echinocereus engelmannii • Cactus Family

The gorgeous flowers of hedgehog cactus resemble those of beavertail cactus (p. 69)—**up to 3" wide with many magenta-rose petals** surrounding clusters of yellow stamens—but there is no confusing the two. Hedgehog cactus, as the name suggests, **has cylindrical, cucumber-like stems covered with long, dangerous spines,** while the flat pads of beavertail cactus are spine-free. Hedgehog cactus usually grows in clusters of 5–15 of the 6–18" spiny cucumbers, forming a clump up to 3' across. The spines also occur in clusters (of 10–18) consisting of 2 or a few long, up-curved, central spines and several short, lateral, horizontal spines. The resulting interlaced network of spines is so dense it may be hard to see the green stems beneath. The flowers are a deeper shade of red-purple than those of beavertail cactus and have a green stigma divided into many finger-like lobes. These magnificent flowers close at night. The fruits are red, fleshy, and edible (remove the spines).

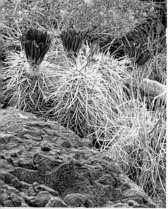

Names: *Echinocereus* means 'hedgehog candle,' in reference to the spiny stems and dazzling flowers. George Engelmann was the first known student of cacti in the U.S. in the early 1900s. Also called torch cactus. **Where found:** also in southern Sagebrush Steppe to 7200'. Sandy or gravelly flats; e.g., Alabama Hills (4000') in May.

red-purple/magenta • many petals • April–June

MOJAVE THISTLE
Cirsium mohavense • Composite Family

Mojave thistle is an ominous, bristly-looking plant, but its rosy flowerheads are exquisitely and delicately beautiful. The stem is thick and tall (to 6') and bears many imposing (to 10"), lobed, spiny leaves. The phyllaries are **sharp spines,** some erect and some sticking out threateningly. The stems, leaves, and bracts are clothed in white felty wool. Being careful of the spines, get right next to this plant and peer into the amazing **2" pink flowerhead**. It's almost like being enveloped in a fireworks display, a **starburst of rosy filaments** streaking all around you. The narrow flower tubes are a light yellow tinged with pink and spotted with darker rose. The reproductive parts are often heavy with stringy, white pollen. Stare into Mojave thistle's dazzling flowerhead awhile and lose yourself in its rose-colored universe.

Names: *Cirsium* means 'swollen,' in reference to the reputed ability of thistles to treat swollen veins. *Mohavense* means 'of the Mojave Desert.' **Where found:** gravelly or rocky slopes and washes; e.g., Alabama Hills (4000') in May.

pink to rose • many spiny disk flowers • April–May

DESERT LARKSPUR
Delphinium parishii • Buttercup Family

Desert larkspur, the most common *Delphinium* species of the desert, brings a touch of cool blue sky to the often hot landscape. **Many (6–75) of the intricate 3/4" flowers branch off the plant's 1/2–3' stem.** The 5 sepals, which are the largest and showiest parts of the flower, are a **soothing sky-blue color** and are usually bent back. The 1/2" nectar spur is sometimes tinged pink or purple. As in all larkspurs, the petals are smaller and less conspicuous than the sepals and are cradled in them, creating a bit of a flower-within-a-flower appearance. The lower 2 petals of desert larkspur are blue and are often finely hairy; the upper 2 petals are white. The 1–3" leaves are deeply cut into many narrow divisions. Most of the leaves are basal, but you may have trouble finding them because they often dry up by blooming time.

Names: *Delphinium* means 'dolphin,' in reference to the shape of the bud. Brothers Samuel and William Parish were American plant collectors of the late 19th and early 20th centuries. **Where found:** among shrubs on dry slopes and flats, washes, pinyon-juniper woodlands; e.g., Alabama Hills (4000') in May.

blue • 5 petal-like sepals (4 true petals) • March–June

WESTERN DESERT PENSTEMON
Penstemon incertus • Snapdragon Family

From the high desert at the base of the Sierra to near the summit of some of the Sierra's highest peaks, penstemons are our nearly constant companions. From royal blue to lavender to white, from pink to rose to red, the delightful tubular blossoms of *Penstemon* species accompany us throughout the entire range of the eastern (and western) Sierra. Western desert penstemon, confined to the desert scrub and lower sagebrush elevations, is one of the showiest and cheeriest. The **1/2–3' shrub, thick with narrow leaves and deep blue 1" flowers,** puts on quite a show in its high desert habitat. The flower tubes have some white markings inside and tend to red-purple outside, but the overall impression is a glorious, rich, saturated blue. The staminode (the 1 stamen without an anther) is densely hairy.

Name: *Penstemon* means '5 stamens,' in reference to the fifth infertile stamen characteristic of this genus. *Incertus* means 'uncertain,' in reference to taxonomic problems with the species. **Where found:** also in southern Sagebrush Steppe to 5500'. Sandy or gravelly flats and slopes, washes, canyons, among sage brush; e.g., along Whitney Portal Road (4000') in the Alabama Hills in May, and along lower part of Horseshoe Meadow Road (5000') in May.

blue • 5 petals united in 2-lipped tube • May–July

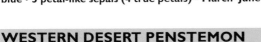

YELLOW THROATS
Phacelia fremontii • Waterleaf Family

With its ³/₄", multicolored blossoms, yellow throats is one of the most delightful floral inhabitants of the high desert. Its **lavender to violet, funnel-shaped flowers with the yellow centers** can bring considerable cheer to sandy or scrubby flats and slopes, especially because the plants often grow in clusters—of a few plants in dry years, of large masses in wet years. The 5 petals are somewhat crepe-papery in texture and are marked with dark purple veins. The upper portion of the 2–12" stem consists of a **caterpillar-like coil thick with flowers,** which have a bit of a skunk-like odor. The leaves are mostly basal and are deeply pinnately lobed.

Names: *Phacelia* means 'cluster,' in reference to the many-flowered, coiled inflorescences of many species including this one. Fremont: see p. 48. **Where found:** also in southern Sagebrush Steppe to 7000'. Sandy or gravelly flats, sagebrush slopes, pinyon-juniper woodlands; e.g., Alabama Hills (4000') in April.

lavender (to blue or violet) • 5 petals united in a bowl • April–May

WILD HELIOTROPE
Phacelia distans • Waterleaf Family

Although wild heliotrope can grow up to 3' tall and frequently grows among rough shrubs, it is quite a delicate-looking plant with its **pinnately compound leaves and its graceful, caterpillar-like coils of ¹/₂" blue flowers.** As with most members of the waterleaf family, the stamens of wild heliotrope stick way out of the flower, creating a rather soft, fuzzy appearance from a distance. Close inspection will reveal beautiful lavender or purple filaments with white, black-edged anthers. The stems are sparsely stiff-hairy.

Names: *Phacelia:* see above. *Distans* means 'distant,' an unclear reference. **Where found:** also in southern Sagebrush Steppe to 6500'. Rocky or sandy flats and slopes, washes, among shrubs; e.g., Alabama Hills (4000') in April, and along lower part of the Sawmill Pass trail (5000') in May.

blue • 5 petals united in bowl • March–May

SAND BLOSSOMS
Linanthus parryae • Phlox Family

Sand blossoms is the perfect name for this plant because the stem is so short (1–2") that the ½–1" **flower seems to bloom right on the sand,** where the plant typically grows. The flowers are strikingly beautiful with their **deep blue (sometimes pale lavender or white) petals, dark purple throats, and bright yellow anthers.** Even in dry years you will usually find sand blossoms growing in small clusters of several plants; in wet years these clusters can form great, dense masses of spectacular color so thick that the ground and the plants' small, needle-like leaves are completely hidden. I hope that everyone has the good fortune to experience the high desert in a wet year (after substantial winter and spring rains); among the great treasures of such a year are the carpets of sand blossoms with their rich, saturated hues.

Names: *Linanthus:* see p. 49. Eva Parry, for whom this plant was named by Asa Gray (see p. 69), was the wife of Charles Parry, a 19th-century American botanist who was part of the Mexican Boundary Survey. **Where found:** also in southern Sagebrush Steppe to 6000'. Sandy or gravelly flats and slopes; e.g., Alabama Hills (4000') in April, and along the Goodale Creek road west of Aberdeen (4100') in April.

blue-lavender (white) • 5 petals in broad funnel • March–May

INDIGO BUSH
Psorothamnus arborescens • Pea Family

Indigo bush is a **1–4' shrub thick with 2–3" spikes of intensely royal blue or deep blue-purple, pea-like flowers.** The ¼–½" flowers are typical of the pea family with their upright banner, 'praying-hands' wings, and inner keel petals. In indigo bush, all these petals are the same rich, saturated blue or blue-purple, which contrasts dramatically with the often red or red-purple calyx. Indigo bush has smooth, white bark, and its 1–2" pinnately compound leaves have ½" leaflets in nearly opposite pairs. The fruits are pointed pods that are dotted with amber, oil-containing glands. The entire plant is strongly aromatic.

Names: *Psorothamnus* means 'scab shrub,' in reference to the blister-like glands speckling the seedpods. *Arborescens* means 'tree-like,' in reference to the shrub growth form. **Where found:** gravelly flats and slopes, washes and canyons; e.g., along Highway 395 between Big Pine and Independence (4000') in April.

blue (blue-purple) • 5 irregular petals • April–June

YELLOW EYES
Lupinus flavoculatus • Pea Family

Yellow eyes is one of the **smaller lupines** but is no less spectacular for its 2–6" stems and its tufted growth form. The ³/₈" **flowers are a gorgeous, deep violet color with a distinctive yellow spot on the banner.** Because the flowers grow in dense terminal clusters and the plants often grow close together, yellow eyes can create extensive patches of vividly colorful groundcover. The palmately compound leaves typical of lupines occur at the tips of ³/₄–2" stems, which often splay out nearly parallel to the ground. The leaflets are finely hairy underneath and fold inward.

Names: *Lupinus* means 'wolf,' illustrating the mistaken belief that plants of this genus 'wolf up' nutrients from the soil. In fact, the contrary is true because peas fix nitrogen and so replenish the soil. *Flavoculatus* means 'yellow-eyed.' **Where found:** also in southern Sagebrush Steppe to 7000'. Sandy or gravelly flats and slopes, pinyon-juniper woodlands; e.g., Alabama Hills (4000') in April.

deep violet or blue • 5 irregular petals • April–June

CHIA
Salvia columbariae • Mint Family

Like its close relative purple sage (p. 125), chia is a fragrant member of the mint family with whorls of rather odd, blue flowers. Chia's **square stems** rise 4–24" above irregularly lobed basal leaves. Sometimes there is a pair or two of opposite stem leaves as well. At the tip of each stem is a ¹/₂–1" **wide, head-like whorl of 10–30 delicately blue, ¹/₂" flowers.** Usually there will be a second whorl of flowers a few inches below the first one, and sometimes a third whorl a few more inches down the stem. Each whorl of flowers presents a dramatic contrast of colors, for the blue petals emerge from dark, reddish-purple, spiky sepals, and under the whole whorl are spine-tipped, green to purple, leafy bracts. The flowers look like some kind of **Dr. Seuss character with ears, arms, torso, and legs.** From these strangely shaped flowers protrude 2 delicate stamens with bright yellow anthers.

Names: *Salvia* means 'save,' in reference to medicinal properties of plants in this genus. *Columbariae* means 'of western North America.' **Where found:** also in Sagebrush Steppe to 6500'. Dry, gravelly flats and slopes; e.g., along Whitney Portal Road in the Alabama Hills (4000') in April.

**blue • 5 irregular petals (look like 4 petals)
• March–April**

MOJAVE ASTER
Xylorhiza tortifolia • Composite Family

Mojave aster is one of the showiest of the desert composites and, in many people's view, one of the loveliest of all the flowering plants of the eastern Sierra. Its **flowerheads are unusually large (up to 2" across) and consist of up to 60 violet to pink (sometimes red-purple or white) rays surrounding a cluster of bright yellow to orange disk flowers.** The rays are tightly crowded and angle up from the disk to form a shaggy bowl. The 1–2¹/₂' plant is bushy. Its lower half is thick with narrow, 1–3" leaves, which have wavy and somewhat prickly edges. The upper half of the plant consists of many nearly leafless stems, each terminating in one of the glorious flowerheads. Because a plant can have scores of these flower-bearing stems, it can look like a forest of blooms rising above a leafy forest floor.

Names: *Xylorhiza* means 'woody root.' *Tortifolia* means 'twisted leaves,' in reference to the wavy edges of the leaves. Also called desert aster. **Where found:** sandy or rocky flats, slopes, washes, canyons; e.g., Alabama Hills (4000') in April.

violet • many ray and disk flowers • March–May

MOJAVE DESERT-PARSLEY
Lomatium mohavense • Carrot Family

Mojave desert-parsley has the **deeply divided, fern-like leaves** and the umbel inflorescence type (i.e., **flowers on radiating spokes**) that you expect from *Lomatium* species. The color of the flowers, though, is unexpected and even a bit shocking. Most *Lomatium* flowers are yellow or white (e.g., see p. 174), but these flowers are an amazing, **unusual rich black-purple to maroon**. If you look closely, you'll see that the tiny reproductive parts are this same deep color. The white, fluffy pollen stands out in vivid contrast with the black-purple background. The thick 4–12" stems rise above delicate, pinnately compound leaves and culminate in several arching spokes, each bearing a tight 1–2" cluster of tiny (¹/₈") flowers. • With their striking color and intricate structure, these flowers are well worth close inspection, though you'll have to get right on the ground to do it. Just watch out for those prickly plant creatures likely to be in the vicinity.

Names: *Lomatium* means 'bordered,' a description of the prominent margins on the wings of the fruit. *Mohavense:* see p. 70. Also called Mojave lomatium. **Where found:** also in southern Sagebrush Steppe to 6000'. Sandy flats; e.g., Alabama Hills (4000') in April.

black-purple • 5 tiny petals • March–May

Great Basin Sagebrush Steppe

4500 – 7500'

Sagebrush Steppe west of Bishop

mule ears at Grant Lake

pinyon-juniper woodlands above Alabama Hills

As you go north along Highway 395 past Big Pine, or as you go west from Highway 395 south of Big Pine up into the eastern foothills of the Sierra, you will move from Mojave Desert Scrub to Great Basin Sagebrush Steppe. The Great Basin Desert covers a huge area between the Sierra–Cascade axis and the Rockies, including most of Nevada and Utah and parts of southern Oregon, Idaho, and Wyoming. It is a higher, colder, and somewhat wetter desert than the hot deserts to the south: the Mojave and the Sonoran. For example, at Bridgeport (6465'), 90 miles north of Bishop along the eastern edge of the Sierra, the average high temperature in July is 83 degrees and the average low temperature in January is 9 degrees. The average annual precipitation is 10".

Although it's not as dry as the Mojave Desert, the Great Basin Desert still presents semi-arid conditions to plants. You won't see many cacti here (Mojave prickly pear is a glorious exception), but you will see lots of gray-green shrubs with small waxy or hairy leaves,

White Mountains, Crawley Lake east of Mammoth
opposite: bitterbrush at base of Tioga Pass road

Piute morning glory along Big Pine Creek

lower limit of pinyon-juniper woodlands

such as sagebrush, bitterbrush, rabbitbrush, shadscale, hopsage, and ephedra.

Because most of these shrubs are wind-pollinated (there always seems to be plenty of wind here!), their flowers are usually small and inconspicuous. Sometimes, when you look out over a flat or slope in this terrain, you wonder whether there are any flowers anywhere, for it can look like an unending monotony of sand or gravel dotted with millions of evenly spaced, gray-green, flowerless shrubs.

But in May and June, these sagebrush plains can come alive with color and bloom. Mule ears, bitterbrush, sulfur flower, phlox, paintbrush, lupine, phacelia, and many other plants with bright, showy flowers can almost completely cover hillsides. And if you look carefully between and beneath the shrubs, you may find incredible miniature gardens of annuals, sometimes carpeting large patches of sand with every color imaginable. That which just a few weeks before and a few weeks later looks like a drab, monotonous sea is now a striking, multi-colored floral masterpiece.

As you look to the west to the massive wall of the Sierra, you will notice a lower timberline where the Sagebrush Steppe turns to small, squat, widely spaced evergreen trees. This line marks the lower limit of the pinyon-juniper woodlands, which in the south (Owens Valley) begin at about 6500' and in the north at about 5500'.

At Lone Pine (the southern end of the region covered in this book), you can drive west up Whitney Portal Road and pass from the Mojave Desert Scrub in the Alabama Hills (at about 4000') into the Sagebrush Steppe (at about 4500') and on into the pinyon-juniper woodlands (at about 6500')—all within a few miles and all before the road even begins its steep switchbacking up to the Mt. Whitney trailhead.

At about 6500' walk a few steps off the road into the woods and you will get a good feel for how open these pinyon-juniper woodlands are. And, of course, the ubiquitous sagebrush dots the ground between the trees. From these woods look east and you will see the Owens Valley desert below you dotted with shrubs, the 'waters' of Owens Lake (actually salt glistening in the sun), and the imposing western face of the Inyo Mountains.

The pinyon-juniper woodlands extend up only about 1000', replaced at about 7500' in the south and at about 6500' in the north by the 'real' forest: the tall and imposing pines and firs of the Mixed Conifer Forest.

There is not much water in this Sagebrush Steppe zone, though of course there are streams and creeks that flow down from the snowfields above. The eastern base of the Sierra is not a land of lakes (those are higher up), though there are a few gorgeous and fascinating examples— notably Crowley Lake (6781'), Mono Lake (7000'), Topaz Lake (5000'), and Washoe Lake (5000'). Mono Lake, with its delicate salt-water ecology, is especially captivating. There's something deeply soul-stirring about the Sierra soaring above those ancient waters.

Owens Lake

Mono Lake

camas lily in Tahoe Basin

Where and When to See the Flowers

When the Alabama Hills and other Mojave Desert spots have passed their prime blooming, head north on Highway 395 or go a couple of miles west up any of the many side roads branching off Highway 395. Some particularly wonderful wildflower displays in the Sagebrush Steppe can be found in the following areas (listed south to north; see map on p. 29):

- the first few miles of Horseshoe Meadow Road as it branches south off Whitney Portal Road

- the first couple of miles of the trail to Sawmill Pass (trailhead is a few miles up the Division Creek Powerhouse road just south of Aberdeen)

- the lower parts of the Bishop Creek road (West Line Street, Route 168) west from Bishop

- June Lake Loop Road (Route 158), especially above Grant Lake

- the lower parts of the Tioga Pass road (Route 120) west from Lee Vining

- the lower parts of Mill Canyon Road west from Walker

- Highway 395 as it borders Topaz Lake

- Route 89 between Topaz Lake and Monitor Pass and between Monitor Pass and Luther Pass

- Route 88 between Minden and Woodfords

- Route 431 (Mt. Rose Highway) between Highway 395 and the base of Mt. Rose.

In May, June, or July of almost any year, you can find glorious Sagebrush Steppe flower displays along any of these roads and trails.

Owens Valley from Sawmill Pass trail

PRICKLY POPPY
Argemone munita • Poppy Family

Coming across a prickly poppy thick with flowers can be a startling experience, for it looks a bit like a helping of fried eggs served on a bed of spiny stems and leaves. Each large flower, up to 5" across, has **6 crinkly, wedge-shaped, white petals surrounding a bright yellow 'yolk' of 150–250 tightly packed stamens.** In the very center of this cluster of stamens is a dash of pepper—the black tipped ovary. The 1–4' plant has **2–6", deeply lobed, spine-tipped leaves.** The stems are covered with short, yellow spines. Even the 2 sepals (which fall off at flowering) and the seed capsules are prickly. • This plant is indeed armed to the teeth, and not just on the outside. It contains **toxic** alkaloids that can cause serious problems if ingested.

Names: *Argemone* means 'cataract,' in reference to the eye affliction that the thick, yellow sap of this plant was thought to cure. *Munita* means 'armed,' in reference to the abundant prickles. **Where found:** also in Mixed Conifer Forest to 10,000'. Sandy flats and slopes, pinyon-juniper woodlands, along roadways; e.g., along Mt. Rose Highway at the base of Mt. Rose (5500') in June, and along the Tioga Pass road (9000') in July.

white • 6 separate petals • June–August

INYO ONION
Allium atrorubens • Lily Family

You may smell Inyo onion well before you see it. If you happen to step on the single, grass-like leaf, it will exude a **strong onion fragrance,** but even so you may have difficulty locating the flowers. The blooms nearly sit on the ground and their **pale pink or white color tends to blend in with the plant's sandy or rocky habitat.** The 2–7" stem bears a large, rounded **cluster of up to 50 papery 1/2" flowers.** The 6 tepals are sharp-pointed and pale pink or white with dark red mid-veins. Under each flower cluster are 2 or 3 tissue-like, pointed bracts about 1/2" long. The single leaf usually extends up higher than the plant stem, though late in the blooming season it may wither away.

Names: *Allium* is Latin for 'garlic.' *Atrorubens* means 'dark red,' perhaps referring to the red-purple tepals of one variety of this species, or to the dark red midveins on the tepals. **Where found:** southern Sagebrush Steppe to 7000'; uncommon. Rocky or sandy flats and slopes, washes, pinyon-juniper woodlands; e.g., above the Alabama Hills (5000') in May.

white (pink) • 6 tepals • April–June

DEATH CAMAS
Zigadenus venenosus • Lily Family

Death camas is well named, for the entire plant is extremely **poisonous** to animals and humans. Studies have shown that even bees can be fatally poisoned by the nectar! Despite its pernicious nature, death camas is a lovely plant with beautiful, fresh white flowers. The many $1/2$" flowers form a **cone-shaped inflorescence** along the top 2–10" of the stout stem, which can reach almost 2'. The **6 white tepals are stalked and are decorated with greenish-yellow glands at their bases.** The 6 stamens with white anthers radiate out from the green ovary. The grass-like basal leaves, which can reach 16" in length, arch gracefully away from the plant stem.

Names: *Zigadenus,* also spelled *Zygadenus,* means 'yoked gland,' in reference to the paired flower glands of another species. *Venenosus* means 'poisonous.' **Where found:** also in Mojave Desert Scrub and in Mixed Conifer Forest to 8500'. Wet areas such as streamsides, moist meadows; e.g., in the Alabama Hills (4000') in May, and along Thomas Creek (6000') in June.

white • 6 separate tepals • April–July

SAND CORM
Zigadenus paniculatus • Lily Family

Sand corm is very similar to death camas (above), but it grows in **dry habitats** instead of wet ones. Like death camas, it has numerous small ($1/4$–$1/2$"), white flowers branching off the upper part of its tall (to 2'), slender stem, and it has long, grass-like leaves. Each blossom has 6 white tepals with a yellowish-green tinge. However, sand corm looks very different than death camas, for its **inflorescence is much looser and sparser and is more cylindrical than conical.** The individual flowers look quite different too, largely because of the stamens. In sand corm they stick way out of the flower and bear **bright yellow anthers,** while in death camas they tend to lie flatter and have creamy white anthers. Sand corm is less dangerous than death camas, but it is still **poisonous.**

Names: *Zigadenus:* see above. *Paniculatus* means 'panicled,' in reference to the branching inflorescence. **Where found:** dry flats often with sagebrush, open woods; e.g., along road paralleling Thomas Creek (6500') in June.

white • 6 tepals • May–July

FALSE SOLOMON'S SEAL
Smilacina stellata • Lily Family

You may have to do a bit of searching for false Solomon's seal because it often hides among tangles of willows or other shrubs alongside mountain streams. When you find it, however, you'll be glad you did, for it's a very attractive plant with interesting, lush leaves and delicate, intricate flowers. The **1–3' stem is sometimes straight but sometimes zigzags between the large (to 8"), clasping leaves**. These parallel-veined leaves are usually somewhat folded in. Out of the axil of the upper leaf rises a **1–6" loose raceme with 5–15 star-shaped ¹/₂" flowers**. The 6 tepals are bright white, contrasting with the yellow anthers. The small berries are green at first and turn red-purple or black.

Names: *Smilacina* means 'little *Smilax*,' which is another genus in the lily family. *Stellata* means 'star,' in reference to the 6-pointed flowers. The common name refers to the strange Star of David marking on the stem of a closely related European plant. **Where found:** also in Mixed Conifer Forest to 8000'. Wet areas along creeks, moist places around trees; e.g., along trail to Baxter Pass (7000') in June, and along the Thomas Creek trail (7500') in June.

white • 6 separate tepals • May–July

SEGO LILY
Calochortus bruneaunis • Lily Family

The *Calochortus* capital of the Sierra is the foothills of the western slope, which teem with yellow, white, lavender, and purple species in all sizes and textures. However, what the eastern Sierra may lack in diversity and number of species, it makes up for in beauty, for several gorgeous species make the eastern edge their home. Sego lily—the state flower of Utah—is certainly one of the most beautiful. The 8–16" stem bears a few grass-like leaves and 1–4 of the bright white (occasionally lavender-tinged) 1–2" flowers. **At the base of each petal is a large yellow splotch upon which is a purplish, spherical nectary. Above the nectary is a red-purple arch**. The 3 sepals also have a yellow splotch and a red-purple arch, but no nectaries. The long, slender anthers are red-purple, blue, or yellow. The 3-parted stigma is red.

Names: *Calochortus* means 'beautiful grass.' *Bruneaunis* refers to the area along the east Bruneau River in Idaho where the species was first described. **Where found:** also in Mojave Desert Scrub and in Mixed Conifer Forest to 10,000'. Sandy flats and slopes usually with sagebrush; e.g., west side of Topaz Lake (5100') in June, and above Onion Valley along the trail to Kearsarge Pass (9300') in July.

white • 3 separate petals • May–July

WRIGHT'S BUCKWHEAT
Eriogonum wrightii • Buckwheat Family

By late August and early September, most flowers of the Great Basin Sagebrush Steppe have finished blooming. Brown is a dominant color here this time of year as leaves and stems dry up and seedpods replace blossoms. There are some late bloomers, however, which are all the more appreciated for their scarcity. Although the flowers of Wright's buckwheat are not large or brightly colored, they put on a wonderful late-season show, for the plant is a **tangle of branching stems bearing many-flowered clusters of pink-tinged white flowers**. Though the 6 'petals' (actually sepals) of each 1/4" flower are mostly papery white, the flowers look pinkish because each sepal has a red midvein, the undersides of the sepals are often red tinged, and the anthers of the protruding stamens are red. The flower stems rise 4–12" above a **dense mat of small, grayish leaves**. The mat of leaves can be 2–3' in diameter.

Names: *Eriogonum:* see p. 47. Charles Wright was a 19th-century plant collector in the American Southwest. **Where found:** also in Mixed Conifer Forest to 9000'. Sandy or gravelly flats; e.g., along Route 89 east of Monitor Pass (6000') in September.

white (pinkish) • 6 petal-like sepals • August–September

DESERT EVENING-PRIMROSE
Oenothera caespitosa • Evening-Primrose Family

Coming upon a desert evening-primrose, especially at dusk, is a joy for the nose and for the eye. The **deliciously fragrant, bright white flowers can be up to 4" across.** The large (to 1' or so), narrow, irregularly toothed leaves form a basal rosette above which the many blossoms rise only a few inches. The stemless plants tend to grow in clumps. Though the enormous flowers are showy even before they open, they are spectacular at dusk when they open wide and fill the air with their sweet aroma. Each flower blooms for only one night, then withers in the light of the next day. Because the flowers turn pink or lavender as they wither, a plant with many flowers can put on a stunning evening show—**fresh, white, open blooms contrasting with drying pink or lavender flowers all on the same plant**. The several varieties of this species have different sizes of flowers and types of leaves (bottom photo shows smooth-leaved variety).

Names: *Oenothera* means 'wine-scented.' *Caespitosa* means 'in dense tufts.' Also called large white evening-primrose. **Where found:** Sagebrush Steppe to 7000'; also in Mojave Desert Scrub. Roadsides, washes, pinyon-juniper woodlands; e.g., along Whitney Portal Road in the Alabama Hills (4500') in April, and along Bishop Creek (5500') in June.

white (fading pink or lavender) • 4 separate petals • April–June

AMERICAN DOGWOOD
Cornus sericea • Dogwood Family

American dogwood is a plant of clean, crisp contrasts. The **broad leaves are rich, dark green, the new stems are deep red, and the large, round-topped clusters of flowers are bright white**. The 5–15' shrub is thick with the pointed, deeply veined leaves and is almost as thick with the showy, dense clusters of flowers. Although the individual flowers are small ($^1/_4$–$^1/_2$"), the clusters can  consist of scores of flowers and can be several inches across. • In some dogwoods, the showy parts are not actually petals but bracts. In American dogwood, however, the conspicuous (though small) white parts are true petals.

Names: *Cornus* means 'horn,' in reference to the hard wood of plants in this genus. *Sericea* means 'silky.' Also called red-stemmed dogwood or red-osier dogwood. **Where found:** also in Mixed Conifer Forest to 9000'. Wet areas such as streamsides, usually forming thickets; e.g., at creek crossing along trail to Baxter Pass (7000') in June.

white • 4 petals • May–July

HAIRY CAULANTHUS
Caulanthus pilosus • Mustard Family

Hairy caulanthus is a most conspicuous plant. The **stems can reach 3$^1/_2$'** in height and the seedpods, like those of most members of the mustard family, are large and showy. However, unlike some mustards, this plant is also conspicuous for its flowers. The **sepals are a rich, chocolaty, dark brownish-purple and form a $^1/_2$" urn** from which the 4 white (sometimes purplish) petals barely emerge. The flowers form a thick cluster at the tip of each stem and extend loosely at intervals down the stem for 1–2'. The 1–6" seedpods usually curve up from the ends of their $^1/_2$–1" pedicels. The leaves in the basal rosette are deeply cut (like dandelion leaves), while the stem leaves are usually narrow and uncut.

Names: *Caulanthus* means 'stalk flower,' in reference to the use of some species as a cauliflower-like vegetable. *Pilosus* means 'soft-hairy.' Also called chocolate drops. **Where found:** also in Mojave Desert Scrub and in Mixed Conifer Forest to 9000'. Dry, sandy flats, pinyon-juniper woodlands; e.g., along Whitney Portal Road above the Alabama Hills (5000') in June.

white (purplish) • 4 petals in cross • May–July

CUT-LEAF THELYPODIUM
Thelypodium laciniatum • Mustard Family

Mustards typically have conspicuous seedpods, and cut-leaf thelypodium is certainly no exception. The plant grows to 3¹/₂', of which as much as 2' can consist of the flower-crammed inflorescence! In bloom the flowers are definitely noticeable, if not showy, with their **narrow, twisted, white petals**. But in fruit the inflorescence becomes a **startling, ragged-looking spike thickly covered with long (to 4"), spreading, thread-like seedpods**. The large basal leaves and smaller stem leaves are usually pinnately lobed or toothed. Cut-leaf thelypodium is a biennial, so all this amazing flowering and fruiting occurs only in its second year of growth.

Names: *Thelypodium* means 'woman foot,' in reference to the appendage at the base of the ovary. *Laciniatum* means 'torn,' probably referring to the rather ragged appearance of the inflorescence when it's covered with hundreds of wiry seedpods. **Where found:** Sagebrush Steppe to 7500'. Rocky hillsides, gravelly flats; e.g., along dirt road paralleling Highway 395 just north of Bishop (4100') in June.

white • 4 separate petals • May–July

GRAND COLLOMIA
Collomia grandiflora • Phlox Family

Grand collomia is placed here in the white-flower section because the flowers often appear more or less white. You may, however, notice a tinge of something else in the petals—sometimes **a touch of pink or orange, sometimes more than just a touch of salmon**. Whatever the color of the flowers, the plant is very showy with a ¹/₂–3' stem topped by a **cluster of flaring, trumpet-like flowers**. The 1–2" flower tubes are narrow and yellowish, opening out into ¹/₂–³/₄", star-shaped bowls. The slightly protruding anthers are a beautiful light blue or turquoise. The leaves are narrow and alternate up the stem.

Names: *Collomia* means 'glue,' referring to the sticky surface of the seeds. *Grandiflora* means 'large-flowered.' Also called large-flowered collomia. **Where found:** also in Mixed Conifer Forest to 8000'. Dry, open slopes; e.g., above Grant Lake on June Lake Loop Road (7400') in June.

white (pink to salmon) • 5 petals united in tube • May–July

DESERT SANDWORT
Arenaria macradenia • Pink Family

Wispy stands of fragile flowers dancing in the breeze—the stems of desert sandwort are so narrow and wiry that they're almost invisible, making the flowers seem to float in the air without any earthly attachment. The ¹/₂" white flowers occur at the tips of the many-branched 8–16" stem, so there are many flowers per plant. At the center of each star-like flower is a glittering, greenish-yellow ovary and 10 delicate, radiating stamens. The leaves occur in opposite pairs along the stem but are so narrow (needle-like) that they are hardly noticeable.

Names: *Arenaria* means 'sand,' in reference to the typical habitat of many species. *Macradenia* means 'large-glanded,' in reference to the 2-lobed nectaries. **Where found:** southern and central Sagebrush Steppe; also in Mojave Desert Scrub. Dry, rocky slopes, sagebrush flats; e.g., along Big Pine Creek (5000') in June.

white • 5 separate petals • May–July

DESERT CEANOTHUS
Ceanothus greggii • Buckthorn Family

On a hot summer day, your nose may discover desert ceanothus before your eyes do. The **clusters of creamy white flowers exude a powerfully sweet fragrance** that can fill the air for quite a distance, especially if the plants are growing in dense thickets as they often do (see top photo). Desert ceanothus is a **shrub up to 6' tall with gray, spineless branches** and twigs. The gray-green leaves are small (¹/₂") and ovate or oblanceolate. Sometimes they are smooth-edged and sometimes slightly toothed. With their spreading, spoon-shaped petals and their protruding reproductive parts, the flowers have a fuzzy appearance, especially when they occur in dense clusters.

Names: *Ceanothus* means 'thorny plant,' which describes some other species in the genus. Josiah Gregg was a 19th-century frontier trader and author. Also called Mojave ceanothus. **Where found:** Sagebrush Steppe to 7500'; also in Mojave Desert Scrub. Dry slopes often with sagebrush, pinyon-juniper woodlands; e.g., great masses along the Sawmill Pass trail (6500') in May.

white (cream) • 5 petals • May–June

VARIED-LEAF PHACELIA
Phacelia heterophylla • Waterleaf Family

The stout ¹/₂–4' stem of varied-leaf phacelia bears leaves most of the way up, then ends in 6–18" of **tight, caterpillar-like flower clusters. The upper stem leaves are unlobed while the lower leaves usually have 2 lateral lobes at the base.** The bowl-like flowers are off-white, yellowish, or pale lavender. The reproductive parts stick way out, creating a fuzzy appearance. The buds look like little yellowish-white pearls. • Varied-leaf phacelia proliferates in disturbed areas and is considered a weed by some people, but its sturdy stem and curls of intricate flowers create a balance of strength and beauty that many find appealing.

Names: *Phacelia:* see p. 72. *Heterophylla* means 'different-leaved,' in reference to the different shapes of leaves on the upper and lower stem. **Where found:** also in northern Mixed Conifer Forest to 9500'. Dry slopes and flats, roadsides; e.g., along Mt. Rose Highway at the base of Mt. Rose (6500') in June.

white (to lavender) • 5 petals united in bowl • May–July

SPREADING DOGBANE
Apocynum androsaemifolium • Dogbane Family

Spreading dogbane is a **low** (¹/₂–1¹/₂'), **much-branched plant** that is thick with broad, **dark green leaves and clusters of** ¹/₄", **fragrant, urn-shaped flowers.** The petals are bright white, often with a tinge of pink. The reddish stems are stringy and tough, ideal for making rope. They are filled with milky sap.

Names: *Apocynum* means 'away from the dog,' in reference to the use of this plant by some cultures as a dog poison. *Androsaemifolium* means 'leaves like *Androsace*,' a genus in the primrose family. **Where found:** also in Mixed Conifer Forest to 8000'. Dry slopes, open woods; e.g., along Bishop Creek (5500') in June.

Related plant: Indian-hemp (*A. cannabinum*, bottom photo) has very similar white, urn-shaped flowers, but they usually have a slight greenish, rather than pinkish, tint. Indian-hemp is a much larger plant (to 6') with ascending pairs of broad leaves. Its range and habitat are similar to those of *A. androsaemifolium*, though Indian-hemp can also be found in Mojave Desert Scrub, e.g., in the Fish Slough area just east of Bishop (4200') in June. *Cannabinum* means 'hemp,' in reference to the use of this plant for high-quality fiber.

white (pinkish) • 5 petals united in urn • June–August

FIELD BINDWEED
Convolvulus arvensis • Morning Glory Family

Field bindweed can become a troublesome, invasive weed in cultivated fields and in the wild, but it does have beautiful, showy flowers. The **stems run along the ground, creating a tangled mat** thick with leaves and flowers. The **dark green leaves resemble fat, round-tipped arrows,** with flaring wings at the base. The **flowers are 1–1½", open, pleated funnels.** They are usually bright white but can be tinged pink or purple (bottom photo). Before the flower unfolds, the petals form a tight spiral like an unopened umbrella.

Names: *Convolvulus* means 'entwined,' in reference to the trailing and twining stems. *Arvensis* means 'of the field,' in reference to the tendency of this plant to become a weed in orchards and fields. **Where found:** Sagebrush Steppe to 5500'. Open fields, roadsides; e.g., along Route 88 from Minden to Woodfords (5500') in June. Alien.

white (pink or purple) • 5 petals united in funnel • May–July

PIUTE MORNING GLORY
Calystegia longipes • Morning Glory Family

In the same family as field bindweed (above) and quite closely resembling it, Piute morning glory has large (1–1½"), funnel-shaped flowers that are usually white but can be pink or lavender. Unlike field bindweed, which often crawls along the ground, Piute morning glory usually forms a **tangled, erect subshrub that can be 3½' tall.** In Piute morning glory the peduncles (leafless flower stems) are up to 8" long and bear only 1 flower, while in field bindweed 1 to several flowers sit atop a short (1–2") peduncle. Although the **leaves in both species are somewhat arrow-shaped, those of Piute morning glory are very narrow and pointed,** while those of field bindweed are broad.

Names: *Calystegia* means 'concealing calyx,' in reference to the large bracts of some species that enclose the base of the flower. *Longipes* means 'long-stalked.' **Where found:** Sagebrush Steppe to 5000'; also in Mojave Desert Scrub. Dry, rocky places; e.g., road along Big Pine Creek (4500') in April, and along dirt road to Baxter Pass trailhead (5000') in May.

white • 5 petals united in funnel • April–June

BLACK LOCUST
Robinia pseudoacacia • Pea Family

Sometimes you have to look up to see wildflowers. Black locust is a **tree** that can reach 50'. It bears **dense, hanging clusters of creamy white flowers**. The ¹/₂" blossoms are typical of the pea family, with an upright banner and 2 vertical wings cradling the 2 keel petals and the reproductive parts. All of the petals are white; the banner has a yellow-green splotch near its base. Even though the flowers are likely to be over your head, you will probably still smell a faint, sweet fragrance in the air. Find a way to get near these blossoms, for up close the **fragrance is magnificent**—deliciously sweet without being cloying. The leaves are divided into 9–17 usually opposite, oval leaflets 1–2" long. The branches have occasional short **spines**. The trunk is slender, grayish, and furrowed.

Names: Jean Robin was a 16th-century herbalist and gardener of the French court. *Pseudoacacia* means 'false *Acacia*,' another genus in the pea family. **Where found:** Sagebrush Steppe to 6000'. Wet areas along creeks, near abandoned houses (originally planted, now naturalized); e.g., along Whitney Portal Road in the Alabama Hills (4000') in April, and along creek near old homestead up Horseshoe Meadow Road (5500') in May. Alien.

white • 5 irregular petals • April–May

SPURRED LUPINE
Lupinus arbustus • Pea Family

It can be difficult to distinguish the many lupines in the Sierra with similar flowers and leaves. Most have blue flowers, so a plant with **white flowers** is easier to narrow down, but several species (including *L. arbustus*) can have white *or* blue flowers,  so even when you come across a white-flowered lupine, you may still have trouble identifying it. Spurred lupine is easier than most to identify because its flowers, as the name suggests, have a **distinctively spurred calyx,** i.e., the calyx looks like it has a sharp elbow. Spurred lupine can grow almost 3' tall and bears many of the palmately compound leaves typical of lupines. The 7–13 leaflets are narrow and often in-folded. The 1–10" inflorescences rise above the leaves, displaying many of the ¹/₂" flowers that are usually arranged in whorls (though they can sometimes be more haphazard). The back of the banner petal is usually hairy.

Names: *Lupinus:* see p. 74. *Arbustus* means 'like a small tree.' **Where found:** also in Mixed Conifer Forest to 10,000'. Dry slopes often with sagebrush; e.g., along trail to Baxter Pass (7000') in July.

white (yellow, blue, or purple) • 5 irregular petals • June–August

HOT-ROCK PENSTEMON
Penstemon deustus • Snapdragon Family

As with all penstemons, the flowers of hot-rock penstemon are tubular with the tube longer than the width of the flaring flower face. Hot-rock penstemon is unusual for a penstemon, however, in at least 2 regards: first, it is the **only white-flowered penstemon in the Sierra;** and second, the flower face on top of the 1/2–3/4" tube looks unbalanced because the **2 upper petals usually appear somewhat shriveled or curled back**. The 4–16" stems are woody and grow in clumps, so you will usually find little forests of this plant, each 'tree' thick with whorls of flowers and opposite pairs of toothed leaves. The entire plant is glandular and sticky to the touch. The white to yellowish flowers are lined with lovely maroon or red-purple nectar guides.

Names: *Penstemon:* see p. 71. *Deustus* means 'burned,' probably in reference to the upper 2 petals, which usually appear dried and brown tinged. **Where found:** also in northern Mixed Conifer Forest to 9000'. Dry, rocky slopes; e.g., along the East Carson River near Markleeville (5700') in June.

white (yellowish) • 5 petals united in 2-lipped tube
• May–July

BUCKSKIN KECKIELLA
Keckiella rothrockii • Snapdragon Family

Buckskin keckiella is a much-branched, leafy shrub 1–2 1/2' tall and usually at least as wide. There are so many stems, and the stems are so thick with small, opposite leaves, that the 1/2" flowers can be somewhat camouflaged. Be sure, however, to take a close look at these fascinating, beautiful flowers. They are distinctly 2-lipped, with the **3 petals of the lower lip reflexed, and the 2 petals of the upper lip forming an arching hood**. The 4 stamens and the 1 staminode (stamen with no anther) curve up under the hood. The petals, especially the back of the hood, are glandular-hairy. The **petals are white, cream, or pale yellow with eye-catching purple or reddish-brown stripes that are especially prominent on the lower lip**.

Names: David Keck was a 20th-century California botanist. Joseph Rothrock was a 19th-century professor of botany at the University of Pennsylvania. **Where found:** also in Mixed Conifer Forest to 10,000'. Dry slopes often with sagebrush, open woods; e.g., along the Sawmill Pass trail (5000') in June.

white (pale yellow) • 5 petals united in 2-lipped tube • June–July

HOREHOUND
Marrubium vulgare • Mint Family

Horehound is a rough-looking mint common to road-sides and other disturbed places. Its **1–2¹/₂' stem is stout and square and covered with white, matted hairs**. The leaves are easily recognizable as mint leaves, being roughly wrinkled, coarsely toothed, and arranged in opposite pairs along the stem. The ¹/₄–¹/₂" **white flowers cluster in dense, doughnut-like circles around the stem** in the leaf axils. Each flower has the typical 2-lipped mint form. In horehound the upper 2 petals are narrow and erect; the lower 3 petals are broader and lobed, forming a sort of lolling tongue or bib. The 4 stamens protrude. Neither the leaves nor the flowers are especially fragrant.

Names: *Marrubium* means 'bitter juice.' *Vulgare* means 'common.' **Where found:** disturbed places, roadsides; e.g., along Jack's Valley Road near Genoa (4800') in May. Alien.

white • 5 irregular petals • May–June

COMMON MALLOW
Malva neglecta • Mallow Family

Common mallow has such a delicately beautiful blossom for such a rough, weedy-looking plant. The ¹/₂–³/₄" flower is typical of the mallow family with its 5 separate, veined petals and its central column bearing both male and female reproductive parts. As with the genus *Sidalcea* (pp. 191, 192), the stamens make up the white, frothy-looking part of the column while the style is a delicate, thread-like structure that branches out of the top of the column. The **petals are white, pink, or pale lavender, usually with darker pink veins.** The ¹/₂–2', **hairy plant stem runs along the ground,** so the plant is usually only 1' or so tall. The rough leaf blades are on long petioles and are round in outline (1–3" in diameter). They are usually toothed and slightly 5–7 lobed. The flowers are on pedicels, which branch out of the leaf axils.

Names: *Malva* is the ancient Greek name for mallow. *Neglecta* means 'overlooked,' probably in reference to the plant's weedy nature. **Where found:** dry, sandy flats, disturbed places; e.g., along Route 89 near Markleeville (5500') in May. Alien.

white (pink) with pink stripes • 5 separate petals • May–June

COYOTE TOBACCO
Nicotiana attenuata • Nightshade Family

Although the common name and genus name are related to the nicotine content of this plant—this and other species were commonly gathered or grown by Native Americans for smoking, and *N. tabacum* is commercial tobacco—oddly enough the **flowers bear quite a resemblance to cigarettes. The 1" flower tube is very narrow, flaring only slightly at the tip into short petal lobes. The tube and lobes are white with a yellowish or greenish tint.** The flowers branch individually off the  upper 1' or so of the stem almost horizontally on short pedicels. There are many 1–4", obovate, pointed basal leaves and some smaller, narrower leaves up the 1–5' stem. • This plant and others in this genus are very **toxic** if eaten.

Names: Jean Nicot, a 16th-century French ambassador to Portugal, introduced tobacco into France in about 1560. *Attenuata* means 'coming to a point,' in reference to the leaves. **Where found:** also in Mixed Conifer Forest to 9500'. Dry slopes, disturbed places; e.g., along the Sawmill Pass trail (5000') in June.

white (yellowish or greenish) • 5 petals united in tube • May–August

PARISH'S YAMPAH
Perideridia parishii • Carrot Family

Yampah is quite common. It has tiny white flowers and at first glance **closely resembles several other Queen Anne's lace–type plants,** so there may be a tendency to overlook it. However, it can put on quite a show, covering meadows or hillsides nearly solidly with soft, breezy, bright clusters of cheer. Like almost all members of the carrot family, the individual flowers are tiny but the clusters of flowers (umbels) are large and dense. Parish's yampah, along with a few other *Perideridia* species, are unusual in the carrot family in having **very narrow, almost needle-like leaflets**. The stems can grow to 2' or so and bear only a few leaves and only 1 or a few rounded umbels of flowers.

Names: *Perideridia* means 'around the neck,' apparently in reference to the bracts under the umbels. Parish: see p. 71. **Where found:** also in Mixed Conifer Forest to 10,000'. Moist or drying meadows, open woods; e.g., along Route 89 near Monitor Pass (7000') in July.

white • 5 tiny petals • June–August

POISON HEMLOCK
Conium maculatum • Carrot Family

Although poison hemlock is a **very large plant (to 10'), with a thick, sturdy stem,** its **delicate, lacy, fern-like leaves and loose umbels of tiny white flowers** give it a gentle appearance that belies its deadly nature. This is the famous hemlock that killed Socrates; ancient Greeks used it to silence radical thinking by terminating the thinkers. All parts of poison hemlock contain alkaloids that are **extremely toxic** to humans and to animals. This plant often has rather ominous **purple spots or streaks on the lower part of the stem,** which can help distinguish poison hemlock from its many close relatives.

Names: *Conium* is the ancient Greek name for the genus. *Maculatum* means 'spotted,' in reference to the purple spots that are usually found on the stems. **Where found:** moist openings in woods, disturbed places; e.g., along Route 89 near Markleeville (6000') in July. Alien.

white • 5 tiny petals • June–August

BLEPHARIPAPPUS
Blepharipappus scaber • Composite Family

Despite its rather cumbersome name, blepharipappus is a particularly graceful and beautiful composite, displaying moderation in structure and subtlety in color. The $^1/_2$–$^3/_4$" flowerheads have **only a few ray flowers** (often 5 but ranging from 2 to 8) and only about 6–25 disk flowers. **Each ray flower has 3 broad, fanned-out lobes, with the middle lobe narrower than the other 2.** As a result, the rays look a bit like darting swallows or swifts with backswept wings. The flowers appear to have black speckles at the center, but close inspection will reveal these to be cylindrical, black anthers. Projecting out from among these anthers are **feathery, bristly, pink-purple styles.** The leaves of this much-branched plant are very small and narrow and occur along almost the entire length of the stem. The plants tend to grow in large clusters.

Names: *Blepharipappus* means 'eyelash pappus,' in reference to the feathery bristles on the seeds. *Scaber,* meaning 'rough,' refers to the short, sticky hairs on the stems and leaves. **Where found:** also in northern Mixed Conifer Forest to 10,000'. Open woods, grassy fields; e.g., along Route 89 near Markleeville (5500') in June.

white • 2–8 ray flowers and 6–25 disk flowers • May–August

OX-EYE DAISY
Leucanthemum vulgare • Composite Family

Each flowerhead of ox-eye daisy is like a whole bouquet by itself—**hundreds of bright yellow disk flowers crammed into a** ¹/₂–³/₄" **button surrounded by 20–40 radiating, bright white rays.** The dramatic **flowerhead can be up to 2¹/₂" in diameter.** And the plant is like a bouquet of bouquets because numerous 1–3' stems rise out of the same creeping rhizome, creating masses of these glorious, white-rayed flowers. Most of the spoon-shaped, toothed leaves are basal, though there are smaller leaves up the stem. • Ox-eye daisy is native to Europe and has escaped from cultivation in the U.S.

Names: *Leucanthemum* means 'white flower.' *Vulgare:* see p. 92. Formerly called *Chrysanthemum leucanthemum.* **Where found:** central and northern Sagebrush Steppe. Fields, roadsides, disturbed places; e.g., gravel bar along the East Carson River near Markleeville (5700') in June. Alien.

white • many ray and disk flowers • May–August

MUGWORT
Artemisia douglasiana • Composite Family

Mugwort, like its close relative big sagebrush (p. 107), is a conspicuous plant despite its **tiny** (¹/₈–¹/₄") **and undramatic flowers.** Unlike daisies and sunflowers and many other composites, mugwort and sagebrush have small flowerheads consisting of only disk flowers. Though the flowerheads in mugwort contain many flowers and there are many **white or pale yellow flower-heads** along the upper 1' or so of the 1–4' stem, they are still scarcely noticeable. It's the **leaves** rather than the blooms that catch our attention, for they are **powerfully and sweetly fragrant.** Early Native Americans (often imitated today) dried the leaves and lit them, creating a sweet smoke used in ritual cleansing and blessing ceremonies. Some of the leaves are narrow and unlobed, but some, especially those lower on the plant, are asymmetrically lobed. They are greenish on the top side and are covered with matted, white hair on the underside.

Names: There is some disagreement about which Artemis the genus was named after, whether goddess or queen. David Douglas was the 19th-century Scottish naturalist for whom Douglas-fir was named. **Where found:** Open slopes, wet areas such as streambanks; e.g., along the Tioga Pass road (7500') in September.

**white (yellow) • many disk flowers
• August–September**

WALLFLOWER
Erysimum capitatum • Mustard Family

Wallflower occurs along the entire length of the Sierra and across a wide elevation range, from sagebrush flats to alpine ridges. Wherever you find it, it may surprise you, for it is **one of the first flowers to bloom**. It's delightful to find this sturdy plant with its **bright yellow flowers** before most other plants have even sprouted; however, this precociousness does have its risks (inset photo). • The 1/2–3' stem bears several narrow leaves with smooth or toothed edges and a **dense, round-topped cluster of the showy 3/4–1" flowers** along its upper 6" or so. Sometimes another cluster or two of flowers branches off the upper stem. The 1–6" seedpods curve up gracefully.

Names: *Erysimum* means 'to help,' in reference to the medicinal uses of some species. *Capitatum* means 'with a head,' in reference to the rounded inflorescences. **Where found:** also in Mixed Conifer Forest and in Alpine to 13,000'. Rocky places, dry flats and slopes; e.g., along Whitney Portal Road above the Alabama Hills (6500') in May, along Mt. Rose Highway at the base of Mt. Rose (6000') in June, and along trail to Morgan Pass (11,000') in July.

yellow • 4 separate petals • May–August

TUMBLE MUSTARD
Sisymbrium altissimum • Mustard Family

Tumble mustard is a highly invasive weed with a clever and effective way of spreading its seeds. After the plant goes to seed and dries, it uproots and rolls in the wind, spreading seeds far and wide as it tumbles across desert or sagebrush flats. • Despite its weediness, everything about this plant's appearance is delicate and wispy. Its **tall (to 5') stem is very slender and much branched, its yellow flowers are tiny (1/4") and barely visible from a distance, and its stem leaves are divided into thread-like lobes**. It also bears larger, broader, pinnately compound basal leaves. The fruits are very slender and very long (2–4") pods.

Names: *Sisymbrium,* meaning 'diffuse,' refers to the slender, much-branched stem. *Altissimum* means 'very tall.' The common name refers to the tumbleweed nature of this plant. **Where found:** also in Mojave Desert Scrub. Roadsides and fields, disturbed places; e.g., lower part of the Sawmill Pass trail (4700') in June. Alien.

yellow • 4 separate petals • June–August

TALL EVENING-PRIMROSE
Oenothera elata • Evening-Primrose Family

Tall evening-primrose is indeed tall—and it's dazzling. The stout stem **can reach 8',** though 3–5' is more usual. The stem bears numerous long, narrow leaves and many **very large (2–4" across), wrinkled, yellow flowers.** During the peak of the bloom, you will probably find the many anthers and/or the long-protruding, 4-parted stigma **heavy with sticky, stringy, yellow pollen.** The flowers open at dusk and wilt the next morning, drying to a reddish or orange color. The stem and the sepals in bud are usually red or red tinged.
• For this and most other *Oenothera* species, go out at dusk not only to see the blooms open but to enjoy their wonderful, warm fragrance.

Names: *Oenothera:* see p. 84. *Elata* means 'tall.' **Where found:** also in Mixed Conifer Forest to 9000'. Moist meadows, roadsides; e.g., along Highway 395 near Washoe Lake (5000') in June, and along the Tioga Pass road (9000') in July.

**yellow • 4 separate petals
• June–August**

NORTHERN SUN-CUP
Camissonia subacaulis • Evening-Primrose Family

When you see the **bright yellow flowers of northern sun-cup lying in their bed of large, fleshy basal leaves,** you can appreciate the common name sun-cup, for the flowers look like little suns about to rise. And, unlike many members of the evening-primrose family, the flowers do 'rise' (i.e., open) in the morning rather than at dusk. Northern sun-cup is also unusual in having no stem. The 1/2–1" flowers bloom directly from a root crown, so the rather swollen-looking 'stem' you see is actually the inferior ovary that is characteristic of the family. With the ovary directly on the ground, the seeds certainly don't have far to go to get planted! The stigma is a green globe. The long leaves lie flat on the ground in a symmetrical rosette. Their petioles are usually red.

Names: *Camissonia:* see p. 47. *Subacaulis* means 'almost a stem,' referring to the plant's having no real stem but rather an inferior ovary that resembles a stem. **Where found:** moist, grassy meadows; e.g., Hope Valley (6500') in June.

yellow • 4 separate petals • June–July

LITTLE WIRY EVENING-PRIMROSE
Camissonia pusilla • Evening-Primrose Family

Although the **flowers of little wiry evening-primrose are very small ($^1/_8$–$^1/_4$") and the plant is only 4–8" tall,** this species is intriguing and will likely catch your eye. The linear leaves are gray-hairy, the wiry stems are usually red, and the flowers are bright yellow. When you look closely at a flower, you will notice the yellow, globe-like stigma typical of *Camissonia* species projecting slightly above the much smaller, yellow anthers. The inferior ovary, characteristic of the evening-primrose family, elongates into a very showy, narrow, cylindrical, red seedpod up to $1^1/_2$" long. When the flower goes to seed, the **petals shrivel and dry red, while the red sepals become reflexed**. As with many small plants, little wiry evening-primrose greatly rewards time and effort spent examining its structural and color intricacies.

Names: *Camissonia:* see p. 47. *Pusilla* means 'very small,' in reference to the flower. **Where found:** Sagebrush Steppe to 10,000'. Sandy flats often with sagebrush; e.g., along the Baxter Pass trail (6500') in May.

yellow • 4 separate petals • May–June

BITTERBRUSH
Purshia tridentata • Rose Family

Almost anywhere you find big sagebrush (p. 107) you will find bitterbrush. Both shrubs are common throughout the Great Basin and in dry parts of the western mountains. Bitterbrush is a **much-branched, 1–8' shrub with gray, glandular stems and many $^1/_2$", pale yellow or creamy white flowers**. Each flower has 5 spoon-shaped petals flaring out from a shallow bowl. Out of this bowl projects a thick cluster of about 25 stamens with bright yellow anthers. The flowers have a strong, **sweet, somewhat spicy fragrance**. The 3-lobed, mitten-like leaves are finely gray-woolly on the undersides and are intermixed with the flowers on the stems. • Bitterbrush must not be too bitter to animals, for it is an important food plant for deer, especially in winter. As with desert peach (p. 116), bitterbrush is often covered by tent caterpillar webs.

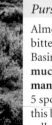

Names: Frederick Pursh was a German botanist who collected plants in North America in the early 19th century. *Tridentata* means '3-toothed,' referring to the 3-lobed leaves. Also called antelope brush. **Where found:** also in Mixed Conifer Forest to 9000'. Dry flats and slopes with sagebrush, openings in woods; e.g., along Mt. Rose Highway at the base of Mt. Rose (6000') in May, and along the Tioga Pass road (7000') in June.

yellow (creamy white) • 5 separate petals • April–June

BIRD'S-FOOT LOTUS
Lotus corniculatus • Pea Family

Bird's-foot lotus is a delightful little pea. Its stems usually run along the ground giving rise every now and then to a **3–12" leafless stalk that bears a whorl of 3–8 flowers at the tip**. Each ¹/₄–¹/₂" flower has a **broad, rounded, bright yellow banner** and 2 wing petals of the same color cupped like praying hands. The banner is sometimes red tinged and sometimes has red streaks at its base. The leaves of bird's-foot lotus are distinctive, growing on their own stalks with 5 narrow leaflets: 3 at the tip of the stalk (1 at the end and 2 at the sides) and a pair of opposite ones at the base of the stalk where it branches off the main stem. • This plant may be **toxic** because it produces cyanide-releasing compounds.

Names: *Lotus* is of uncertain meaning, though it may be derived from a word meaning 'to cover.' *Corniculatus* means 'horned,' probably in reference to the spiked calyx or to the pair of leaflets at the base of the petioles. Also called bird's-foot trefoil. **Where found:** also in Mixed Conifer Forest to 9000'. Dry flats, roadsides, disturbed places; e.g., along Route 89 near Markleeville (5500') in June, and along Bishop Creek (9000') in July. Alien.

yellow • 5 irregular petals • June–August

YELLOW SWEET-CLOVER
Melilotus officinalis • Pea Family

One of the many peas that have been introduced to the Sierra from Eurasia, yellow sweet-clover can take over meadows and roadsides, but it is really quite a beautiful plant with interesting flowers. Near the top of the 1–6' plant are several leaf stems, each bearing a palmately compound leaf with 3 toothed leaflets. Out of the axils where the leaf stalks join the main plant stem rise **slender, leafless stems each bearing a 2–6" spike of ¹/₈–¹/₄" reflexed flowers**. The **lemon yellow flowers are sweetly fragrant**, especially on hot days.

Names: *Melilotus* means 'honey lotus,' in reference to the flowers' sweet fragrance. *Officinalis*, or 'medicinal,' refers to the many uses of the plant in folk remedies. **Where found:** Sagebrush Steppe to 6000'. Dry flats and slopes, disturbed places; e.g., along Route 89 near Markleeville (5500') in June. Alien.

yellow • 5 irregular petals • June–July

WOOLLY MULLEIN
Verbascum thapsus • Snapdragon Family

Woolly mullein is probably known more for its leaves than for its flowers. The long (to 1¹/₂'), broad leaves almost completely conceal most of the length of the stem, but the most noted— and sometimes very appreciated—attribute is the soft, downy hairs on the leaves. It is these **plush, soft leaves that led some people to nickname this plant 'mountain toilet paper.'** The top 1' or so of this tall (to 6') plant is a **slender spike of many tightly packed, ¹/₂–1", yellow flowers**. The petals are thick and fleshy, and the upper 3 filaments are covered with white or yellow hair.

Names: *Verbascum* may mean 'bearded,' in reference to the hairy filaments. *Thapsus* was the name of an ancient Mediterranean town. The common name mullein comes from the Latin *mollis*, 'soft.' **Where found:** sandy or gravelly flats, disturbed places; e.g., along Bishop Creek (5000') in July. Alien.

yellow • 5 irregular petals • July–September

MOTH MULLEIN
Verbascum blattaria • Snapdragon Family

Moth mullein is very similar in growth form to its close relative woolly mullein (above), but **without the 'toilet paper' leaves**. The leaves of moth mullein are long and broad but lack the soft hairs. The lower part of the 1–4' stem is cloaked with leaves, but most of the stem is leafless and bears many of the ¹/₂" yellow flowers. Unlike woolly mullein, these flowers are not tightly crammed into the spike, but occur individually at intervals. The most noticeable and delicately beautiful feature of the flower is its stamens—the **filaments are densely covered by feathery, purple hairs**. • Moth mullein flowers open in the morning and usually wilt by afternoon.

Names: *Verbascum:* see above. *Blattaria* is derived from *blatta,* meaning 'moth.' The 'moth' references in the scientific and common names may come from the resemblance of the stamens and styles to the antennae and tongue of a moth, or they may refer to the attractiveness of this flower to moths. **Where found:** dry flats, disturbed places; e.g., along Highway 395 near Washoe Lake (5000') in July. Alien.

yellow • 5 irregular petals • July–August

GIANT BLAZING STAR
Mentzelia laevicaulis • Loasa Family

Giant blazing star is a perfect name for a plant with such an **enormous, dazzling flower—up to 6" across!** With its **pointed, satiny, lemon yellow petals and its dense cluster of long, up-curving, yellow stamens,** it really does look like a fiery sun blazing forth heat as well as light. The stout, white stem can be as tall as 4' and is dense with large (2–10"), triangular, ragged leaves that clasp the stem. The flowers occur only at the tips of branches and at the top of the main stem. The green sepals are narrow and pointed and show through between the petals.

Names: *Mentzelia:* see p. 57. *Laevicaulis* means 'smooth-stemmed,' in reference to the hairless, white stem. **Where found:** also in Mixed Conifer Forest to 9000'. Sandy or gravelly flats, washes, roadsides; e.g., Highway 395 at Topaz Lake (5000') in July, and the Tioga Pass road (8000') in August.

**yellow • 5 separate petals
• June–September**

WHITE-STEMMED STICKLEAF
Mentzelia albicaulis • Loasa Family

White-stemmed stickleaf does indeed have **white-felty stems and leaves that will stick to you,** but its alternative name, little blazing star, describes its even more noticeable feature—its **shiny, bright yellow flowers** that seem like intensely burning, satiny suns. The cluster of protruding, yellow reproductive parts and the often orange flower tube add even more brightness to the $^1/_4$–$^1/_2$" flowers. The 4–16" stems bear long (1–4"), strongly saw-toothed leaves. The flowers sit atop conspicuous cylindrical ovaries.

Names: *Mentzelia:* see p. 57. *Albicaulis* means 'white-stemmed.' The common name refers to the barbed hairs on the leaves that cling to almost anything. Also called little blazing star. **Where found:** also in Mojave Desert Scrub. Sandy or gravelly flats, washes, open woods; e.g., Route 89 between Markleeville and Monitor Pass (6000') in June, and Highway 395 north of Conway Summit (7000') in June.

Related plant: Nevada stickleaf (*M. dispersa*, bottom photo) has similar shiny, yellow flowers and a similar whitish stem. The leaves, however, are smooth margined or only slightly toothed. It has a habitat and range similar to that of *M. albicaulis*, e.g., along Mt. Rose Highway at the base of Mt. Rose (6000') in June. *Dispersa* means 'wide-spreading.'

yellow • 5 separate petals • March–July

FLOWER BASKETS
Mentzelia congesta • Loasa Family

With its 5 separate, shiny yellow petals, its clump of protruding, yellow stamens, and its orange flower tube, flower baskets is easily recognized as a *Mentzelia*. However, it does have a unique feature, to which its common name alludes, that distinguishes it from all other *Mentzelia* species. **Several of the ¹/₂" flowers are held within a 'basket' of toothed bracts** more or less fused together. These **papery bracts are white at the base and green at the tips** where the teeth are. The bracts and flowers are crowded together, so it is hard to see the cylindrical inferior ovaries typical of the *Mentzelia* genus. The 1–3" leaves are thick and usually lobed or toothed.

Names: *Mentzelia:* see p. 57. *Congesta* means 'crowded,' in reference to the several flowers within each cradle of bracts. **Where found:** Sagebrush Steppe to 9000'. Sandy slopes often with sagebrush; e.g., along the Sawmill Pass trail (6000') in May.

yellow • 5 separate petals • May–June

WESTERN SWEET-CICELY
Osmorhiza occidentalis • Carrot Family

Though western sweet-cicely is a tall plant (1–4') with large, rather rough leaves, the **loose umbels of tiny flowers** give it a delicate, lacy look. The **flowers are pale yellowish green,** giving the impression that they're not quite 'ripe'—that somehow they'll mature into a brighter yellow. The **leaves are pinnately lobed into (usually) five 1–4" saw-toothed leaflets,** with the largest leaflet at the tip of the petiole. The flower stalks project up above the leaves and branch into an umbel with 5–12 rays. The leaves and roots have a **soft anise fragrance.** The ¹/₂–1" fruits are narrow, pointed, and hairless (most *Osmorhiza* species have bristly-hairy fruits).

Names: *Osmorhiza* means 'sweet root,' referring to the licorice-scented roots. *Occidentalis* means 'western.' Also called sweet-anise. **Where found:** also in Mixed Conifer Forest to 9000'. Open woods; e.g., along the Thomas Creek trail (7000') in July.

yellow-green • 5 tiny petals • May–August

MOJAVE PRICKLY PEAR
Opuntia erinacea • Cactus Family

As with most cacti, the flowers of Mojave prickly pear are a startling contrast to the plant's ominous, spiny appearance. Whereas the flat pads bristle with **clusters of 5–12 long (to 5"), needle-thin, needle-sharp, whitish spines,** the **large (2–3" across), lemon yellow flowers** that perch on these pads have thin, **translucent petals** that seem almost liquid. It's as if pale yellow jellyfish settled on this cactus for a rest. The plant forms clumps up to 1½' tall and several feet wide. Most plants have yellow flowers that turn reddish with age, though occasionally you'll find plants whose flowers are red throughout the bloom. The large, green, globular stigma is surrounded by a cluster of yellow stamens.

Names: *Opuntia:* see p. 58. *Erinacea* means 'hedgehog-like.' **Where found:** Sagebrush Steppe to 7000'; also in Mojave Desert Scrub. Dry flats and slopes with sagebrush, open woods; e.g., along lower part of the Baxter Pass trail (6000') in May, and along Highway 395 near Walker (5400') in June.

**yellow (occasionally red) • many petals
• May–June**

YELLOW POND-LILY
Nuphar luteum • Waterlily Family

Yellow pond lily is a stunning flower, all the more so when it rises out of the murky, black waters of some stagnant, muck-bottomed pond. The flowers are about 2" wide and **yellow** all over: the **7–9 leathery, petal-like sepals that form the flower cup,** the many narrow petals mostly hidden by the many stamens, and the compound stigma forming the central disk-like structure are all the same yellow (sometimes red tinged). The leaves are almost as amazing as the flowers. They are **very large—to 1½' long and almost as broad—and heart shaped, with a waxy green surface. And they float!** On some ponds, the leaves almost completely cover the water, forming a shiny, green background for the many flowers rising a few inches above the water.

Names: *Nuphar* is an Arabic name for this genus. *Luteum* means 'yellow.' Formerly called *Nuphar polysepalum*. **Where found:** also in central and northern Mixed Conifer Forest to 8000'. Wet sites such as ponds, slow-moving streams; e.g., pond in Lundy Canyon (7800') in July.

**yellow • many petals and petal-like sepals
• June–August**

BALSAMROOT
Balsamorhiza sagittata • Composite Family

Balsamroot is one of the cheeriest plants of spring and early summer, bursting into full sunshine while most other plants are still remembering winter. The **flowerheads are up to 3" across and blaze a bright yellow.** They are usually solitary on their own 1–2' stems and seem to lean in the direction of the sun as if in friendly greeting. The **basal leaves boast 4–12", triangular or heart-shaped blades that arch out away from the plant** on 6–12" stalks. Although they are slightly gray-green from the soft hairs on their surface, these leaves are much greener than those of mule ears (below), a close relative and frequent companion with which balsamroot could be confused.

Names: *Balsamorhiza* means 'balsam root.' *Sagittata* means 'arrow-shaped,' a description of the leaves. **Where found:** also in Mixed Conifer Forest to 8500'. Dry slopes often with sagebrush, open woods; e.g., along Mt. Rose Highway at the base of Mt. Rose (6500') in May, and along the Tioga Pass road (7000') in June.

yellow • many ray and disk flowers • April–July

MULE EARS
Wyethia mollis • Composite Family

Mule ears is quite similar to balsamroot (above), but a bit bigger, a bit later-blooming, and quite a bit more plentiful in the northern part of our area. It has the same bright yellow flowerheads (to 4" across) and long (to 1¹/₂'), broad leaves, but after that the differences begin to show more than the similarities. The **leaves of mule ears are covered with matted, white hairs** and so are much grayer than the leaves of balsamroot; **the leaf bases taper smoothly to the stem,** rather than having a heart shape; and **the leaves are oriented vertically** instead of horizontally. **Mule ears can cover entire volcanic hillsides,** whereas balsamroot usually occurs only in patches. As well, the blooms of mule ears arrive on the scene a couple of weeks later than balsamroot's. These 2 bright composites often grow together, and during the time they both are in bloom they can fool you if you don't know what to look for.

Names: Nathaniel Wyeth was a 19th-century American explorer. *Mollis:* see p. 100. **Where found:** also in northern Mixed Conifer Forest to 10,000'. Dry, open hillsides (mostly volcanic); e.g., along Mt. Rose Highway at the base of Mt. Rose (6500') in June, with balsamroot.

yellow • many ray and disk flowers • June–August

KANSAS SUNFLOWER
Helianthus annuus • Composite Family

Kansas sunflower is a somewhat coarse plant that **can reach 7' tall**. It bears many broad leaves and **large (2–4" wide) flowerheads**. It's hard to believe that such a tall and robust plant with such sizable flowers could be an annual. Perhaps that's why the species name makes a special point of it! • The showy flowerheads have 15 or more bright **yellow, narrow, pointed rays surrounding a button of many reddish-brown or purplish (rarely yellow) disk flowers**. This button alone, about 1" across, is bigger than entire flowerheads of many other composites. The 4–8" leaves are broadly oval (or heart shaped) and slightly toothed. The leaves on the lower stem are in opposite pairs.

Names: *Helianthus* means 'sun flower.' *Annuus* means 'annual.' **Where found:** dry or moist flats, disturbed places; e.g., along dirt roads just north of Bishop (4100') in July.

yellow • many ray and disk flowers
• June–September

COMMON TARWEED
Madia elegans • Composite Family

Although this plant does not have a very promising common name, the epithet *elegans* is certainly more hopeful. And indeed, of the many showy yellow composites in the eastern Sierra, this bloom is one of the most elegantly beautiful. The ¹/₂–3' plant is usually thick with flowerheads, each of which is up to 1¹/₂" across. The **8–16 ray flowers look like many more than this because each ray is 3-lobed. The rays are bright yellow except for a red, orange, or purple splotch at the base. The disk flowers are yellow with black anthers.** As the common name suggests, the leaves and phyllaries are tacky-sticky.

Names: *Madia* is the Chilean name for tarweed. *Elegans* means 'elegant.' **Where found:** dry, grassy fields; e.g., along Route 88 near Minden (4700') in August.

yellow • many ray and disk flowers
• July–September

SINGLE-STEMMED GROUNDSEL
Senecio integerrimus • Composite Family

If you come across a rather **scraggly-looking yellow composite** that seems to have a few rays missing, you have probably come across a *Senecio*. If the phyllaries are black-tipped, you can be sure of it (though not all *Senecio* species have black-tipped phyllaries). Single-stemmed groundsel has **a single, stout 1–3' stem that rises above 2–10", spoon-shaped basal leaves** with long petioles. There are a few smaller stem leaves as well. A loose cluster of 6–20 flowerheads, each on its own stem and each only about 1/2" wide, tops the stem. The flowerheads consist of **8–13 narrow, widely spaced, yellow rays** surrounding a yellow disk. The rays often droop, giving the plant a bit of a tired look.

Names: *Senecio* means 'old man,' in reference to the white pappus. *Integerrimus* means 'complete' or 'entire,' probably describing the single stem supporting the cluster of flower-heads. The name groundsel means 'ground-swallowing,' in reference to these plants' tendency to spread rapidly. Also called tower butterweed. **Where found:** also in Mixed Conifer Forest to 10,000'. Meadows, open woods; e.g., along Mt. Rose Highway at the base of Mt. Rose (6500') in May.

yellow • several ray flowers • May–August

RAYLESS DAISY
Erigeron aphanactis • Composite Family

It's amazing sometimes how eye-catching and attractive composites can be even without their showiest attributes—their ray flowers. The 1/2" flowerheads of rayless daisy are like **shiny brass buttons,** all the more attention-grabbing for their contrast with the **white-hairy leaves and stems**. The stems are 3–10" tall and are covered with short, stiff, white hairs. The 1–3" tongue-like leaves are similarly attired. You will often find the flowerheads nodding before the disk flowers open.

Names: *Erigeron* means 'early old age,' in reference to the white-downy plants of some species (the idea being that they appear old even early in their life). *Aphanactis* means 'invisible,' probably in reference to the absent rays. The common name daisy derives from a Middle English word for 'day's eye.' **Where found:** also in Mojave Desert Scrub. Sandy or gravelly flats often with sage-brush; e.g., along west side of Topaz Lake (5100') in June.

yellow • many disk flowers • May–July

CURLY GUMWEED
Grindelia squarrosa • Composite Family

Curly gumweed has the name and the look of a rather unpleasant plant—it grows in disturbed sites and it has **hard, varnished leaves and flowerheads with stiff, prickly, hooked phyllaries**. To top it off, the **flowerheads are gooey with a thick, resinous gum**. It's no surprise to find that these plants are unpalatable to animals and so thrive where other plants (the competition) have been overgrazed. Despite all these less than alluring qualities, curly gumweed does have its charm. The varnished leaves and the sticky phyllaries often glisten in the sunlight, and the 1–2" flowerheads are like miniature suns: the 20–30 narrow, bright yellow rays radiate up at an angle from the tight yellow button of scores of disk flowers. Even before the bloom, the plant is worth a close look, for the spiny, hooked phyllaries create an interesting architecture with a satisfying symmetry.

Names: D.H. Grindel was a 19th-century Latvian botanist. *Squarrosa* means 'with parts spreading' or 'rough,' in reference to the short tips of the reflexed phyllaries. **Where found:** also in Mojave Desert Scrub. Roadsides, ditches, disturbed places; e.g., along back roads between Highway 395 and Kingsbury Grade (4700') in July. Alien.

yellow • many ray and disk flowers • June–October

BIG SAGEBRUSH
Artemisia tridentata • Composite Family

When you visualize the American West, big sagebrush is probably part of your picture, for it is the most abundant shrub in this area of the country. You can probably smell that sweet sagebrush fragrance now just by hearing its name. Big sagebrush is as dominant in the Great Basin Desert (Sagebrush Steppe) and in the northern Mojave Desert as creosote bush (p. 57) is in the southern Mojave Desert. In many places in the Great Basin you can find sagebrush plains with acres and acres nearly solid with this plant. It is the state flower of Nevada. • Among the several species of sagebrush, big sagebrush is distinct for its **silvery gray, hairy leaves, which are wedge-shaped and 3-toothed at the tip**. The plant can grow 7' tall in places with a little moisture, but it is much shorter in drier conditions. The narrow peduncle, up to 1' long, bears **many very small ($^1/_8$–$^1/_4$"), pale yellow flowerheads** comprising only a few inconspicuous disk flowers. The flowers bloom late in summer.

Names: *Artemisia:* see p. 95. *Tridentata* means '3-toothed.' **Where found:** also in Mojave Desert Scrub. Dry flats and slopes; e.g., along practically the entire length of Highway 395, blooming July through September or October.

yellow • 4–6 disk flowers • July–October

BUDSAGE
Artemisia spinescens • Composite Family

All species of sagebrush have rather inconspicuous heads of disk flowers, but budsage may have the least showy flowers of all *Artemisia* species. Its pale yellow flowerheads are small (¹/₄") and are somewhat obscured by surrounding leaves. The **clusters of flowerheads look a bit like small, yellow cauliflower heads nestled in beds of greens**. The plant too is small (¹/₂–2') but attractive, with its soft-hairy, palmately divided leaves, its white stems, and its yellow flowers. The **old flower-bearing branches become modified into stiff spines,** while the old bark becomes furrowed and shredded. • Budsage is a widespread and dominant plant through much of the Great Basin and Mojave Desert.

Names: *Artemisia:* see p. 95. *Spinescens* means 'spiny,' in reference to the stiff spines on the old branches. Also called spiny sagebrush. **Where found:** Sagebrush Steppe to 5000'; also in Mojave Desert Scrub. Sandy or gravelly flats usually with other shrubs; e.g., along the Goodale Creek road west of Aberdeen (4500') in April.

yellow • 2–10 disk flowers • April–May

DUSTY MAIDENS
Chaenactis douglasii var. *douglasii* • Composite Family

Dusty maidens is one of the many surprisingly showy rayless composites. Each ¹/₂" flowerhead consists of **many tightly packed, tubular disk flowers that are usually yellow but can be rose tinged or pure white** (bottom photo). Out of each narrow flower tube projects a cylindrical reproductive structure with the stamens at its base and the pistil at its tip. At first the top of the pistil is a straight thread; later in the blooming period it opens into a gracefully arching, 2-parted stigma. The ¹/₂–1¹/₂' stems and the **lacy, pinnately divided leaves are covered with gray, cobwebby hairs.** The entire plant is sticky and aromatic.

Names: *Chaenactis:* see p. 52. Douglas: see p. 95. Also called Douglas' pincushion. **Where found:** also in Mixed Conifer Forest to 10,000'. See p. 233 for an alpine variety of *C. douglasii.* Dry flats and slopes, open woods; e.g., along the Clear Creek road paralleling Highway 50 (5000') in May, and along Horseshoe Meadow Road (7000') in June.

yellow (pink or white) • many disk flowers • May–August

YELLOW SALSIFY
Tragopogon dubius • Composite Family

Salsify is dramatic in all its phases—bud, bloom, and seed. The bud is a long, bulging beak that eventually opens into a **2–3" flowerhead with many narrow, lemon yellow, pointed rays**. Adding to the spiky appearance of the flowerhead are the 8–13 green, **sharply pointed phyllaries that extend beyond the rays**. When yellow salsify goes to seed, it becomes an **enormous, feathery globe of parachuted seeds**. A close inspection of the flowerhead will reveal an intricate structure—red-brown anthers and thread-like, forked stigmas. The plant grows to 4' and has a few 8–20" grass-like leaves. • The flowerheads open in mid-morning and close again by afternoon.

Names: *Tragopogon* means 'goat's beard,' probably in reference to the white pappus. *Dubius* means 'doubtful,' which perfectly describes the meaning of this epithet! **Where found:** Dry flats, roadsides, disturbed places; e.g., along Route 88 near Woodfords (6000') in July. Alien.

yellow • many ray flowers • June–August

RABBITBRUSH
Chrysothamnus nauseosus • Composite Family

The most common and widespread of the many medium-sized, gray-green shrubs at the base of the eastern Sierra are various species of sagebrush (especially big sagebrush, p. 107) and rabbitbrush. These plants often create **acres of shrubby seas** where you have to look closely to find anything else growing. • Whereas the disk flowers of sagebrush are minute and barely noticeable, those of rabbitbrush are conspicuous and showy. Each **flowerhead of rabbitbrush consists of several ¹/₄–¹/₂", narrow, tubular, bright yellow flowers**. The leaves of both sagebrush and rabbitbrush are covered with gray, woolly hairs, but whereas big sagebrush leaves are distinctively 3-lobed, rabbitbrush leaves are narrow and unlobed. • Rabbitbrush **blooms in fall,** bringing splashes of gold to an otherwise mostly drab landscape. Even in winter, this plant can bring color to the high desert (top photo), for its dried flowerheads retain some of their yellowish tinge.

Names: *Chrysothamnus* means 'gold bush,' in reference to the yellow flowerheads. *Nauseosus,* or 'nauseating,' refers to the bitter leaves and stems. Also called rubberbush because of the high rubber content in the leaves. **Where found:** also in Mojave Desert Scrub and in Mixed Conifer Forest to 11,000'. Sandy flats and slopes, open woods; e.g., along Mt. Rose Highway at the base of Mt. Rose (6000') in September.

yellow • many disk flowers • September–October

SPINELESS HORSEBRUSH
Tetradymia canescens • Composite Family

Sometimes it seems that the dry flats and slopes of the Sagebrush Steppe are nothing but gray-green shrubs with brushy flowerheads of yellowish disk flowers. Not only are there many such species, but some of them, such as big sagebrush (p. 107) and rabbitbrush (p. 109) are extremely common and widespread. *Tetradymia* species are also **shrubs with flowerheads of yellow disk flowers,** but in the eastern Sierra they are much less common than sagebrush and rabbitbrush. • Whereas the flowers tend to dominate the plant in rabbitbrush, in *Tetradymia* species the **phyllaries may be more conspicuous than the flowers**. They form **long, swollen, gray-felty 'vases'** that contrast dramatically with the bright yellow flowers. These white vases are particularly noticeable and swollen-looking in this species of *Tetradymia*. As its common name indicates, spineless horsebrush is distinguished from other species in the genus (e.g., see p. 61) by having **spineless** stems.

Names: *Tetradymia:* see p. 61. *Canescens* means 'gray-hairy,' in reference to the leaves and phyllaries. **Where found:** also in Mixed Conifer Forest. Dry flats and slopes often with sagebrush, open woods; e.g., along Kingsbury Grade about 5 miles west of Highway 395 (6000') in July.

yellow • several disk flowers • July–September

GREEN EPHEDRA
Ephedra viridis • Ephedra Family

All of the plants in this book are true flowering plants (angiosperms), except this one. Plants in the ephedra family are gymnosperms—relatives of pines and junipers. Although the ephedras have no actual flowers, they do bear attractive **flower-like cones.** The shrubby plants have **jointed stems,** and at the stem joints (nodes), you will find **clusters of small (¼") cones as well as a pair of tiny, scale-like leaves,** which soon dry brown or black. Because the leaves are reduced to tiny scales, the green stems are photosynthetic. • Green ephedra is a 1½–4' shrub with green or **yellow-green, mostly erect, broom-like stems.** Male plants (shown in both photos) have 2–5 thick, yellow-green cones per node. Female plants have 2–6 narrower cones per node. • The antidepressant and decongestant drug ephedrine is derived from *Ephedra* species. A tasty tea can be made by boiling the stems.

Names: *Ephedra* is the ancient Greek name for horsetail (genus *Equisetum*), which *Ephedra* species resemble. *Viridis* means 'green.' **Where found:** Sagebrush Steppe to 7000'. Sandy flats usually with sagebrush; e.g., along the Goodale Creek road west of Aberdeen (4200') in April.

yellow cones • no petals • April–May

ASPEN ONION
Allium bisceptrum • Lily Family

Aspen onion is well named, for usually you'll find it in the damp soil **under aspen trees.** This is an unusual habitat for an onion—only a few species that occur in the eastern Sierra or the Great Basin grow in moist or wet places. • The flowers of aspen onion **range from pale pink to rose to lilac,** often with a streak of darker rose down the midvein of each tepal. There are typically 15–40 flowers in an umbel, and because the pedicels can be up to 3 times as long as the flowers, the umbel can be rather large and showy. There are usually **2 or more leaves,** which aren't quite as tall as the plant stem. Though they are the grasslike leaves typical of onions, they are unusual in that they **remain green throughout the bloom** (most onion leaves shrivel up before or as the flowers open).

Names: *Allium:* see p. 81. *Bisceptrum* means '2 scepters,' in reference to the pair of toothed appendages atop each ovary. **Where found:** also in Mixed Conifer Forest to 9000'. Wet areas along creeks, frequently in aspen groves; e.g., under aspens along creek near Silver Lake on June Lake Loop Road (7200') in June.

pink (rose or lilac) • **6 separate tepals**
• **May–July**

BLUE DICKS
Dichelostemma capitatum • Lily Family

If you have spent any time in the Sierra's western foothills in spring, you will probably be familiar with blue dicks, for it is common and widespread there on grassy slopes and flats. You may be surprised to find it on the east side of the Sierra growing on dry, gravelly flats with sagebrush; you may be even more surprised to learn that it occurs throughout the Mojave Desert! • The **slender 1–3' stem is topped by an umbel of 2–15 small (¹/₂"), pink-purple or blue-purple flowers.** Because the pedicels are very short, the flowers are usually crowded close together. **Under the umbel (enclosing it in bud) is a papery, purplish bract.** The 6 tepals flare out of a flower tube that is cylindrical and a bit pinched. The 2 (sometimes 3) basal leaves are long (6–16") and grass-like, though they often wither shortly after the flowers bloom.

Names: *Dichelostemma* means 'cleft garland,' in reference to the forked stamen appendages. *Capitatum* means 'head,' in reference to the tight umbel of several flowers. Also known as desert hyacinth. **Where found:** also in Mojave Desert Scrub. Gravelly flats often with sagebrush and other shrubs; e.g., lower part of the Sawmill Pass trail (4800') in April.

pink-purple or blue-purple • **6 tepals**
• **April–May**

DAGGER POD
Phoenicaulis cheiranthoides • Mustard Family

Despite its aggressive-sounding common name, dagger pod is a deliciously gentle-looking plant of subtle contrasts. The 1–6" tongue-like leaves, which form dense basal clusters, are covered with soft, gray hairs. Rising above these leaves are several 2–8" stems from which branch many ¼–½" flowers. The delicate pink (sometimes rose-purple) petals and the soft yellow, slightly protruding anthers provide a graceful complement to the pale green leaves. The common name refers to the **long (to 3"), sharp-edged and pointed seedpods that usually extend horizontally from the stem**. • Dagger pod is an early bloomer, one of the first to flower among the rocks of the Sagebrush Steppe.

Names: *Phoenicaulis* means 'visible stem.' *Cheiranthoides* means 'resembling *Cheiranthes,*' which was the former name for some species now included in *Erysimum* (wall-flowers), another genus in the mustard family. **Where found:** also in Mixed Conifer Forest to 10,000'. Rocky places; e.g., hills west of Bishop (5500') in April, and along the Thomas Creek trail (7000') in May.

pink (lavender) • 4 separate petals • April–May

HOLBOELL'S ROCK-CRESS
Arabis holboellii • Mustard Family

There are many species of *Arabis* in the eastern Sierra, all with small, 4-petaled flowers and long, narrow seedpods. Holboell's rock-cress is an especially lovely plant with beautiful flowers and intriguing seedpods. As do most *Arabis* species, Holboell's rock-cress has a dense cluster of basal leaves and smaller, less conspicuous leaves at intervals along the plant stem, although sometimes these hairy, gray-green leaves can extend thickly quite far up the ½–3' stem. The ½" flowers are a delicate pink-purple or rose. Unlike many *Arabis* species whose flowers and fruits are held upright or horizontally, the **pedicels of Holboell's rock-cress reflex soon after the flowers open, so the flowers spend most of their blooming hanging down close to the stem. The long (to 3") seedpods hang almost parallel to the stem**.

Names: *Arabis:* see p. 62. Carl P. Holboell was a 19th-century Danish ornithologist. **Where found:** also in Mixed Conifer Forest. Rocky places; e.g., along Highway 395 at Topaz Lake (5050') in April, and along the Thomas Creek trail (8000') in June.

pink • 4 separate petals • April–June

STANSBURY'S PHLOX
Phlox stansburyi • Phlox Family

The 'flames' of Stansbury's phlox burn bright in **pink, rose, and white, often with all colors on the same plant**. The **pinwheel flowers can be up to 1" across** flaring out of a very long (to 1¹/₂"), very narrow tube. The petals are slightly spoon-shaped and sometimes have slightly notched tips. The 4–12" stems are somewhat woody at the base and usually sprout from horizontal underground stems, giving the plant the appearance of a low, rounded shrub thick with flowers. The narrow leaves are deep green and hairy. • You will usually find this phlox growing up through other shrubs, but its dense display of bright flowers makes it extremely noticeable no matter how entangled it is with other plants.

Names: *Phlox* means 'flame,' probably in reference to the brightly colored flowers of many species. Cpt. Howard Stansbury led the U.S. Government survey of the Great Salt Lake area of Utah in 1850. This plant is sometimes considered the same as *P. longifolia*. **Where found:** also in Mixed Conifer Forest to 10,000'. Sandy slopes usually with sagebrush, open woods; e.g., along Mill Canyon Road west of Walker (5700') in May.

pink (sometimes white) • 5 petals united in pinwheel
• May–June

DEDECKER'S CLOVER
Trifolium macilentum var. *dedeckerae* • Pea Family

Dedecker's clover may be the most beautiful clover you will ever see. The **large flowerheads (to 1¹/₂") are densely packed with 10–20 flowers that range from pink to rose to white—often on the same flower**. The mixture of these soft colors is delightful; the **mop-head form of the flowerhead** (all the flowers are reflexed) is intriguing and a bit comical. The leaves consist of the 3 leaflets typical of clover, but the leaflets are unusually narrow, forming an upside-down T or Y. They are a deep green and are shallowly toothed. • With its fascinating form and delicious blend of colors, Dedecker's clover is truly a sight to see and admire. This plant is also **rare,** so count yourself fortunate if you find it.

Names: *Trifolium* means '3-leaved.' *Macilentum* means 'lean.' Mary DeDecker, an expert on the flora of the eastern Sierra Nevada, passed away in 2000. Her love of the flowers and her dedication to the eastern Sierra environment inspired many of us, and she will be sorely missed. **Where found:** also in Mixed Conifer Forest to 11,000'. Rocky slopes and rock ledges, open woods; e.g., along Horseshoe Meadow Road (7000') in June.

pink • 5 irregular petals • June–July

RED CLOVER
Trifolium pratense • Pea Family

Although red clover usually grows in disturbed places and has a rough, somewhat weedy look to it, its large head of bright red or red-purple flowers and its unusual leaves will certainly catch your eye. The hairy ¹/₂–2' stem bears several typical clover leaves with long petioles. Each leaf blade is divided into 3 elliptic, ¹/₂–1¹/₂" leaflets. What's **unusual about these leaflets is the white chevron marking across the middle.** The **1" flowerhead is ovoid and tightly packed with scores of ¹/₄–¹/₂", red-purple flowers,** looking a little like tiny spectators jammed into an amphitheater with closely tiered seats.

Names: *Trifolium:* see p. 113. *Pratense* means 'of a meadow.' **Where found:** northern Sagebrush Steppe. Grassy fields, roadsides, disturbed places; e.g., along Highway 395 just north of Coleville (5100') in June. Alien.

red • 5 irregular petals • May–July

HUMBOLDT RIVER MILKVETCH
Astragalus iodanthus • Pea Family

The eastern edge of the Sierra is replete with *Astragalus* species, many of them with flowers some shade of blue-purple or red-purple. These species can be difficult to distinguish when in bloom, but often become easier to identify once they go to seed. Humboldt River milkvetch is a prostrate plant with clusters of 10–25 pink-purple or whitish flowers at the end of each stem. Each leaf has 13–21 roundish leaflets arranged in 6–10 opposite pairs with 1 terminal leaflet. The leaflets are blue-green, softly white-hairy and blunt-tipped. The distinguishing characteristic of this *Astragalus* is the **odd seedpod.** It is yellow-green with red mottling, which isn't that unusual, but it is also **incurved to form the letter C or, in some cases, an almost complete circle.** In a genus with many unusual seedpods, those of the Humboldt River milkvetch still manage to stand out.

Names: *Astragalus:* see p. 66. *Iodanthus* means 'violet-flowered.' **Where found:** dry slopes usually with sagebrush; e.g., west side of Topaz Lake along Highway 395 (5050') in April.

pink-purple (violet) • 5 irregular petals • April–May

CASE'S MILKVETCH
Astragalus casei • Pea Family

Case's milkvetch has several attributes that distinguish it from the many other *Astragalus* species in the eastern Sierra. Although its **pink-purple banner with the white splotch** is quite similar to that of Humboldt River milkvetch (p. 114), its **wings and keel tips are quite different—white, not the same pink-purple as the banner**. The 4–16" plant is also distinctive in that it has wiry stems and **widely spaced, needle like leaflets**. The 1–2" swollen seedpods are bronze with red splotches and are straight or slightly curved, with a sharp beak. Clusters of 8–25 of the ¹/₂–³/₄" flowers branch off the ends of the gray-green stems, which have appressed hairs.

Names: *Astragalus:* see p. 66. E.L. Case was a 19th-century American plant collector who accompanied John Gill Lemmon (see p. 179) on several expeditions in Nevada. **Where found:** Sagebrush Steppe to 7000'. Sandy or gravelly flats, washes; e.g., along the Sawmill Pass trail (6500') in May.

pink-purple with white-tipped wings • 5 irregular petals • May–June

WILD ROSE
Rosa woodsii • Rose Family

Wild rose is a **shrub up to 6' tall that often forms thickets**. It is also one of the most sensuously stimulating of all the plants of the eastern Sierra. It delights the eye and nose and provokes the skin and tongue. What more could you hope for! • The flowers develop from deep rose torpedos when in bud (bottom photo) to 1¹/₂–2¹/₂" **crinkly-petaled blooms that vary in color from rose to pale pink**. The petals provide a lush background for the **dense cluster of yellow stamens and pistils**. The fragrance of these flowers is strong but delicately sweet. The stems, which usually have a few prickly thorns, are heavy with compound leaves that are composed of 5–9 toothed leaflets. The fleshy rind of the rose hip is a great source of vitamin C and is a real jolt to the taste buds.

Names: *Rosa* is the ancient Latin name for roses. Alphonso Wood was the 19th-century author of *Class-Book of Botany,* the first American book to use dichotomous botanical keys. Also called interior rose. **Where found:** also in Mixed Conifer Forest to 10,000'. Wet areas; with willows along creeks, damp places in open woods; e.g., along the Baxter Pass trail (6000') in June.

rose (pink) • 5 separate petals • June–August

DESERT PEACH
Prunus andersonii • Rose Family

The flowers and fruits of desert peach resemble those of its namesake, the domestic peach. The ¹/₂" bowl-shaped blossoms are a **pastel rose to pink color with clusters of delicate, protruding stamens with pale yellow anthers**. The fruits are like small (¹/₂"), dry, pulpy peaches. Desert peach is a **2–6' shrub with spine-tipped, white or gray branches**. The ¹/₂–1" oval leaves are a beautiful shiny green that provides a striking background for the colorful flowers, though sometimes the flowers cluster so thickly you can hardly see the leaves. The flowers are gently fragrant, as attractive to bees as to people. After the flowers have gone, you are likely to see these shrubs teeming with tent caterpillars.

Names: *Prunus* is the ancient Latin name of plum. C.L. Anderson was a physician and naturalist in Nevada and California at the beginning of the 20th century. **Where found:** also in Mojave Desert Scrub. Rocky slopes and flats, canyons, open woods, often with sagebrush; e.g., along Mill Canyon Road west of Walker (5700') in April, and along Mt. Rose Highway at the base of Mt. Rose (6000') in May.

pink to rose • 5 separate petals • March–May

ROSY PENSTEMON
Penstemon floridus • Snapdragon Family

When you first see rosy penstemon, you may not know whether to ooh and aah or break into laughter. It is a striking plant (1–4' tall) full of stunning flowers: **1¹/₂" tubes of a dazzling pink-rose color**. The flowers arch gracefully away from the main stem, usually in pairs or whorls, on short pedicels. The saw-toothed leaves are in opposite pairs on the lower stem; the upper 1' or so of the stem is devoted almost solely to the gorgeous flowers. This is definitely an ooh-and-aah plant! But when you look at the flowers closely, it's hard not to laugh because they look for all the world like blowfish or grinning walruses. The flowers are quite **potbellied** (though one variety of rosy penstemon is less inflated) and the **petals of the lower lip are often folded down,** making each flower look as if it wears a grin or pout.

Names: *Penstemon:* see p. 71. *Floridus* means 'full of flowers,' in reference to the long inflorescence. **Where found:** sandy or gravelly flats, open woods; e.g., along Big Pine Creek (7000') in June.

pink • 5 petals united in 2-lipped tube • May–July

OWENS VALLEY PENSTEMON
Penstemon patens • Snapdragon Family

The flowers of Owens Valley penstemon and the plant itself are smaller and more delicate than most of the other *Penstemon* species in the eastern Sierra. Off the slender 8–16" plant stem branch several short stems, each of which bears a **cluster of 3–5 flowers.** The **narrow ¹/₂" flower tube flares only slightly into a small face.** The flowers are **shiny red-purple or violet with small, yellow markings inside.** The blue-green leaves are the only aspect of this plant that isn't delicate. They are thick and fleshy and cluster at the base of the plant. There are a few smaller leaves without petioles up the stem.

Names: *Penstemon:* see p. 71. *Patens* means 'spreading,' probably in reference to the tendency of this species to put up several stems from an underground root crown. **Where found:** also in southern Mixed Conifer Forest to 10,000'. Sandy or rocky flats often among sagebrush, open woods; e.g., along Big Pine Creek (6000') in June.

red-purple • 5 petals united in 2-lipped tube • May–July

APPLEGATE'S PAINTBRUSH
Castilleja applegatei • Snapdragon Family

Of all the species of paintbrush in the Sierra, Applegate's paintbrush may be the most variable, both in appearance and in distribution. It has at least 4 recognized subspecies; it grows from low elevation to near timberline on both sides of the Sierra; it frequents sagebrush flats, open woods, and even rock ledges; and it varies in color from **bright red to orange to yellow (sometimes even on the same plant).** Throughout all this variability, however, a couple of aspects generally remain constant: the **edges of the leaves are wavy,** and the **entire plant is glandular-sticky.** The leaves are usually 3-lobed and the colored bracts are usually 3-lobed or 5-lobed, but sometimes the leaves and/or the bracts are unlobed.

Names: *Castilleja:* see p. 67. Elmer Applegate was a student of Oregon flora who died in the mid-20th century. **Where found:** also in Mixed Conifer Forest to 11,000'. Dry slopes, rock ledges, open woods; e.g., west side of Topaz Lake (5000') in April, and the sagebrush slope along Route 89 between Highway 395 and Monitor Pass (6500') in July.

red (orange or yellow) bracts • 5 petals united in 2-lipped tube • April–August

LONG-LEAVED PAINTBRUSH
Castilleja linariifolia • Snapdragon Family

One of several red paintbrushes of the eastern Sierra, long-leaved paintbrush is, as its name suggests, distinguishable by its **leaves**. They **are very narrow (almost needle-like) and quite long (to 3")**. They are usually folded or rolled inward and can have 2 or 3 lobes, though often they are unlobed. The colored bracts are usually red or red-purple, though they can be yellow. Unlike many paintbrush species, whose flowers are mostly concealed by the colorful bracts, in long-leaved paintbrush the **yellowish beak that is formed by the upper 2 petals is easily seen because it sticks out well beyond the calyx and the bracts.** • Long-leaved paintbrush, which grows to 3' tall, is the state flower of Wyoming. This makes 3 state flowers that frequent the Sagebrush Steppe of the eastern Sierra; see also sego lily (p. 83) and big sagebrush (p. 107).

Names: *Castilleja:* see p. 67. *Linariifolia* means 'leaves like *Linaria*,' which is the toadflax genus also in the snapdragon family. Also called Wyoming paintbrush. **Where found:** also in Mojave Desert Scrub and in Mixed Conifer Forest to 10,000'. Dry flats often with sagebrush, rocky slopes, open woods; e.g., the Alabama Hills (4000') in June, and along Bishop Creek (8000') in July.

red, yellow • 5 petals united in 2-lipped tube • June–August

COPELAND'S OWL'S-CLOVER
Orthocarpus cuspidatus • Snapdragon Family

Copeland's owl's-clover resembles a slender pine cone with colorful, overlapping scales. The 4–16" stem ends in a **spike of broad, rounded bracts with pointed, pink-purple tops**. Projecting out between the bracts, looking a bit like divers poised on the ends of diving boards, are the flowers. Whereas in their close relatives, the paintbrushes, the flowers are mostly atrophied and are usually mostly hidden by the bracts, in the owl's-clovers the flowers are relatively small but colorful and highly visible. In Copeland's owl's-clover, the 1/2" flowers consist of a **pink beak (the joined upper 2 petals) projecting above and beyond a swollen, white sac** (the lower 3 petals). The leaves are quite distinct from the bracts, being longer and much narrower. They are often reddish. It is not unusual to discover fields of Copeland's owl's-clover (top photo), especially on volcanic slopes.

Names: *Orthocarpus* means 'straight fruit.' *Cuspidatus* means 'with a sharp, stiff point.' Edwin Copeland was a 20th-century California authority on ferns. **Where found:** also in Mixed Conifer Forest to 9000'. Dry flats often with sagebrush, open woods; e.g., along Route 89 north of Monitor Pass (7000') in July.

pink to rose • 5 petals united in 2-lipped tube • June–August

DWARF MONKEYFLOWER
Mimulus nanus • Snapdragon Family

The monkeyflowers in the eastern Sierra and the adjoining high desert run the color gamut from yellow to pink to rose, purple, and scarlet. Dwarf monkeyflower blooms are **red-purple, but they are unusual for a monkeyflower in that the purple has a slightly bluish tinge to it**. Although its flowers are a fair size ($^1/_2$"), this plant is indeed a **dwarf, reaching only about 4" above the ground**. Its $^1/_2$–1" leaves tend to form clustered beds for the showy flowers. Providing a wonderful contrast and complement to the bluish-magenta petals are the 2 yellow ridges in the flower throat on a background of velvety rose-purple. If you love all sorts of purple, dwarf monkeyflower is the flower for you!

Names: *Mimulus:* see p. 67. *Nanus* means 'dwarf.' **Where found:** also in Mixed Conifer Forest to 8000'. Sandy or gravelly flats, open woods; e.g., along Route 88 below Carson Pass (7700') in July.

red-purple • 5 petals united in 2-lipped tube • June–August

STICKY YELLOW THROATS
Phacelia bicolor • Waterleaf Family

Sticky yellow throats and the alternative common name, trumpet phacelia, are wonderful descriptions of this lovely flower. The $^1/_2$" **yellow flower tubes flare out into broad pink or purple faces,** and these flower tubes (as well as the narrow, green calyx lobes) are covered with **glandular, sticky hairs**. As in most *Phacelia* species, the flowers are arranged in tight, coiled cymes at the tips of the 2–16" stems and their branches. The plants can spread horizontally several feet, producing dense patches of the beautiful, multicolored flowers. The leaves are pinnately compound and irregularly toothed or lobed.

Names: *Phacelia:* see p. 72. *Bicolor* translates as '2-colored.' Also called trumpet phacelia. **Where found:** also in Mojave Desert Scrub and in Mixed Conifer Forest to 11,000'. Sandy flats and slopes; e.g., in the Alabama Hills (4000') in May, and above Grant Lake on June Lake Loop Road (7400') in June.

pink or pink-purple • 5 petals united in tube • May–July

FLAX-LEAVED MONARDELLA
Monardella linoides • Mint Family

Flax-leaved monardella resembles its relative pennyroyal (p. 208), but it tends to be a taller plant (to 2¹/₂') and has quite a distinctive **silvery green hue to its stems and leaves** (the result of fine, appressed, silvery hairs). Like pennyroyal, the narrow, ovate leaves are in opposite pairs and have small, perpendicular, leaf-like structures at the base. The leaves are also strongly aromatic. At the tip of each stem is a 1–1¹/₂" head of many flowers cradled by a **cup composed of erect, ovate, papery bracts. These bracts are usually white or straw-colored, often with rose or purple tinges.** The flowers within are pink-purple, lavender, or white. The stamens protrude conspicuously.

Names: Nicholas Monardes was a 16th-century Spanish physician and botanist. *Linoides* means 'like *Linum*,' the flax genus, in reference to the similar leaves. **Where found:** also in southern Mixed Conifer Forest to 10,000'. Dry flats, pinyon-juniper woodlands; e.g., along the Sawmill Pass trail (5500') in June.

pink-lavender (white) • 5 petals united in 2-lipped tube • May–June

SHOWY MILKWEED
Asclepias speciosa • Milkweed Family

Showy milkweed is well named, for it is an imposing plant **2–6' tall** with large (to 1¹/₂"), spectacular flowers. The **tongue-like petals are pink or rose and are strongly bent back. Above these petals project 5 white to pink, curved horns** about as long as the petals. The long (to 8"), broad, felty leaves occur in opposite pairs along the full length of the stem. Even in bud the flowers are showy, looking like a bunch of pink, furry grapes. In fruit, the rough 3" pods are filled with flat seeds tufted with long, silky hairs. Many of us can remember childhood days helping handfuls of these seeds get airborne.

Names: *Asclepias* honors Asklepios, the Greek god of healing, in reference to the medicinal properties of some species. *Speciosa* means 'showy.' Also called pink milkweed. **Where found:** Sagebrush Steppe to 6500'. Grassy fields, roadsides; e.g., along Highway 395 just north of Bishop (4100') in July.

Related plant: Narrow-leaf milkweed (*A. fascicularis*, bottom photo) has similar flowers with reflexed petals, but the flowers are smaller and paler. Its leaves are very long and narrow and occur in whorls on the stem. The seedpods look like erect green beans. Narrow-leaf milkweed has a similar range and habitat as *A. speciosa*, e.g., Alabama Hills (4500') in July. *Fascicularis* means 'clustered.'

pink • 5 separate petals • May–July

COBWEB THISTLE
Cirsium occidentale • Composite Family

Cobweb thistle, like most thistles, is an imposing and even somewhat scary plant. Its stout
stem can reach 10' tall, though 5–6' is more
usual, and its 4–16" lobed leaves and the phyllaries beneath the flowerheads are tipped with
sharp spines. The stem has numerous branches,
at the ends of which are the **deep red flowerheads. These flowerheads are 1¹/₂" across and**
about the same high, so they appear squarish.
Most of the phyllaries stick out horizontally or
bend outward, resulting in an involucre that is
broader than the flowerhead above. The main
distinguishing feature of cobweb thistle is, as
the name suggests, the **silvery gray, felty, cobwebby covering over the entire plant except
for the flowers**.

Names: *Cirsium:* see p. 70. *Occidentale* means 'of the
West.' **Where found:** also in Mojave Desert
Scrub. Dry flats often with sagebrush, disturbed
places; e.g., along Highway 395 near Topaz Lake
(5100') in June.

red • many disk flowers • June–August

BULL THISTLE
Cirsium vulgare • Composite Family

All thistles are similar in that they have brush-
like flowerheads of long, tubular disk flowers;
spiny phyllaries under the flowerheads; and
large, lobed, spine tipped leaves. What can help
distinguish the many thistle species are the
shape and color of the flowerheads and the
shape and orientation of the phyllaries. Bull
thistle has **red-purple flowers that tend to fan
out a bit, creating a flowerhead that is more
mushroom-like than rectangular or square**.
The **phyllaries are small and narrow** (e.g.,
compared to the much bigger and thicker phyllaries of cobweb thistle, above) and tend to
curve up more than down or out. The leaves are
green and narrow and are tipped with fine
spines. The plant is typically 2–4' tall, though it
can reach 6' or so.

Names: *Cirsium:* see p. 70. *Vulgare:* see p. 92.
Where found: dry flats, disturbed places; e.g.,
along Highway 395 near Washoe Lake (5000') in
July. Alien.

red-purple • many disk flowers • June–August

YELLOWSPINE THISTLE
Cirsium ochrocentrum • Composite Family

Thistles are known for their rather nasty, spiny natures, but yellowspine thistle may be the nastiest, spiniest of them all! You can hardly see its thick, 1–3^1/$_2$', much-branched stem because it's cloaked in leaves that are almost more spine than leaf. The **white-felty leaves are armed with long, sharp, yellow spines that point in all directions**. The lower leaves can be up to 1' long, creating a spiny skirt for the plant; the much smaller upper leaves occur at intervals along the upper branches. Under the 1–1^1/$_2$" flowerheads are phyllaries whose **yellow spines stick mostly straight out**. **The flowers are pink or lavender or sometimes white**. Like the leaves, the stem is covered with a white, felty mat of appressed hairs.

Names: *Cirsium:* see p. 70. *Ochrocentrum* means 'yellow-spined.'
Where found: Sagebrush Steppe to 6000'. Dry flats, disturbed places; e.g., along the Sawmill Pass trail (5000') in May. Alien (from central U.S.).

pink (white) • many disk flowers • May–June

WILD IRIS
Iris missouriensis • Iris Family

Wild iris has gorgeous and complicated flowers that may take some careful examination to figure out. The largest (to 2^1/$_2$" long and 1" wide), showiest parts are actually the **3 sepals, which are a rich blue or blue-purple streaked with a network of white and yellow veins**. These are the outside parts that **hang down and out like the tongues of panting dogs**. The 3 petals, the erect structures inside the sepals, are usually paler blue or lilac and lack veins. Between the petals are 3 other conspicuous structures, the pistils, which arch over the stamens and spring up to an erect posture after picking up pollen from landing bees (or sometimes other pollinators). Each 1–2' stem bears 1 or 2 flowers. The grasslike leaves usually reach about as high as the flower, or sometimes higher. • Overgrazed fields are often thick with irises because cattle and sheep tend to leave these plants alone.

Names: *Iris* means 'rainbow,' describing the multicolored flowers. *Missouriensis* means 'of Missouri.' Also known as blue flag. **Where found:** also in Mixed Conifer Forest to 10,000'. Damp, grassy fields; e.g., along Highway 395 near Bridgeport (6500') in June, and grassy edges of Frog Lake on trail to Winnemucca Lake (9000') in July.

blue-purple (lilac) • 3 petal-like sepals and 3 petals • May–July

CAMAS LILY
Camassia quamash • Lily Family

Camas lily flowers are such a deep blue or blue-purple and **grow in such masses (sometimes acres) in wet meadows that you might mistake them for ponds or even lakes**. They bloom in early spring before much else has appeared, so the 'lakes' are nearly solid camas. From up close the 1–2" flowers may be still more beautiful, with their 6 narrow, pointed, **blue purple tepals, bright green ovary, and even brighter yellow anthers**. The buds are no less spectacular, glistening with an almost iridescent turquoise. The stems are 1–2' tall; the grass-like leaves are about as long.

Names: *Camassia* and *quamash* mean 'sweet,' in reference to the importance of the bulbs as a major food source for the Northwest Indians. **Where found:** northern Sagebrush Steppe. Wet meadows; e.g., Hope Valley (6500') in June.

blue-purple • 6 separate tepals • May–June

SILVER LUPINE
Lupinus argenteus • Pea Family

All lupines have distinctive, palmately compound leaves and racemes of irregular, pea-like flowers. In most species, including silver lupine, the flowers are blue with a splotch of white or yellow on the banner. Silver lupine is a **1–3' (occasionally up to 5'), bushy perennial**. The stems and leaves are covered with **appressed, silvery hairs,** giving the plant a silvery-satiny appearance. The compound leaves consist of 5–9 very narrow, somewhat in-folded, ¹/₂–2" leaflets. **Rising above the leaves are 2–10" racemes of many ¹/₂" blue-purple flowers**. The banner has a white or yellow central splotch often speckled with tiny, black dots. The back of the banner is usually silvery-hairy.

Names: *Lupinus:* see p. 74. *Argenteus* means 'silvery,' in reference to the appressed silver hairs covering various parts of the plant. **Where found:** dry sagebrush flats and slopes; e.g., along Mill Canyon Road west of Walker (5400') in June.

blue (blue-purple) • 5 irregular petals • May–August

INYO BUSH LUPINE
Lupinus excubitus • Pea Family

Inyo bush lupine is a typical lupine in most ways, with its palmately compound leaves and its long (to $1^{1}/_{2}'$) stalks of bluish, pea-like flowers whose banners have a patch of another color. However, it does have some characteristics that in combination help distinguish it from other *Lupinus* species you are likely to meet in the eastern Sierra: its $^{1}/_{2}"$ **flowers are more violet than blue,** the flowers usually occur in whorls, **the patch on the banner is bright yellow** (turning red-purple with age), and the plant is a **subshrub or shrub that is usually 2–3' tall but can reach 5' or more**. The flowers have a sweet fragrance. The seedpods are gray-silky and 1–2" long. The leaf blades are divided into 7–10 narrow leaflets.

Names: *Lupinus:* see p. 74. *Excubitus* means 'elbow out,' perhaps in reference to the deeply notched calyx. **Where found:** southern Sagebrush Steppe; also in Mojave Desert Scrub. Dry flats often with sagebrush; e.g., along road to Sawmill Pass trailhead (4200') in April, and lower Horseshoe Meadow Road (5000') in June.

violet (lavender) • 5 irregular petals • April–June

WINTER VETCH
Vicia villosa • Pea Family

Winter vetch is a **sprawling 2–5' vine** that forms tangles with the other 'weeds' in abandoned fields and other disturbed places. Calling it a weed might lead you to dismiss it as only an unpleasant intruder, but close inspection will show it to be an intriguing plant with charming flowers. Branching off the rough-hairy plant stem are several leaf stems, each bearing 12–18 narrow leaflets. Each leaf stem ends in a **tendril,** which you will usually find twined around some other plant. The flower stems rise out of the leaf axils and are crowded with many slender $^{1}/_{2}"$ blooms. There is a graceful elegance in the way these **flowers sweep down off one side of the stem**. Each flower is a delicious **blue-purple or violet,** often with tinges of red-purple or magenta toward its base.

Names: *Vicia* is the old Latin name for vetch. *Villosa* means 'soft-hairy,' in reference to the hairs on the stems and leaves. **Where found:** dry flats, disturbed places; e.g., along **Route 88** close to Woodfords (5000') in September. Alien.

blue-purple • 5 irregular petals • June–September

BECKWITH'S VIOLET
Viola beckwithii • Violet Family

Beckwith's violet, with its spectacular 1–1¹/₂" multi-colored blossoms, is one of spring's loveliest floral gifts. The flowers come in 2 types, each with its own dazzling color combination. The **upper 2 petals of both types are an amazing, velvety purple-maroon; the lower 3 petals are either blue-purple or white with purple veins**. The center of both types is white and yellow. To see a patch of Beckwith's violet with the 2 types of flowers intermingled is truly a stunning sight. These plants are only 2–8" tall, so the flowers are either on the ground or only a few inches above it. The leaves are deeply divided and somewhat fan-shaped.

Names: *Viola* is the ancient Latin name for violets. Lt. E.G. Beckwith led one of the Pacific Railroad surveys through northern Nevada. Also called Great Basin violet. **Where found:** also in northern Mixed Conifer Forest to 9000'. Dry flats usually with sagebrush; e.g., along the Thomas Creek trail (6500') in May.

blue-purple (white) and maroon • 5 petals united in tube • May–June

PURPLE SAGE
Salvia dorrii • Mint Family

The rocky high desert terrain, the miles of shrubs of purplish flowers, the **strong minty-sage fragrance**—all you need is a horse and an Old West attitude and you too can 'ride the purple sage.' Purple sage is a 1–2¹/₂' shrub with pale green, ovate leaves and flower stems bearing 1–3 whorls of the ¹/₂" flowers at intervals along the stem. The **calyx of the flowers is often red or red-purple, a dramatic contrast to the usually violet or blue-purple petals**. As in most mints, the petals emerging from the flower tube are irregular with the middle petal of the lower lip considerably larger than the others. This enlarged petal serves as a wonderful landing pad for bees. The pistil and the 2 stamens are slender and delicate and protrude from the flower tube, giving the flowers a wispy, slightly disorganized appearance.

Names: *Salvia:* see p. 74. C. Herbert Dorr was a 19th-century plant collector in the Nevada Territory near Virginia City. Also called Great Basin blue sage. **Where found:** also in Mojave Desert Scrub and in Mixed Conifer Forest to 10,000'. Dry, rocky flats and slopes, washes, rock outcrops, open woods; e.g., along lower part of the Sawmill Pass trail (4800') in May, and along the Baxter Pass trail (6500') in June.

violet (to blue-purple or rose) • 5 irregular petals • April–June

SELF-HEAL
Prunella vulgaris • Mint Family

Like some of the gentians (e.g., see p. 200), self-heal is a blue to violet floral gem that often hides in the grass of damp meadows. Its square 4–20" stem terminates in a strange, **1–2", red-purple 'pine cone' packed tightly with scale-like sepals.** The sepals are decorated with sparse, stringy white hair. Emerging from these sepals are the fascinating 1/2" flowers with the typical mint form: **2 erect upper petals (in this case united to form a sort of awning),** 2 lateral petals, and a larger lower petal. In self-heal, the **lower petal is a white or violet, fringed bib, while the 2 lateral petals are small, violet wings.** There are several opposite pairs of oval, toothed leaves along the stem. Just below the spike of flowers is an opposite pair of narrow, pointed, leaf-like bracts.

Names: *Prunella* is derived from a German word for 'quinsy,' one of many afflictions this plant has been used to treat. *Vulgaris* means 'common.' **Where found:** moist, grassy meadows; e.g., east side of Mt. Rose (7000') in July.

violet • 5 irregular petals • July–August

LOW PHACELIA
Phacelia humilis • Waterleaf Family

Low phacelia has small (1/4–1/2") flowers and the plants are 'humble'—**only 2–8" tall**—but there are many flowers on each plant crammed into **tight caterpillar-like cymes,** a feature typical of *Phacelia* species. With so many flowers per plant and often many plants growing together, low phacelia can **carpet large areas with its deep blue-purple flowers.** The narrow calyx lobes and the ovate, 1 1/2" leaves are covered with short, stiff hairs. The stamens, tipped with black anthers, stick out of the flowers, contributing to their overall fuzzy appearance.

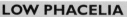

Names: *Phacelia:* see p. 72. *Humilis* means 'low.' **Where found:** dry flats often with sagebrush; e.g., along Mt. Rose Highway at the base of Mt. Rose (6500') in June.

blue-purple (violet) • 5 petals united in bowl • May–July

NOTCH-LEAF PHACELIA
Phacelia crenulata • Waterleaf Family

Although most *Phacelia* species have their flowers in dense, coiled cymes, few have such **dense and conspicuous cymes** as does notch-leaf phacelia: 1–3" long and crammed with scores of flowers. Usually these cymes are **curled at the tip and straight the rest of their length, looking a bit like furry sea horses!** The ¹/₂" pale blue petals sit atop the silvery-hairy, glandular sepals. The thin, blue or lavender stamens stick well out of the flowers, adding to the furry look of the plants. The **1–5" leaves are wavy edged and/or irregularly lobed**. The stems are usually reddish.

Names: *Phacelia:* see p. 72. *Crenulata* means 'minutely notched,' in reference to the leaves. **Where found:** Sagebrush Steppe to 7000'; also in Mojave Desert Scrub. Sandy or gravelly slopes; e.g., along the Sawmill Pass trail (5200') in May.

**blue (lavender) • 5 petals united in bowl
• May–June**

DESERT DWARF PHACELIA
Phacelia curvipes • Waterleaf Family

Of all the lovely blue-flowered or purple-flowered *Phacelia* species of the eastern Sierra, desert dwarf phacelia may be the most striking. Probably not at first, for the plant is small and lies almost flat on the ground, but when you look at it up close, it dazzles you with its interesting shapes and intense color. The 1–3" entire or lobed leaves are soft-hairy and frequently have a slight suggestion of purple edging. They usually rise up at an angle (sometimes nearly erect) from the ground. The ¹/₄–¹/₂" **flowers are at the ends of short pedicels and usually lie almost directly on the ground, sometimes partly concealed by the leaves**. The bowl-shaped **flowers are a dramatic contrast of colors: white in the center with intense blue-purple or violet petal lobes**. This is a plant and flower well worth getting on your hands and knees for!

Names: *Phacelia:* see p. 72. *Curvipes* means 'curved.' **Where found:** southern Sagebrush Steppe; also in Mojave Desert Scrub. Sandy or gravelly flats; e.g., lower part of the Sawmill Pass trail (4700') in April.

**blue-purple (violet) • 5 petals united in bowl
• April–May**

STAR LAVENDER
Hydrophyllum capitatum • Waterleaf Family

When you first see star lavender, you will probably see a thick cluster of leaves but no flowers. The 2–5", **deeply lobed leaves** either rise vertically (top photo) or hang horizontally, in each case **mostly concealing the globe-shaped clusters of flowers beneath**. The flowers may take some effort to find, but they are worth the search. The individual 1/4–1/2" bowl-shaped blooms are usually a pale purple or lavender with a bright green ovary and long, delicate, lavender stamens with black anthers. The **buds are round, fuzzy balls that look a little like a nest of tiny, cottony eggs**.

Names: *Hydrophyllum* means 'water leaf.' *Capitatum* means 'head,' in reference to the shape of the inflorescence. Also called cat's breeches. **Where found:** northern Sagebrush Steppe. Dry flats often with sagebrush; e.g., along Highway 50 east of Lake Tahoe near Spooner Lake (7000') in May.

blue-purple • 5 petals united in a bowl • May–July

HEAVENLY BLUE
Eriastrum densifolium • Phlox Family

Heavenly blue is a showy plant with striking yet delicate flowers. The plant is woody at the base, growing 1/2–2' tall and often several feet wide. It has a spiky appearance, but this is caused by the very narrow, needle-like leaves and bracts, not by any actual spines or thorns. The 1/2–1" flowers grow in dense clusters. The long flower tubes flare into 5-pointed stars with long-protruding, slender reproductive parts. The **stars can be deep blue but usually are a softer silvery blue with darker blue veins**. Even from a distance, and despite their soft hue, the blue-silver flowers will catch your eye, for they occur in dense patches and their color is unusual and intriguing.

Names: *Eriastrum* means 'woolly star.' *Densifolium* means 'thick-leaved.' Also called giant wool star. **Where found:** southern Sagebrush Steppe; also in Mojave Desert Scrub. Sandy or gravelly flats and slopes; e.g., along Horseshoe Meadow Road (5000–6500') in June, and along the lower part of the Sawmill Pass trail (5000') in June.

blue (silvery) • 5 petals united in tube • June–August

BLUE FLAX
Linum lewisii • Flax Family

Blue flax is an interesting mixture of solidity and fragility, of strength and delicacy. The 1–2¹/₂' **stems are slender but tough and wiry,** and the 1–1¹/₂" flowers make a strong statement in **deep sky blue or steely silvery blue,** yet the **petals fall off with the slightest touch** or whisper of a breeze. Each flower, then, is short-lived, but each stem bears many clusters of flowers that bloom at different times, so each plant is in bloom for several weeks. • Blue flax has 2 different types of flowers: one has long pistils and short stamens, the other short pistils and long stamens. Long pistils are compatible only with long stamens, and short pistils only with short stamens. Because all the flowers on any given plant are the same type, they must cross-pollinate with flowers on a plant of the opposite type. This adaptation, called *heterostyly,* prevents self-pollination and increases genetic variation.

Names: *Linum* means 'flax.' Meriwether Lewis, of the Lewis and Clark expedition, has many species and a genus named after him. **Where found:** also in Mojave Desert Scrub and in Mixed Conifer Forest to 11,000'. Dry slopes and ridges; e.g., along Route 88 near Woodfords (5700') in June.

blue • 5 separate petals • May–July

SQUAW CARPET
Ceanothus prostratus • Buckthorn Family

Squaw carpet forms **extensive leaf mats, sometimes several yards across, that gracefully flow along the contours of the ground.** The small (1"), stiff, prickly, **holly-like leaves** are woven so tightly together that usually no ground is visible through the mat. The leaves are adapted to hot, dry environments by means of their small size, waxy surfaces, and pores (stomates) present only on the undersides away from direct exposure to the sun. The flowers, typical of the buckthorn family, are rather strange with 5 spoon-shaped petals radiating out from a puckered center. The **deliciously fragrant, light blue or lavender flowers** give way to **deep red, fleshy, sectioned fruits** (inset photo) that are at least as striking and appealing as the flowers.

Names: *Ceanothus:* see p. 87. *Prostratus* means 'prostrate,' in reference to the ground-hugging growth form of this species. Also called mahala mat. **Where found:** northern Sagebrush Steppe. Dry flats, open woods; e.g., along Mt. Rose Highway near the base of Mt. Rose (6500') in May.

blue (lavender) • 5 petals united at base • May–June

ROCKY MOUNTAIN ASTER
Aster ascendens • Composite Family

Wherever we may be in the eastern Sierra, from the hottest, sun-scorched desert flat to the coldest, windswept alpine ridge, the showy, daisy-like composites (with their radiating rays and button-like disk) are there with us. They are our constant companions, soothing us with their familiar symmetry and cheering us with their bright exuberance. They really seem to love being flowers, holding nothing back in color or in form. Rocky Mountain aster is a prime example of this exuberance; the ½–2' plant is practically all flowers. **The narrow, toothed leaves are barely noticeable, so the many large (to 1½") flowerheads have the stage all to themselves. The delicate yet intense violet rays perfectly complement the bright yellow button of disk flowers.** The involucre under the flowerhead is covered with knobby phyllaries.

Names: *Aster* means 'star,' in reference to the star-like flowerhead. *Ascendens* means 'ascending,' in reference to the erect stems. **Where found:** Sagebrush Steppe to 6500'. Sandy or gravelly flats, disturbed places; e.g., along Highway 395 near Topaz Lake (5100') in August.

violet • many ray and disk flowers • July–September

BACHELOR'S BUTTON
Centaurea cyanus • Composite Family

Bachelor's button is a very attractive and unusual composite both for its color and for its form. Most composites are yellow, white, pink, or purple, but bachelor's button is very definitely blue. The 1½–2" flowerheads consist of **20–25 flaring, light blue to deep blue flowers that appear to be rays but turn out instead to be showy disk flowers.** The green phyllaries under the flowerheads are distinctively tipped with tiny, white or black teeth.

Names: *Centaurea* is the ancient Greek name for the genus. *Cyanus* means 'blue.' Also called cornflower. **Where found:** grassy fields, open woods, disturbed places; e.g., along Route 88 near Woodfords (5600') in June. Alien.

Related plant: Blue sailors (*Cichorium intybus,* bottom photo) is another blue composite. Many of the 1½–2", windmill-like flowers are clustered along the 1–3' stem. Blue sailors has only ray flowers and has dandelion-like leaves. It grows in similar habitats and elevations as bachelor's button, e.g., along Route 89 near Markleeville (5500') in August. *Cichorium* is an old Arabic name. *Intybus* means 'endive,' in reference to the use of the leaves in salads. Also called chicory. Alien.

blue • 20–25 ray-like disk flowers
• May–September

DAVIDSON'S FRITILLARY
Fritillaria pinetorum • Lily Family

Although Davidson's fritillary is very well camouflaged with its mottled flowers, when you find it, you'll marvel at its beauty and complexity. Several of the **1–1¹/₂" starfish-like flowers** cluster along the upper part of the 4–16" stem, which also bears 4–20 narrow leaves. Both the stem and the leaves are glaucous, i.e., covered with a fine, blue-gray film. Scrape off this film with a fingernail, and you'll see the green beneath. It's difficult to decide exactly what color the flowers are. They tend toward **yellow-green mottling at the center with brown-purple spots that turn to splotches and then solid color at the tips of the pointed tepals.** The arching 3-parted stigma is pinkish; the 6 large, tongue-like anthers are intense red. These amazing flowers sometimes extend more or less horizontally from the stem and sometimes are more erect.

Names: *Fritillaria* means 'dice box,' probably in reference to the checkered flowers. *Pinetorum* means 'of pine forests.' **Where found:** also in northern Mixed Conifer Forest to 10,000'. Dry slopes often with sagebrush, open woods; e.g., Agnew Lake trailhead on June Lake Loop Road (7200') in May.

brown-purple (yellow-green mottling) • 6 separate tepals • May–July

BROWN'S PEONY
Paeonia brownii • Peony Family

The blooms of Brown's peony are certainly beautiful, but perhaps 'startling' is a more appropriate adjective. The 1¹/₂–2" flowers consist of **5–10 rounded, brown-maroon petals** with yellowish edges surrounding a **dense cluster of bright yellow stamens.** In the center are 2–5 fleshy, green pistils. Under the flower (or actually over it, because the **flower hangs down from the end of its drooping stem**) are 5 stiff, brownish-purple sepals. As striking as the flowers may be in bloom, they are even more so in seed, for the pistils enlarge and enlarge until they're **2–4" swollen 'sausages'** (top photo). The weight of these amazing seedpods, even with the petals and stamens having fallen off the plant, is enough to pull the pods and sepals almost all the way to the ground. The large, smooth leaves are deeply lobed.

Names: *Paeonia* is derived from Paeon, Greek physician to the gods. *Brownii* is of uncertain origin, though it may honor Robert Brown, 19th-century Keeper of Botany at the British Museum. **Where found:** also in northern Mixed Conifer Forest to 10,000'. Sagebrush flats, open woods; e.g., above Red Lake along Route 88 near Carson Pass (8000') in June.

brown (maroon) • 5–10 separate petals • May–June

Mixed Conifer Forest

7500 – 11,500'

near Mammoth

wildflower meadow

high-elevation forest

Although the entire east side of the Sierra is drier than the west side, at the higher elevations on the east side the rainshadow effect is diminished. Winters bring heavy snows and summer afternoons are sometimes dampened by brief showers.

At about 7500' in the south and at about 6500' in the north, the open woodlands of drought-tolerant juniper and pinyon pine are replaced by denser stands of many of the same evergreen trees that grow on the west side. At these lower elevations of the Mixed Conifer Forest zone, you will encounter lodgepole pine, pondersosa pine, Jeffrey pine, cedar, white fir, and red fir. Although some species of sagebrush occur at these elevations, you have left behind the Sagebrush Steppe for the lush conifer forests.

The narrow stream-cut canyons of the lower elevations are now replaced by broad, glacier-carved, U-shaped canyons. Now you encounter the deep blue lakes, rushing streams, and glorious, open wildflower meadows for which the Sierra Nevada is famous. Sometimes these meadows are great masses of one color, but more often they are glorious, multicolored tapestries of various combinations of yellows, oranges, reds, pinks, blues, purples, whites, and greens.

Although in wet areas of the lower zones you can sometimes find lush gardens, it is here along creeks

above & opposite: Mosquito Flat

autumn's blossom

aspen forest near Conway Summit

high mountain meadow plants

foxtail pine along trail to Kearsarge Pass

and in soggy meadows in the Mixed Conifer Forest that you will encounter almost impenetrable wildflower jungles with rainbows of flowers on plants sometimes taller than you are.

It is also here in these wet areas that you will find great groves of aspen (often mixed with willow, alder, and cottonwood) that will ignite the landscape with yellow, orange, bronze, and gold flames in September and October.

For particularly dazzling fall colors, drive up any of the canyons to the west of Highway 395 in the Yosemite area, most notably Lundy Canyon, Bloody Canyon, and Tioga Canyon. In the north, drive west from Highway 395 toward any of the passes, e.g., Monitor Pass, Luther Pass, Carson Pass, Spooner Summit, and Mt. Rose Summit. Hope Valley and Spooner Lake (and Marlette Lake, which is a 5-mile hike from Spooner Lake) are especially dramatic. Aspen leaves are October's blossoms.

At about 9500' in the south and 8500–9000' in the north, the forest begins to thin a bit and the sky seems to draw closer. In this zone of subalpine forest you will continue to see lodgepole pine, but now you will meet some different trees—mountain hemlock, western white pine, and whitebark pine joined in the south by limber pine and foxtail pine.

As you approach timberline at about 11,500' in the south and about 10,500' in the north, the trees become stunted and gnarled until they are little more than wind-ravaged shrubs. This intriguing, bonzai-like growth form is known as *krummholz,* or *elfin forest.* Go just a little higher and you will leave the last of even these dwarfed trees behind, and you will enter the open and exposed world of the miniature alpine plants (next section).

Where and When to See the Flowers

July and August are the peak months for wildflowers of the Mixed Conifer Forest zone. Although Highway 395 reaches the lower parts of this zone in a few places, you will need to head west from the highway to experience this blooming in its full splendor. Here are some especially wonderful wildflower areas reached by paved road (listed south to north; see map on p. 29):

- along the upper parts of Horseshoe Meadow Road (off Whitney Portal Road from Lone Pine)

- Onion Valley (Market Street from Independence)

- Big Pine Creek (Crocker Road from Big Pine)

- Bishop Creek (West Line Street/Route 168 from Bishop)

- Mosquito Flat (the Rock Creek road from Tom's Place)

- June Lake Loop Road (Route 158, 6 miles south of Lee Vining)

- Tioga Pass (Route 120 from Lee Vining)

- Sonora Pass (Route 108, 17 miles north of Bridgeport)

- Monitor Pass (Route 89 from Topaz Lake)

- Carson Pass (Route 88 from Minden)

- Mt. Rose Highway (Route 431, 10 miles south of Reno).

Hanging Basket Lake near timberline

garden along trail to Winnemucca Lake

Minarets from Mammoth

west of Mosquito Flat

aspen trees in Lundy Canyon

Some of the most spectacular wildflower displays that require some—or a lot of—hiking include the trails to the following areas:

- Morgan Pass and Mono Pass (both from Mosquito Flat)

- Mt. Whitney

- Baxter Pass

- Sonora Peak (from Sonora Pass)

- Winnemucca Lake (from Carson Pass)

- Grass Lake (near Luther Pass)

- Mt. Rose.

Take a leisurely stroll or a strenuous hike or just wander a little from your car, and in mid-summer you can find sensational wildflower gardens all through the Mixed Conifer Forest zone.

McGee Creek, Crowley Lake

west of Mosquito Flat

high Sierra south of Yosemite

LEICHTLIN'S MARIPOSA LILY
Calochortus leichtlinii • Lily Family

A patch of Leichtlin's mariposa lily is a dazzling sight, for the flowers are not only large (1¹/₂–2¹/₂" across) but extraordinarily bright. The **silky, white petals** seem to glow even on the darkest day, and the yellow centers shine with a sunny cheer. The ¹/₂–2' stem is very slender and the 4–6" grass-like leaves wither early, so in the peak of blooming the flowers often seem to float above the ground. Although the shiny white petals are lovely, the markings and colors toward the center of the flower may be the biggest attraction. At the **base of each petal is a black-purple spot below which thick, stringy, yellow hair** covers the nectaries. In the center of the flower are 6 fascinating, **arrow-shaped, white anthers and a delicate, creamy, 3-branched stigma**. Leichtlin's mariposa lily is indeed a 'beautiful grass'—the kind of flower that almost makes you want to be a bee!

Names: *Calochortus:* see p. 83. Max Leichtlin was a 19th-century German horticulturalist. **Where found:** northern Mixed Conifer Forest to 11,000'; also in Sagebrush Steppe. Sandy or gravelly slopes, grassy fields; e.g., along Route 89 near Markleeville (5500') in June, and on the east side of Mt. Rose (9000') in July.

white • 3 separate petals • June–August

CORN LILY
Veratrum californicum • Lily Family

In late spring or early summer when you come across an open meadow still soggy from the recent snowmelt, the ground will be a checkerboard of bare ground and tips of new shoots. Many of these shoots will probably be grasses; most likely some (or many) will be corn lily. As the days pass, the corn lily shoots will emerge and enlarge, rapidly becoming **tightly wound bundles of large, deeply veined leaves** (top photo). If you return to this same meadow over the summer, you'll be amazed at how fast corn lily grows, eventually becoming a **stout 3–6' stem thick with huge leaves up to 1¹/₂' long and ¹/₂' wide and with many branches bearing an incredible number of 1" greenish-white flowers**. Since corn lily usually grows in masses, the resulting flower display can be truly astonishing. • Do not eat any part of this plant—the entire plant is **toxic** to humans and many animals.

Names: *Veratrum* means 'dark roots.' *Californicum* means 'of California.' **Where found:** Mixed Conifer Forest to 11,000'. Streambanks, wet meadows; e.g., along Mt. Rose Highway just below the pass (8500') in July, and along the Tioga Pass road (9500') in July.

white (greenish) • 6 separate tepals • July–August

WESTERN TOFIELDIA
Tofieldia occidentalis • Lily Family

If you tiptoe around the edges of a boggy meadow in mid-summer (being careful not to disturb the plants or the ground), you may be amazed at the density and variety of flowering plants. Many are tall and robust with large leaves and bright, showy flowers. Not all the floral treasures in this lush place are quite so flashy, however. In this flamboyant, raucous wildflower jungle, western tofieldia is a quiet breath of serenity. Western tofieldia is not tiny, growing 1–3' tall, but its 2–8" grass-like leaves are less conspicuous than those of most of its neighbors. Its **flowers *are* tiny** ($^1/_8$–$^1/_4$"**), forming 1–1$^1/_2$" tight clusters at the tips of the stems**. The **white tepals** continue the low-key theme, blending in with the background. The flowers do have **yellow anthers,** however, which provide a dash of zing.

Names: Thomas Tofield was an 18th-century British botanist. *Occidentalis:* see p. 102. **Where found:** Mixed Conifer Forest to 11,000'. Wet meadows, bogs; e.g., above Onion Valley on trail to Kearsarge Pass (9500') in July, and along trail to Morgan Pass (11,000') in August.

white • 6 separate tepals • June–August

SIERRA REIN-ORCHID
Platanthera leucostachys • Orchid Family

When you think of orchids, you probably visualize one of the enormous, sensuous, exotic flowers of the tropics. Sierra rein-orchid is certainly nothing like that image, but it does have its own subtle beauty. The stout stem (usually 1–2' though sometimes over 3' tall) ends in a **long spike packed with scores of flowers**. Each $^1/_2$" flower has **3 bright white sepals and 3 petals of the same color**. The upper sepal forms a sort of erect hood while the other 2 sepals form horizontal wings. The upper 2 petals are erect, bordering the hood, while the lower petal forms a protruding tongue. The back of this lower petal forms the $^1/_4$–$^1/_2$" **hanging, curving spur** that gives 'rein'-orchid its name. The largest of the plant's grass-like leaves are basal, and smaller leaves extend up the stem.

Names: *Platanthera* means 'wide anther.' *Leucostachys* means 'white spike,' referring to the inflorescence. Formerly called *Habenaria dilatata*. **Where found:** also in Sagebrush Steppe. Seeps, boggy meadows, streambanks; e.g., along the Tioga Pass road (8500') in July.

white • 3 petal-like sepals and 3 petals • July–August

NUDE BUCKWHEAT
Eriogonum nudum var. *nudum* • Buckwheat Family

Eriogonum is the largest genus in California, and many of its species in the Sierra are difficult to distinguish. Most have oval basal leaves and leafless or nearly leafless stems bearing umbels or heads of tiny flowers. In most species the flowers are white, off-white, or yellow. In all members of the buckwheat family, the flowers have no true petals—what appear to be petals are actually petal-like sepals. • Nude buckwheat has all these typical *Eriogonum* characteristics, but it is **taller than most other species (1–5')**, its **stems are blue-green,** its large basal leaves are dark green with long petioles, and its **spheres of tiny white flowers are tight and relatively small (¹/₂" across).** For all these reasons, nude buckwheat is easier than most *Eriogonum* species to distinguish, even though it has 13 varieties (see, for example, p. 53).

Names: *Eriogonum:* see p. 47. *Nudum:* see p. 53. **Where found:** also in Sagebrush Steppe. Sandy or gravelly flats, open woods; e.g., along the Tioga Pass road (8500') in July, and along trail to Gardisky Lake near Saddlebag Lake (10,000') in August.

white • 6 separate petal-like sepals • July–September

SPURRY BUCKWHEAT
Eriogonum spergulinum • Buckwheat Family

Spurry buckwheat is unusual for an *Eriogonum* in that the **flowers are borne individually rather than in umbels or heads.** The plants, though, tend to grow in masses, sometimes filling a field nearly solidly. The flowers are so small (¹/₈–¹/₄") and the stems are so slender that from a distance all you can see is a shimmering pink haze floating over the ground. When you get closer, you may be surprised to find that the 'petals' (actually petal-like sepals) are white. It is **these white sepals with the red stripe down the center, the red or orange anthers, and the reddish-brown stems that create the cloud of pink.** The stems can be 1¹/₂' tall but often are much shorter. The ¹/₄–1" leaves are narrow and basal.

Names: *Eriogonum:* see p. 47. *Spergulinum* means 'scatter net,' probably referring to the tendency of this species to grow in great masses, filling fields with a network of its slender, wiry, branching stems. **Where found:** sandy flats; e.g., around Frog Lake on trail to Winnemucca Lake (9000') in September.

white with red veins • 6 petal-like sepals • July–September

BREWER'S BITTERCRESS
Cardamine breweri • Mustard Family

Brewer's bittercress has a fresh, crisp look about it, with its thick, deep green leaves and its small (¹/₄–¹/₂"), **bright white flowers**. The fact that it **often has its 'feet' in standing water** (in boggy meadows or at the edges of creeks) probably contributes to this clean image. The ¹/₂–2' stem bears many flowers on short pedicels, followed by slender, ¹/₂–1", **cylindrical, nearly erect seedpods**. The leaves are distinctive with a **broad, terminal leaflet and 2 much smaller, lateral leaflets below**.

Names: *Cardamine* means 'heart subdue,' in reference to the medicinal qualities of some species. William Brewer was a professor of agriculture at Yale and the botanist on several expeditions in California in the 1800s. **Where found:** streambanks, seeps, boggy meadows; e.g., along the Tioga Pass road (8500') in July.

Related plant: Lyall's bittercress (*C. cordifolia*, bottom photo) has quite similar, though slightly larger, bright white flowers, but its leaves are different—rounded or kidney shaped and up to 4" wide. It occurs in similar wet habitats in the Mixed Conifer Forest but is limited to the northern parts of the zone; e.g., along the Thomas Creek trail (7000') in June. *Cordifolia* means 'heart-shaped leaves.'

white • 4 separate petals • June–August

SHIELDLEAF
Streptanthus tortuosus • Mustard Family

It is quite easy to understand why this plant was given its common names, for the amazing leaves do look like warriors' shields and the ¹/₂" flowers do resemble exquisite little jewels. The ¹/₂–3' stem bears several 'conventional' leaves (petioled and oblong) near its base, but the **upper stem leaves are very unusual and dramatic. They are 1–2" across, thick, and round and completely surround the stem as if they were large beads threaded on a necklace.** In the fall their impact is even greater, for they turn a dazzling bronze. Above the last of the shield-like leaves rises a 6–12" raceme bearing many of the rather strange flowers, each of which consists of **4 wavy, crepe-papery white, yellow or purple petals projecting from a swollen, vase-like purple, green or yellow calyx.** The superior ovary becomes a very long (to 6"), slender seedpod (silique) that arches gracefully off the stem.

Names: *Streptanthus* means 'twisted flower.' *Tortuosus* means 'much twisted,' also in reference to the twisted sepals and wavy, crinkly petals. Also called jewel flower. **Where found:** also in Sagebrush Steppe. Sandy or rocky slopes, rock ledges, open woods; e.g., along road to South Lake (8500') in July.

white (purplish or yellow) • 4 petals forming a cross • June–August

DIFFUSE GAYOPHYTUM
Gayophytum diffusum • Evening-Primrose Family

With all the large, showy flowers in the evening-primrose family (see pp. 168, 181, 182, 231), diffuse gayophytum is quite a surprise. Its **wiry, 1–12", branching stems bear tiny (¹/₈–¹/₄") flowers** that could easily be overlooked, especially early in the morning before they open. But these delicate 4-petaled flowers reward careful observation, especially over a period of several hours. There is a satisfying symmetry, not only to the cross-like arrangement of the petals, but also to the blooming cycle. The flowers start **deep red in bud, then turn to white in bloom, then fade back to red or pink in 'old age,' which is less than 24 hours!** The narrow leaves are scattered on the stem. The ¹/₂" seedpods are narrowly cylindrical and slightly knobby.

Names: Claude Gay was the 19th-century French author of *Flora of Chile. Diffusum* means 'spreading,' in reference to the branching stems. **Where found:** also in Sagebrush Steppe. Sandy flats, open woods; e.g., along Route 89 near Grass Lake (7700') in July.

white (fading pink) • 4 separate petals • July–September

DEER'S TONGUE
Swertia radiata • Gentian Family

Now this is an astonishing plant! Deer's tongue has a thick, hollow stem that can grow **up to 6' or even 7' tall.** Hundreds of big (1–2"), gorgeous, intricate flowers swarm over most of the length of this stem. Each flower has **4 greenish-white petals decorated with red-purple spots.** At the base of each petal is a **pair of roundish, pink nectar glands partly concealed by wispy white or pink hairs.** Adding to the drama is the swollen, green ovary in the center of the flower surrounded by fleshy, green stamens tipped with yellow anthers. The basal leaves are large (up to 1¹/₂' long and ¹/₂' wide); smaller leaves are in whorls high up the stem. With all this amazing size and intricacy, it may not surprise you to learn that it can take 2 or even 3 years of growth before the flowering stem is produced and that, after profuse blooming, the plant dies.

Names: Emmanuel Sweert was a 16th-century Dutch herbalist. *Radiata* means 'radial,' probably in reference to the radially symmetrical flowers, though it could also refer to the whorled leaves. Also called monument plant. **Where found:** Mixed Conifer Forest to 10,000'; also in Sagebrush Steppe. Dry flats, open woods; e.g., Onion Valley (9200') in July, and along trail to Winnemucca Lake (9000') in July.

greenish-white • 4 petals united in saucer • July–August

STEER'S HEAD
Dicentra uniflora • Poppy Family

When you discover steer's head in the high Sierra, you may forget where you are for a moment and imagine you are trudging across some remote desert in the blazing sun. Steer's head looks remarkably like the **sun-bleached skull of some unfortunate miniature steer** that perished in the desert heat and was left to bake for time immemorial. The inner 2 petals form the snout, and the outer 2 petals curve back to form the horns. Despite its riveting appearance, steer's head can be hard to spot. The ¹/₂" flowers are at the tips of 1–3' stems and so lie practically on the ground, where their pinkish-white color blends easily into their gravelly or rocky habitat. In addition, they bloom early in the season, perhaps before you're likely to be out botanizing. The leaves are lacy and are borne on their own stems.

Names: *Dicentra* means 'twice spurred,' in reference to the outer petals. *Uniflora* means 'single flower,' in reference to the single flower per stem. **Where found:** gravelly or rocky places; e.g., near Winnemucca Lake (9000') in June.

white (pink-tinged) • 4 petals • May–July

THIMBLEBERRY
Rubus parviflorus • Rose Family

Thimbleberry is a delicious-looking plant both in flower and in fruit. The 1–5' shrub has 3–12" wide, **maple-like leaves** and vivid 1–3" flowers. Its **petals are bright white,** creating a lovely counterpoint to the deep green leaves and the dense cluster of yellow stamens and pistils. The **petals are crinkled and curve up to form graceful bowls.** Often thimbleberry will form thickets under trees, creating a beautiful tangle of showy leaves and flowers. The fruit is no less beautiful and even more delicious—a red, raspberry-like thimble of juicy delight.

Names: *Rubus* is the ancient Latin name for bramble. *Parviflorus* means 'small-flowered,' which is puzzling, for the flowers of thimbleberry are among the largest of any *Rubus* species. **Where found:** Mixed Conifer Forest to 8000'. Thickets along streambanks, partial shade in woods; e.g., around Grass Lake (7700') in July.

white • 5 separate petals • June–July

MOUNTAIN STRAWBERRY
Fragaria virginiana • Rose Family

You are out walking in the woods and come to a small opening where the ground is slightly damp, and then you see, crowded together on the forest floor, **deep green and roughly toothed leaves with 3 leaflets**. You get excited, for you know right away that these are the distinctive leaves of mountain strawberry. You notice the pretty, 1/2–1", white flowers with clusters of yellow reproductive parts. You do appreciate their beauty, but to be honest you are happy that most of the flowers have already gone. You're salivating, you're searching, you're smelling a warm sweetness in the air. Then you see what you've been seeking; there they are, partially hidden under the leaves—**perhaps the lushest and sweetest of all the berries** of the eastern Sierra. You've found the succulent red berries of mountain strawberry, and you won't be leaving this spot for a while. Just be sure to leave some for the animals!

Names: *Fragaria* means 'fragrant.' *Virginiana* means 'of Virginia.' **Where found:** damp, grassy meadows, partial shade of woods; e.g., around Grass Lake (7700') in June, and along trail to Morgan Pass (10,500') in July.

white • 5 separate petals • May–July

STICKY CINQUEFOIL
Potentilla glandulosa • Rose Family

Several species and numerous subspecies of *Potentilla* grow in the eastern Sierra, and all have the typical *Potentilla* flowers—5 separate, rounded petals surrounding a dense cluster of yellow reproductive parts. All of these cinquefoils also have compound leaves, either palmately compound or pinnately compound. Most cinquefoils in our area have bright yellow flowers. Sticky cinquefoil is the only one that **consistently has white or pale yellow flowers**. The plant grows to 3' and has **pinnately compound leaves** with several pairs of toothed, opposite leaflets and 1 terminal leaflet. Only some subspecies of sticky cinquefoil are actually sticky.

Names: *Potentilla* means 'potent,' in reference to the medicinal qualities of some species. *Glandulosa* means 'glandular,' in reference to the sticky-hairy stems and leaves of some subspecies. The common name cinquefoil means '5-leaved,' in reference to the leaves of some species which have 5 leaflets. **Where found:** also in Sagebrush Steppe. Dry slopes, open woods; e.g., Mosquito Flat (10,230') in July.

white (cream or pale yellow) • 5 separate petals • June–September

DUSKY HORKELIA
Horkelia fusca • Rose Family

It's easy to see why this *Horkelia* is called *fusca*. Even though the **wedge-shaped petals are bright white, the clusters of flowers have an overall reddish-brown appearance**. The sepals are this dark color, and because only a few of the 5–30 flowers per cluster bloom at a time, the clusters usually have many unopened flowers whose sepals are on display. The 1/2" flowers have the 5 separate petals typical of the rose family. They also have the characteristic central cluster of reproductive parts, but this cluster is not as obvious as in most rose-family members, for the reproductive parts are small and do not stick out of the flower tube. The leaves are mostly basal and are pinnately compound with 10–30 feathery leaflets. The 1/2–2' stems are reddish and rise, nearly leafless, well above the basal leaves.

Names: Johann Horkel was a 19th-century German plant physiologist. *Fusca* means 'dusky,' in reference to the dark reddish-brown sepals. **Where found:** also in Sagebrush Steppe. Dry meadows, open woods; e.g., along trail to Gardisky Lake near Saddlebag Lake (10,000') in July.

white • 5 separate petals • May–August

MOUSETAIL IVESIA
Ivesia santolinoides • Rose Family

The 1/4–1/2" white flowers of mousetail ivesia are typical of the rose family, with rounded petals that are slightly separated and usually allow a glimpse of the sepals beneath, and with a central cluster of protruding reproductive parts. However, the stems and leaves of this plant are quite distinctive. The 1/2–2' **stems are extremely slender and much branched,** creating a delicate, wiry web on which the many flowers rest. If these stems are unusual, the leaves are extraordinary. As the name 'mousetail' suggests, **each basal leaf is so slender and so densely packed with tiny, overlapping leaflets that it really does look like a mouse's tail.** When you look at one of these 'tails' up close and try to count all the leaflets, you may be amazed—there can be as many as 160!

Names: There is some disagreement about the origin of the genus name. It may honor either E. Ives, a 19th-century pharmacologist at Yale University, or Lt. Joseph Ives, leader of the Colorado Exploring Expedition of 1857 and 1858. *Santolinoides* means 'resembling *Santolina*,' a genus in the composite family whose plants have similar pinnately divided leaves. **Where found:** Mixed Conifer Forest above 9000'; also in Alpine to 12,000'. Sandy or gravelly flats, rocky places; e.g., along trail to Kearsarge Pass (9500') in July.

white • 5 separate petals • July–August

BITTER CHERRY
Prunus emarginata • Rose Family

Bitter cherry can attain tree size (up to 30'), but much more often it is a **3–10' shrub that forms thickets** on dry hillsides. In the peak of its bloom, it can create a thicket you may not mind being ensnared by, for the many clusters of 3–12 flowers are strikingly beautiful and sweetly fragrant. Each ¹/₂" flower is lovely with its **clean white petals** and its fuzzy-looking cluster of long-protruding reproductive parts. The tongue-like **leaves are finely toothed and often folded inwards**. The stems are usually silvery gray, and the fruits are bright red cherries that look much better than they taste!

Names: *Prunus.* see p. 116. *Emarginata* means 'with a shallow notch at the tip.' **Where found:** Mixed Conifer Forest to 9000'; also in Sagebrush Steppe. Open scrub, rocky slopes, open woods; e.g., around Silver Lake on June Lake Loop Road (7200') in June.

Related plant: Western chokecherry (*P. virginiana*, bottom photo) has very similar flowers but instead of forming roundish clusters, they form long, narrow, drooping plumes. The fruits are edible, though astringent. Western chokecherry has a similar range and habitat as bitter cherry, e.g., along the Thomas Creek road (7000') in May. *Virginiana:* see p. 143.

white • 5 separate petals • May–June

DESERT SWEET
Chamaebatiaria millefolium • Rose Family

From a distance, desert sweet intrigues with its distinctive, lacy leaves; from up close, it fascinates and soothes with its intricate and inviting flowers. Desert sweet is a **1–7' shrub** that is thick with 1–3", **twice pinnately divided leaves that resemble miniature Christmas trees.** Each leaf has numerous 'branches' (leaflets), each of which bears many 'needles' (tiny leaflets). The 'branches' tend to be longest in the middle of the leaf, tapering off at the base and at the tip. The leaves are rough to the touch and are very **strong smelling when crushed.** Each ¹/₂" flower consists of **5 white, rounded petals surrounding a rose-colored center** that is rimmed by scores of slender, long-protruding stamens with yellow anthers.

Name: *Chamaebatiaria* means 'like *Chamaebatia,*' the mountain misery genus (also in the rose family), whose plants have fern-like leaves. *Millefolium* means 'a thousand leaves,' in reference to the finely divided leaves. Also called fern bush. **Where found:** Mixed Conifer Forest to 11,000'; also in Sagebrush Steppe. Dry flats frequently with sagebrush, rocky places, open woods; e.g., along Horseshoe Meadow Road (8000') in July, and along road to Mosquito Flat (9000') in July.

white • 5 separate petals • May–August

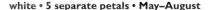

SERVICEBERRY
Amelanchier alnifolia • Rose Family

Although its flowers are 'only' white rather than some flashy rainbow hue, serviceberry blooms will probably grab your attention anyway, because of both their color and their form. They are a remarkably **clean, bright white, especially in contrast to the shrub's dark green leaves**. And although the flowers have 5 separate petals surrounding a central cluster of many reproductive parts (typical of the rose family), they have a bit of an odd, ragged look to them because all or some of the **petals are somewhat twisted**. Serviceberry is a shrub several feet tall with 1–2" leaves that are oval and slightly toothed and 1" flowers that grow in clusters. The deep blue fruits are edible.

Names: *Amelanchier* is the Latinized version of the old French common name. *Alnifolia* means 'alder-like leaves.' **Where found:** northern Mixed Conifer Forest to 8000'; also in Sagebrush Steppe. Open woods often with aspen, rocky places; e.g., along Route 88 east of Carson Pass (7500') in June.

white • 5 separate petals • May–July

PINE LUPINE
Lupinus albicaulis • Pea Family

Many species of lupine grow in the eastern Sierra, and many are tall and shrub-like. Although at first pine lupine might look like just another of the shrub-like species to you, close inspection will reveal some distinguishing characteristics. The 1–3' plants are thick with leaves, but the flower stalks rise ¹/₂–1¹/₂' above them, displaying the flowers in all their unobscured glory. The **flowers sometimes are in whorls around the stalk and sometimes are more haphazardly arranged**. The ¹/₂" flowers are **white** (sometimes blue-purple) with a yellow patch at the base of the banner. Unlike spurred lupine (p. 90), which is quite similar in many respects, the **calyx of pine lupine is not spurred**. The palmately compound leaves have 5–10 narrow, widely separated leaflets that are usually in-folded. The leaflets do not radiate all the way around the petiole—there is a noticeable gap at one point.

Names: *Lupinus:* see p. 74. *Albicaulis:* see p. 101. **Where found:** Mixed Conifer Forest to 10,000'. Dry slopes, open woods; e.g., along Route 88 above Red Lake just east of Carson Pass (8200') in June.

white (sometimes purple) • 5 irregular petals • June–August

CARPET CLOVER
Trifolium monanthum • Pea Family

As the specific epithet *monanthum* indicates, carpet clover is an unusual clover in that the **flowers grow singly, or in loose clusters of 2–6,** instead of in dense, many-flowered heads. As the common name suggests, the plant forms **thick, ground-hugging mats**. The 1/2" flowers are creamy white, though the tip of the keel and the banner petal are often tinged with purple or lavender. The 1/8–1/2" leaflets are oval and toothed and form the 3-leaflet clusters typical of clovers. Although the flowers can be rather hidden in the mat of leaves, carpet clover is delightful, for the leaf mat is lush and the flowers have a delicate charm.

Names: *Trifolium:* see p. 113. *Monanthum* means 'one-flowered.'
Where found: also in Sagebrush Steppe and in Alpine to 12,000'. Streambanks and seeps, wet meadows, open woods; e.g., along trail to Morgan Pass (10,500') in July.

white • 5 irregular petals • June–August

RICHARDSON'S GERANIUM
Geranium richardsonii • Geranium Family

Finding a meadow filled with Richardson's geranium is a real pleasure both for the 'forest' type of person and for the 'tree' type of person. These plants can create a pleasing floral landscape to enjoy from a distance, and they can offer intricate and beautiful details to the person willing to examine them closely. The 1–3' stems bear many 2–10", somewhat **maple-like leaves** with 3–7 pointed lobes. Each palmate lobe is itself lobed or toothed. Rising a little above this thicket of leaves are the pedicels with the showy 1–1 1/2" flowers at their tips. Careful inspection of the flowers reveals a **pale pink tinge** to the generally white petals, which are also streaked with dark red-purple veins. There are 10 delicate, often pink stamens. Look carefully at the stems and you will notice that they are covered with tiny, bristly hairs tipped with yellow glands. Whether you look with pattern-perceiving eyes from afar, or with discriminating eyes from up close, Richardson's geranium is pure delight.

Names: *Geranium* means 'crane,' in reference to the beak-like fruit. John Richardson was a 19th-century Scottish botanist. **Where found:** Mixed Conifer Forest to 9000', also in Sagebrush Steppe. Moist meadows, open woods; e.g., around Grass Lake (7700') in June.

white (pale pink) • 5 separate petals • June–August

BUSHY LINANTHUS
Linanthus nuttallii • Phlox Family

Although the individual flowers of bushy linanthus are quite beautiful with their **creamy white petals and cluster of bright yellow stamens,** it is the profusion of flowers on the ¹/₂–1' shrub that is the real show. This **round shrub can be several feet in diameter and can be almost completely covered with the ¹/₂" flowers.** To see one of these linanthus quilts draped over a hillside is a floral treat everyone should be fortunate enough to experience. The ¹/₂" leaves, as with all *Linanthus* species and many other members of the phlox family, are deeply lobed into needle-like segments that appear to be in whorls around the stem.

Names: *Linanthus:* see p. 49. Thomas Nuttall was a 19th-century naturalist and author. **Where found:** Mixed Conifer Forest to 11,000'; also in Sagebrush Steppe. Dry flats, open woods; e.g., Mosquito Flat (10,230') in July.

white • 5 petals united in tube • May–August

SPREADING PHLOX
Phlox diffusa • Phlox Family

Spreading phlox puts on a spectacular show, **carpeting the ground with mats of white, pink, or purplish flowers** (sometimes all 3 color variations are on the same plant). The flowers tend to start white and turn pink or purple after pollination. The ¹/₂–³/₄" blossoms are so profuse and closely packed that, during the peak bloom, you may not even realize that there are leaves and stems beneath the floral carpet. If you do find a gap in the flowers, you will discover that spreading phlox has ¹/₂" needle-like leaves and a thick, woody, prostrate stem. Each flower is a delicate pinwheel whose rounded petals flare out of a very narrow tube in which are nestled slender stamens with yellow anthers. • Spreading phlox is an **early bloomer,** reaching its peak before most of its neighbors regardless of whether it's growing in the Sagebrush Steppe or on a high Sierra ridge. The flowers are sweetly fragrant.

Names: *Phlox:* see p. 113. *Diffusa* means 'spreading,' in reference to the flowing mat growth form. **Where found:** Mixed Conifer Forest to 11,000'; also in Sagebrush Steppe. Dry flats, open woods; e.g., above Grant Lake on June Lake Loop Road (7000') in June, and along the Thomas Creek trail (9000') in June.

white (pink or lavender) • 5 petals united in tube • May–July

SLENDER PHLOX
Phlox gracilis • Phlox Family

In a family of plants whose flowers typically have long, narrow tubes, you might expect several other species to be called *gracilis*, but *Phlox gracilis* is the only one. It is an apt name for this flower, for the tiny ¹/₄" **star flares out of a very slender tube ¹/₈" or less in width and up to ¹/₂" long.** One of the identifying characteristics of slender phlox, however, is that you probably won't even see this **flower tube, for it's mostly concealed by the erect, prickly sepals that surround it.** As with many *Phlox* species, a close look at the blossom will reveal delicate and interesting coloration. Slender phlox has white or pink petal lobes flaring out of a yellowish tube that is filled with orange anthers. The **petals are usually notched.** The 2–8" plant can be much branched or simple. The narrow leaves are glandular-sticky.

Names: *Phlox:* see p. 113. *Gracilis* means 'slender.' **Where found:** Mixed Conifer Forest to 10,000'; also in Sagebrush Steppe. Grassy fields, sandy flats; e.g., along the Thomas Creek trail (7500') in May.

white (pink) • 5 petals united in tube • April–July

WHITE HEATHER
Cassiope mertensiana • Heath Family

If you wander among the granite boulders and slabs near timberline in the eastern Sierra, you may come across the marvelous bells of white heather. You may even find yourself wishing for a breeze so the bells will stir to music, for they look like they're right on the verge of song. White heather is a **low (4–12"), evergreen shrub that loves the rocks,** frequently finding shelter on rock ledges or in cracks. The **leaves are tiny, forming leathery, overlapping scales pressed tightly against the stem.** The resulting stems resemble tightly woven braids. The ¹/₄" **flowers are hanging, white bells** dangling from arched red pedicels. Between each bell and its pedicel are 5 narrow, red sepals, like 5 outspread scarlet fingers.

Names: Cassiope was the mother of Andromeda in Greek mythology. Franz Karl Mertens was a German botanist of the late 1700s and early 1800s. **Where found:** also in Alpine to 12,000'. Rock ledges and around rocks, moist subalpine meadows; e.g., along trail to Baxter Pass (10,000') in August.

white • 5 petals united in bell • July–September

LABRADOR TEA
Ledum glandulosum • Heath Family

Labrador tea is a 1–4' shrub that is thick with both leaves and flowers. There is a wonderfully satisfying symmetry to this plant, for both the flowers and the leaves are densely clustered. The **shiny, yellow-green leaves form graceful rosettes that perfectly complement the thick clusters of flowers**. Each ¹/₂" flower is white with a tinge of yellow-green, partly owing to the conspicuous ovary of that color. The 8–10 stamens stick way out of the flower bowls, giving the flowers and the clusters a distinctly fuzzy look. The leaves are finely white-hairy underneath. • **Rub a leaf** and you will discover that its shininess is the result of glands that emit quite a **strong fragrance**. The leaves have been used to make a tea, but this use should be avoided because concentrated doses are **toxic**.

Names: *Ledum* is the ancient Greek name. *Glandulosum* means 'glandular,' in reference to the sticky, aromatic leaves. **Where found:** also in Alpine to 12,000'. Boggy meadows, edges of ponds and lakes; e.g., above Mosquito Flat near Heart Lake (10,500') in August.

white (yellow-green) • 5 petals united in bowl • June–September

GREEN-LEAF MANZANITA
Arctostaphylos patula • Heath Family

This manzanita can be a delight or a curse, depending on whether you are on a leisurely outing to enjoy wildflowers or on a rigorous hike trying to push your way through its tangled shrubs. Green-leaf manzanita is a **1–3' shrub with very thick and hard wood**. It can form almost inpenetrable thickets on dry hillsides. The **stems, however, are a beautiful sleek and shiny red-purple**. The **oval leaves are bright green, thick, and stiff, and are often tipped up on edge like a rigid hand about to give a karate chop**. The ¹/₂", urn-shaped, white (sometimes pink-tinged) flowers form hanging clusters. The round, brownish fruits are tasty, though mealy. • Manzanitas are among the first plants to bloom in spring.

Names: *Arctostaphylos* means 'bear's grapes.' *Patula* means 'spreading.' The common name manzanita is Spanish for 'little apple.' **Where found:** Dry slopes, open woods; e.g., along Mt. Rose Highway (7000') in June.

Related plant: Pinemat manzanita (*A. nevadensis*, bottom photo) has smaller leaves and flowers. This low shrub sprawls across dry slopes and rocks throughout the Mixed Conifer Forest zone, e.g., along Route 88 below Carson Pass (8000') in June. *Nevadensis* means 'of the Sierra Nevada.'

white (pink tinge) • 5 petals united in urn • May–June

PINE DROPS
Pterospora andromedea • Heath Family

Coming across pine drops in the woods may catch you by surprise. It is a plant full of paradoxes and touched with mystery. Its **stem is tall (1–4') and stout,** yet its flowers are small ($^1/_4$") and gracefully droop off the stem. The white, puckered flowers seem pure and innocent like a first kiss, yet the **sticky, cold, clammy, red stem** seems far from innocent. You may not be surprised to discover that pine drops has **no green leaves,** choosing instead to feed off other plants. In fall, the now reddish-brown stems are heavy with their swollen seedpods. These stems often remain standing for years after the plants die, haunting the forests with their memories (photo at right).

Names: *Pterospora* translates as 'winged seed.' Andromeda was the daughter of Cassiope in Greek mythology. The 'pine' in the common name refers to this plant's typical habitat under pine trees. **Where found:** under trees; e.g., along Thomas Creek (7000') in July.

white • 5 petals united in urn • June–August

ROCK STAR
Lithophragma glabrum • Saxifrage Family

The 'music' from this particular rock star may be considerably more serene than that from most! The $^1/_2$" flowers gracefully branch off the plant's slender, wand-like, $^1/_2$–1$^1/_2$' stem. The flowers have a dainty look to them, for their **petals are soft white or pink and are delicately lobed into 4–7 fringe-like segments.** The leaves are mostly basal and are deeply lobed or palmately compound. In addition to the few (1–7) flowers along the upper part of the stem, you will often find **small, round, red, hairy bulbils** as well. These are a nonsexual backup method of reproduction—they will drop and sprout to form clones of the parent plant.

Names: *Lithophragma* means 'rock hedge,' in reference to the rocky habitats of many species. *Glabrum* means 'smooth,' in reference to the hairless leaves. **Where found:** also in Sagebrush Steppe. Gravelly flats, open woods; e.g., along road to South Lake (8000') in June.

white (pink) • 5 separate petals • June–July

SMOOTH GRASS-OF-PARNASSUS
Parnassia californica • Saxifrage Family

The flowers of smooth grass-of-Parnassus will definitely catch your attention, even though they usually grow along creeks and seeps where they are surrounded by many, more colorful neighbors. Only a single 1–1¹/₂" flower sits atop each ¹/₂–2' stem, so each blossom is displayed to its full advantage. The **flowers open widely, and the petals are a delicious creamy white with greenish veins.** There is a hint of soft greenish yellow at the center of the flower, which turns out to be **5 stamens that are without anthers but are delicately fringed. The other 5 stamens with anthers stick up out of the flower bowl.** The 1–2" basal leaves are round or elliptic.

Names: *Parnassia* refers to Mt. Parnassus in Greece, although *Parnassia* species don't grow there. *Californica* means 'of California,' where these plants do grow. **Where found:** creekbanks, grassy meadows; e.g., along the Tioga Pass road (8500') in August.

white • 5 separate petals • July–September

ALUMROOT
Heuchera rubescens • Saxifrage Family

It always amazes me to see the dainty **wisps of alumroot's tiny (¹/₄") flowers rising out of apparently solid rock.** These plants are adept at growing in the smallest cracks on even sheer rock walls, so you will often find the flower stems sticking out nearly horizontally. The petals are white, but the flowers have a pinkish look to them because the sepals are conspicuously red tinged. Even though the 6–12" stems bear many clusters of flowers, the flowers are usually not the first thing you notice about alumroot. The **leaves are much more dramatic—they are broad (1–2"), round, and scalloped.** Sometimes alumroot grows in large colonies, cloaking a rock ledge with dense masses of the showy leaves. Perhaps only after you recover from being stunned by the leaves will you notice the fragile sprays of flowers dancing in the breeze.

Names: Johann von Heucher was an 18th-century German professor of medicine. *Rubescens* means 'becoming red,' in reference to the pinkish tinge of the sepals and sometimes the petals. **Where found:** also in Sagebrush Steppe. Rock ledges, crevices in rocks; e.g., along trail to Baxter Pass (8500') in June, and along trail to Morgan Pass (11,000') in July.

white • 5 separate petals • June–August

BROOK SAXIFRAGE
Saxifraga odontoloma • Saxifrage Family

Brook saxifrage is one of the more difficult flowers to photograph, for the blossoms are small (¹/₄") and they dance in the slightest breeze. The slender, pliant plant stems rise ¹/₂–1¹/₂' above the basal leaves and end in a **much-branched, open panicle** that holds scores of flowers up to the vagaries of the wind. The flowers are intriguing and striking with their **stalked, fan-shaped, bright white petals, reflexed red sepals, and red anthers**. As in many species of *Saxifraga*, the fruit (enlarged ovary) is dramatically 2-beaked. The basal leaves are round or kidney shaped and scalloped with sharp teeth.

Names: *Saxifraga* means 'stone-breaker,' in reference to the rocky habitat of some species. *Odontoloma* means 'toothed,' in reference to the leaves. **Where found:** wet meadows, streambanks; e.g., around Frog Lake along trail to Winnemucca Lake (9000') in August.

white • 5 separate petals • July–September

BOG SAXIFRAGE
Saxifraga oregana • Saxifrage Family

Bog saxifrage is a typical *Saxifraga* in several ways: its leaves are basal; its flowers branch off a tall, leafless stem; its flowers are small (¹/₄–¹/₂") with white, spatula-shaped petals; and its ovary is split into 2 beaks that swell prominently when the plant goes to seed. However, bog saxifrage is easy to distinguish from other *Saxifraga* species primarily because of its **thick, fleshy, glandular stem**. In addition, its flowers are on very short pedicels, seeming to be attached directly to the main stem, and its **3–10", tongue-like leaves are not scalloped or toothed, but smooth edged**. As the common name suggests, if you are standing near bog saxifrage, your shoes and socks are probably getting wet!

Names: *Saxifraga:* see above. *Oregana* means 'of Oregon.' **Where found:** northern Mixed Conifer Forest to 8000'. Bogs, meadows, seeps; e.g., along the Thomas Creek trail (7000') in June.

white • 5 separate petals • June–July

TOAD-LILY
Montia chamissoi • Purslane Family

When you see one toad-lily flower, you are likely to see several, because toad-lily spreads by runners that stretch along the ground. If you look carefully down in the grass between the flowers, you can find these **slender, often reddish runners rooted every 1' or so**. The 2–12" stems rising from the runner bear opposite pairs of small, egg-shaped leaves and clusters of 2–8 flowers. Each ¹/₄–¹/₂" flower has **shiny white petals that glisten in the sun**. Protruding from the flower tube are **5 slender stamens tipped with red anthers**. As with almost all members of the purslane family, toad-lily has only 2 sepals forming a cup under the petals.

Names: Giuseppe Monti was an 18th-century Italian botanist. L.A. von Chamisso: see p. 47. Formerly called *Claytonia chamissoi*. **Where found:** also in Sagebrush Steppe. Seeps, wet meadows; e.g., along the Thomas Creek trail (7000') in June, and east of Saddlebag Lake (10,500') in September.

white • 5 separate petals • June–September

MAGUIRE'S CATCHFLY
Silene bernardina • Pink Family

As with most members of the pink family, the 5 petals of Maguire's catchfly are pinked, i.e., deeply lobed or fringed. However, **whereas in most *Silene* species the petals have only 2 lobes or have 2 larger lobes and 2 smaller lobes, in Maguire's catchfly the petals have 4 almost equal lobes**. These lobes are very narrow, creating a flower with a very delicate, fringed appearance. As in all *Silene* species, the calyx is a conspicuous cylinder out of which the petals flare into a flat pinwheel. This calyx tube is sticky-glandular and is marked by 10 prominent, red-purple, parallel veins. The ¹/₂–2' plant bears many 1–3" linear leaves in its lower parts and many ¹/₂" white flowers in its upper parts.

Names: Silenus was the constantly intoxicated foster-father of Bacchus, the Roman god of wine. This name and the common name catchfly refer to the sticky secretions of many species, most noticeable on the calyx. *Bernardina* is of uncertain origin; contrary to what you might guess, the species was not first described in the San Bernardino Mountains. **Where found:** also in Sagebrush Steppe. Rocky slopes, open woods; e.g., along trail to Kearsarge Pass (9500') in July.

white • 5 separate petals, each 4-lobed • June–August

MOUNTAIN CHICKWEED
Stellaria longipes • Pink Family

Mountain chickweed is one of those elusive flowers that seems to have magical powers of instantaneous propagation. You may have to get down on your hands and knees and part the grass to find a chickweed flower, but once you locate one, all of a sudden they seem to be everywhere! • This plant is only 4–12" tall and the flowers are ¹/₄–¹/₂", delicate, 10-armed stars. Although each of these 'arms' appears to be a separate petal, it turns out that chickweed has only 5 petals, each one very deeply 2-lobed. The tiny red anthers contrast deliciously with the bright white petals. The 5 triangular, green sepals are usually visible between the petals. The leaves are narrow and pointed.

Names: *Stellaria* means 'star,' in reference to the flaring petals and sepals. *Longipes* (see p. 89) refers to the long, slender peduncles. **Where found:** wet meadows, seeps, streambanks; e.g., along the Thomas Creek trail (7000') in June, and along the Tioga Pass road (8500') in July.

white • 5 separate petals (each 2-lobed) • July–August

TOBACCO BRUSH
Ceanothus velutinus • Buckthorn Family

Tobacco brush is a 3–6' shrub that can form extensive thickets on dry hillsides, often growing with whitethorn (p. 156) and the manzanitas (p. 150). Together these evergreen shrubs can almost completely blanket dry, open (often logged or burned) slopes, making it extremely difficult to walk off trail in these areas. • Tobacco brush has the clusters of small, fragrant flowers typical of *Ceanothus* species. The ¹/₄" flowers are a creamy white. Distinguishing tobacco brush from other *Ceanothus* species are the broad, shiny leaves that, when crushed, exude a powerful spicy fragrance. The fragrance and the shiny appearance are caused by a highly flammable oil that can greatly aid the spread of fire. This feature is adaptive because the plant depends on fire to germinate its seeds and kill off competing plants. Tobacco brush survives fires by having extensive root crowns just beneath the ground which can resprout quickly after the above-ground parts of the plant burn.

Names: *Ceanothus:* see p. 87. *Velutinus* means 'velvety,' in reference to the undersides of the leaves, which are covered with fine hairs. **Where found:** dry, open slopes; e.g., along Highway 50 near Spooner Summit (7100') in August.

white • 5 petals united at base • June–August

WHITETHORN
Ceanothus cordulatus • Buckthorn Family

Whitethorn is a **1–4' shrub that often associates with other fire-adapted, evergreen shrubs,** such as tobacco brush (p. 155) and the manzanitas (p. 150), on dry, sun-beaten slopes to form almost impenetrable thickets. This chaparral vegetation covers more than 10% of California, mostly in the western foothills but also extending into the Mixed Conifer Forest. • Whitethorn's clusters of small, white flowers are sweetly fragrant—small wonder plants in this genus are often called California lilac. The ¹/₂–1" leaves, like those of many *Ceanothus* species, are stiff and evergreen. As the common name suggests, a slope of whitethorn is especially difficult to negotiate, for most of its **branches end in sharp points.**

Names: *Ceanothus:* see p. 87. *Cordulatus* means 'somewhat heart-shaped,' in reference to the leaves, which are usually elliptic or ovate but can be a bit heart shaped. Also called snowbush. **Where found:** Mixed Conifer Forest to 9500'. Dry slopes, open woods; e.g., along the Tioga Pass road (8000') in June.

white • 5 petals united at base • May–July

MACLOSKEY'S VIOLET
Viola macloskeyi • Violet Family

Roses are red, violets are blue, but violets are yellow and even white, too! Macloskey's violet is the **only white violet in the Sierra,** though its ¹/₂" flowers do have touches of violet (actually more red-purple) in the showy veins on the middle petal of the lower lip. The 2 lateral petals of the lower lip are often bearded toward the base. The 1–5" plants spread by runners, forming thick patches of flowers in moist or wet areas. The broad leaves are round or kidney shaped. As do many of its relatives, Macloskey's violet hedges its bets with pollinators by producing a second bud-like flower that never opens but self-pollinates. This strategy, called *cleistogamy,* may not be very trusting and is certainly not conducive to genetic diversity, but sometimes you just can't rely on others when your very survival is on the line!

Names: *Viola:* see p. 125. George Macloskey was a professor of natural history at the College of New Jersey, Princeton. **Where found:** also in Sagebrush Steppe. Wet meadows, streambanks, seeps; e.g., edges of Grass Lake (7700') in July.

white • 5 petals united at base • June–August

BUCKBEAN
Menyanthes trifoliata • Buckbean Family

You'll have to slog into **very wet meadows or even into shallow ponds** to find buckbean, but it will be worth temporary sogginess, for the flowers are fascinating and strikingly beautiful. The 1/2–1 1/2' stem ends in a raceme of many of the 1/2–1", bright and shiny white flowers. The buds and sometimes the petals are pink-tipped. The most striking aspect of the flowers is their **elegant, fringed appearance created by thread-like, erect, white hairs that line the top side of the petals.** The short anthers are black (often covered with bright yellow-orange pollen), and the pistil is long, stout, and fleshy. The basal leaves with 3 broad leaflets were used historically as a hops substitute in the making of beer.

Names: *Menyanthes* may mean 'month flower,' in reference to the approximate flowering time, or it may be derived from *menanthos* ('moon flower'), the Greek name for a related plant. *Trifoliata* means '3-leaved,' describing the 3 leaflets of each leaf. **Where found:** Mixed Conifer Forest to 9000'. Bogs, ponds, wet meadows; e.g., marshy edges of Grass Lake (7700') in June.

white • 5 petals united in tube • June–August

RED ELDERBERRY
Sambucus racemosa • Honeysuckle Family

Although you will sometimes see red elderberry growing over 10' tall, in the eastern Sierra it more commonly forms a **1–2' mat that cascades down open, rocky slopes.** The **dense, dome-shaped clusters of tiny (1/8"), creamy white flowers** are often so thick on the plant that they form a nearly solid blanket over the rocks. The leaves are distinctive for both their shape and their smell. They are pointed, saw-toothed, and rather **crinkly, and they have a strong smell when crushed that many people find unpleasant.** The red berries are **poisonous,** though when they are cooked, they can make a delicious syrup that is safe to consume.

Names: *Sambucus* comes from a Greek word for a musical instrument made of elderberry wood. *Racemosa* means 'in a raceme,' in reference to the dome-shaped clusters of flowers. **Where found:** Mixed Conifer Forest to 10,000'. Moist slopes, rocky places; e.g., along Route 88 just east of Carson Pass (8500') in July.

white • 5 petals united in tube • June–August

BLUE ELDERBERRY
Sambucus mexicana • Honeysuckle Family

Although the individual flowers of blue elderberry are quite similar to those of red elderberry (p. 157), the two shrubs have several distinct differences, both in flower and in fruit. First, the **flower clusters of blue elderberry are flat-topped and broader than high,** while those of red elderberry are more dome shaped and higher than broad. Second, as the common names indicate, the berries are completely different colors—blue-black as opposed to bright red. Third, although both plants have pinnately compound leaves with several opposite pairs of pointed leaflets, the **leaflets of blue elderberry are usually asymmetrical at the base.** The leaves of both species have a rather unpleasant smell when crushed, though those of red elderberry are stronger smelling. Usually blue elderberry shrubs reach at least 5–6' in height (and can be over 25'), while red elderberry, especially at high elevations, is shorter, often flowing along close to the ground.

Names: *Sambucus:* see p. 157. *Mexicana* means 'of Mexico.' Formerly called *Sambucus caerulea.* **Where found:** Mixed Conifer Forest to 10,000'; also in Sagebrush Steppe. Streambanks, open woods; e.g., creekbank along road to Onion Valley (7500') in June, and along the McGee Creek trail (9000') in July.

white • 5 petals united in tube • June–August

DWARF CHAMAESARACHA
Chamaesaracha nana • Nightshade Family

Though it isn't rare to find a ground-hugging plant with large flowers, such a plant may still catch you by surprise because we tend to associate small plants with small flowers. The flowers of dwarf chamaesaracha will probably startle you, then, for they are large (1" across) and showy and usually lie on or very near the ground. **The 2–10" plant stem crawls along the ground and is usually hidden by the broad, oval, 1–2" leaves. The flowers, too, are often partially hidden by the leaves.** The 5 petals are united to form a bright white saucer with yellow-green splotches at the base, against which are displayed thick, creamy yellow anthers.

Names: *Chamaesaracha* means 'low *Saracha,'* a South American genus also in the nightshade family. *Nana* means 'dwarf.' Also called green-spotted nightshade. **Where found:** Mixed Conifer Forest to 9000'; also in Sagebrush Steppe. Sandy slopes, open woods; e.g., along the Thomas Creek trail (8000') in May.

white • 5 petals united in bowl • May–June

CALIFORNIA VALERIAN
Valeriana californica • Valerian Family

At first glance you may think that California valerian is one of the many white-flowered members of the carrot family (like Queen Anne's lace), for it **appears to have round-topped umbels of tiny flowers**. However, closer examination of the flower clusters will reveal that they are **not true umbels,** for the short stems of the individual flowers do not all originate at the same point on the stem, but instead are staggered. Also, California valerian has very **distinctive leaves** that are unlike those of any carrot family genus. They are **relatively broad with pinnate lobes and a larger terminal lobe**. The 1–2' plant stems have numerous leaves toward the base and only a few on the upper parts. • Valerian root is an important herb used for calming, and it is an ingredient in many herbal sleep aids.

Names: *Valeriana* means 'strength,' in reference to the many medicinal uses for plants in this genus. *Californica:* see p. 51. **Where found:** also in Sagebrush Steppe. Moist slopes, open woods; e.g., along the Thomas Creek trail (7000') in June, and grassy edges of Frog Lake on trail to Winnemucca Lake (9000') in July.

white • 5 tiny petals • June–September

SODA STRAW
Angelica lineariloba • Carrot Family

The *Angelica* species are particularly lovely members of the carrot family. Their **round-topped or spherical clusters of tiny flowers are large and beautifully symmetrical and are crowded with flowers, yet exude a soft airiness**. The 'spokes' that carry the small umbels of flowers (which together make up the large 'bouquet') are long enough to keep the small umbels separated slightly, allowing some sky to show through and allowing the spokes to be clearly seen. Most *Angelica* species have pinnately lobed leaves, and usually the leaf segments are a bit round or oval. Soda straw has **unusual leaves that have very narrow, linear segments**. When soda straw goes to seed, the bouquet changes from soft white to greenish.

Names: *Angelica* means 'angelic,' in reference to the uses of plants in this genus for medicine. *Lineariloba* means 'linear-lobed,' in reference to the narrow leaf segments. The common name refers to the slender, hollow plant stem. **Where found:** southern and central Mixed Conifer Forest; also in Sagebrush Steppe. Open slopes, rocky places; e.g., Onion Valley (9200') in July.

white • 5 tiny petals • June–August

COW-PARSNIP
Heracleum lanatum • Carrot Family

Cow-parsnip is indeed a Hercules of a plant! Its **stem is stout, though hollow, and can reach 10' (though 5–6' is more usual); its maple-like leaves are 6–16" long and nearly as wide; and its umbel of flowers can be up to 1' across**. Rather ironically, the individual flowers are tiny ($^1/_8$–$^1/_4$"). The flowerhead is formed by 15–30 umbrella-like spokes, each of which bears scores of flowers on mini-umbels of short pedicels. The resulting flowerhead can be nearly solid with blooms. If you decide to stick your nose into the flowers to get a sniff, don't be surprised if you're ambushed by a clever white spider who lies in wait perfectly camouflaged (inset photo).

Names: *Heracleum* is derived from 'Hercules,' probably in reference to the large stature of some species. *Lanatum* means 'woolly,' in reference to the soft, white hairs covering the stem. **Where found:** Mixed Conifer Forest to 8500'; also in Sagebrush Steppe. Streambanks, wet meadows; e.g., along the Thomas Creek trail (8000') in June, and along the trail to Winnemucca Lake (9500') in July.

white • 5 tiny petals • July–September

RANGER'S BUTTONS
Sphenosciadium capitellatum • Carrot Family

Ranger's buttons is a wonderful name for this plant because the $^3/_4$", spherical **umbels of flowers do resemble cloth buttons**. Each 'button' is at the end of a thick 1–4" spoke, and is crammed with scores of tiny ($^1/_8$"), white or sometimes pinkish flowers. The resulting loose inflorescence of tightly packed balls **resembles the spider ride at the fair, with round cars at the ends of long arms whirling around a central point**. The hollow 2–5' plant stem has scattered leaves branching off its lower portion. The leaves are large and deeply pinnately lobed into narrow segments. The peduncles (up to 1$^1/_2$' long), which bear the 'spokes,' and the petioles both emerge from sheaths. Ranger's buttons, like several of its carrot-family relatives, is **poisonous**.

Names: *Sphenosciadium* means 'wedge umbrella,' in reference to the umbels of flowers. *Capitellatum* means 'having little heads,' also in reference to the small, spherical umbels. **Where found:** also in Sagebrush Steppe. Wet meadows, streambanks; e.g., Onion Valley (9200') in July, and along trail to Morgan Pass (10,500') in July.

white • 5 tiny petals • July–September

DIRTY SOCKS
Polygonum bistortoides • Buckwheat Family

Visit a **grassy meadow in the eastern Sierra early in the summer when it's still soggy from snowmelt,** and you may find it filled with the sight and smell of dirty socks in full bloom. The sight can be stunning when the bright white of the dirty socks intermingles with the blue of camas lily (p. 123) and the yellow of buttercups (e.g., p. 175). The smell can also be stunning, but it may not be as pleasant! Some people claim that your reaction to the aroma of dirty socks has to do with your gender as well as your sartorial habits. The **½–2' stem terminates in one dense thumb of scores of tiny (⅛") white to pink flowers.** The narrow, leathery, 6–16" leaves are mostly basal.

Names: *Polygonum* means 'many knees,' in reference to the swollen stem nodes of some species. *Bistortoides* means 'like bistort,' in reference to *P. bistorta*, a species of the eastern U.S. Also called bistort and lady's thumb.
Where found: wet meadows; e.g., Hope Valley (6500') in July, and along the Tioga Pass road (9500') in July.

white • 5 tiny petals • May–August

NEVADA LEWISIA
Lewisia nevadensis • Purslane Family

With its succulent leaves and sepal cup of 2 fleshy sepals, Nevada lewisia (like most *Lewisia* species and most other members of the purslane family) looks fresh and juicy and appetizing. Nevada lewisia has a **basal rosette of narrow, cylindrical, succulent leaves above which rises a 1–4" stem bearing only 1 flower.** This ¾–1¼" flower consists of a variable number of white petals (6–10), often with a pinkish tinge and greenish veins. The sepals underneath the petals are the typical 2 cradling 'hands.' The bud is often red or pink. The clustered 6–15 stamens have yellow anthers.

Names: Lewis: see p. 129. *Nevadensis:* see p. 150.
Where found: moist meadows, seeps, open woods; e.g., along Route 88 east of Carson Pass (8500') in July.

Related plant: Three-leaf lewisia (*L. triphylla,* bottom photo) has similar white flowers with a variable number of petals (5–9), but it has distinctive leaves in pairs or in 3s. It also occurs in wet habitats throughout the Mixed Conifer Forest zone, e.g., along trail to Winnemucca Lake (9000') in July. *Triphylla* means '3-leaved.'

white • 6–10 separate petals • June–August

MARSH MARIGOLD
Caltha leptosepala • Buttercup Family

Marsh marigold is one of the great joys of spring in the Sierra, for well before much else is in bloom these large (to 2" across), spectacularly bright flowers light up meadows and seeps with their cheer. The **5–11 white, petal-like sepals with the cluster of sparkling reproductive parts in the center** seem like radiant smiles welcoming in the new wildflower year. Each plant has at least one 4–12" stem that bears 1 flower at its tip. The **basal leaves are distinctive—they are round or kidney shaped, 1–3" wide, and fleshy green.** • To get close to marsh marigolds in bloom you will probably have to get your feet wet and cold, for these plants love marshy meadows or even standing water that can be frigid in early spring.

Names: *Caltha* means 'bowl-shaped,' which describes the flower. *Leptosepala* means 'thin-sepaled,' in reference to the ray-like sepals. **Where found:** streambanks, seeps, wet meadows; e.g., along Thomas Creek (7500') in June.

white • 5–11 separate petal-like sepals • May–July

EATON'S DAISY
Erigeron eatonii • Composite Family

Eaton's daisy is a delightful white-rayed composite that keeps a bit of a pink or purple secret. The 15–75 narrow rays in the large (to 1¹/₂" wide) flowerhead are an **intense pink or purple when they first open up.** Though the **mature rays are white, they are sometimes pink tinged,** especially at the tips, and **they are almost always pink or purple underneath.** The 3–12" stem bears numerous narrow, alternating leaves and is topped by only 1 of the showy flowerheads. The yellow button of disk flowers resembles a raised crown.

Names: *Erigeron:* see p. 106. Daniel Eaton was a 19th-century botany professor at Yale University. **Where found:** northern Mixed Conifer Forest to 9500'; also in Sagebrush Steppe. Grassy flats, dried clay or rocks; e.g., along Route 89 near Monitor Pass (7000') in June.

Related plant: Coulter's daisy (*E. coulteri*, bottom photo) is a similar daisy with many white rays and a yellow central disk. It is a taller plant (1–4'), but with somewhat smaller flowerheads, and it grows in wet meadows and along streambanks throughout the Mixed Conifer Forest zone, e.g., east side of Mt. Rose (8000') in July. John Coulter was an American professor of botany in the late 1800s and early 1900s.

white • many ray and disk flowers • June–July

YARROW
Achillea millefolium • Composite Family

Although yarrow does have the ray flowers and disk flowers characteristic of daisy-like composites, it doesn't look much like a daisy. First, instead of having separate, large, showy flowerheads, yarrow's **flowerheads are very small (¹/₄"), and scores of them form tight clusters**. Second, each individual flowerhead of yarrow consists of only 3–8 tiny, rounded rays surrounding a tiny central cluster of 13–40 beige disk flowers. If you didn't know yarrow was a composite, you might not guess it. • The 1–4' stem and the **fern-like leaves** are covered with white, woolly hairs. The leaves **emit a medicinal smell when crushed** and do have many medicinal uses.

Names: *Achillea* is in reference to Achilles, the legendary Greek hero who was said to have used yarrow medicinally. *Millefolium* means 'thousand-leaved,' in reference to the much-divided leaves. **Where found:** also in Sagebrush Steppe. Grassy meadows, open woods; e.g., along the Tioga Pass road (9000') in September.

white (pink) • few rays, many tiny disk flowers • June–September

PEARLY EVERLASTING
Anaphalis margaritacea • Composite Family

Pearly everlasting is both pearly and everlasting, or at least it seems that way. The ¹/₄–¹/₂", **spherical flowerheads are a lustrous pearly white** when they are young, so they do bear quite a resemblance to pearls. These 'pearls' are actually not flowers but papery bracts. As the plant matures, these bracts spread out, revealing tiny, yellow disk flowers that then enlarge somewhat. **When the flowers and bracts dry up, the bracts retain their structure and their pearly appearance** well into autumn and even into winter. The ¹/₂–4' stems usually form sizable clusters, so there is often quite a significant display of these 'jewels.' The 1–4" leaves are narrow and green on top but grayish underneath.

Names: *Anaphalis* is the old Greek name for this genus. *Margaritacea* means 'pearly.' **Where found:** Mixed Conifer Forest to 9500'. Open woods, rocky slopes, disturbed places; e.g., along trail to Winnemucca Lake (9000') in July.

white bracts around tiny, yellow disk flowers • many disk flowers • June–August

DRUMMOND'S THISTLE
Cirsium scariosum • Composite Family

In the thistle world of stout-stemmed, towering plants, Drummond's thistle is an anomaly. It has the typical spiny leaves and bristly flowerheads, **but it usually has no stem, so the flowerheads rest right on the rosette of leaves that lies flat on the ground**. The 1–2" flowerheads are unusual, too, for they are **not the typical red, pink, or purple but instead are creamy white (drying brown)**. The 4–16" leaves are deeply pinnately divided, with very sharp spines. • Drummond's thistle is highly variable, sometimes having short stems (occasionally even up to 3') and sometimes having purplish flowers. Some botanists call the extreme variations separate species.

Names: *Cirsium:* see p. 70. *Scariosum* means 'thin, membranous, and not green,' in reference to the phyllaries. Also called dwarf thistle and elk thistle. **Where found:** also in Sagebrush Steppe. Grassy clearings; open woods; e.g., along Route 88 east of Carson Pass (7500') in July.

white • many disk flowers • June–August

CURL-LEAF MOUNTAIN MAHOGANY
Cerocarpus ledifolius • Rose Family

Curl-leaf mountain mahogany is a much-branched **shrub or tree up to 30' tall**. Its stiff, resinous, evergreen leaves make it well suited for the hot, dry conditions of the Great Basin and eastern Sierra. This tree can present a dramatic array of colors, especially when seen against the backdrop of  a typical bright blue Sierra sky, for its bark is usually silver and its **oval leaves often turn yellow or red** as the season progresses. As the common name suggests, the leaves usually roll under at the edges. The flowers are unusual for a member of the rose family because they have **no petals**. The 15–25 stamens create a rather inconspicuous, fuzzy-looking cluster of white in the leaf axils. Much more striking are the **fruits, with their long, silky plumes** (the styles).

Names: *Cerocarpus* means 'tailed fruit.' *Ledifolius* means 'leaves like *Ledum*,' the Labrador tea genus (p. 150). **Where found:** also in Sagebrush Steppe. Dry, rocky slopes often with sagebrush; e.g., along trail to Baxter Pass (7000') in May, and along the Thomas Creek trail (8000') in May.

white reproductive parts • no petals • April–May

YELLOW LADIES' TRESSES
Spiranthes porrifolia • Orchid Family

Yellow ladies' tresses is difficult to find because it grows in boggy areas that you might tend to avoid, it often hides among grasses, and it's uncommon. It is, however, well worth seeking, for it is a lovely plant with a unique inflorescence. The ¹/₂–2' stem rises above narrow basal leaves, and there are also a few smaller stem leaves. The upper 2–6" is a **slender spike thick with scores of yellowish ¹/₄–¹/₂" flowers that appear braided in a tight spiral**. Each flower consists of 3 petals and 3 similar sepals. The upper sepal and the upper 2 petals are fused together, the lateral 2 sepals stick out horizontally, and the lower petal hangs down. This lower petal is broader and longer than the other perianth parts.

Names: *Spiranthes* means 'coiled flowers.' *Porrifolia* means 'leaves like leek.' **Where found:** Mixed Conifer Forest to 8000'; also in Sagebrush Steppe. Wet meadows, grassy marshes, seeps; e.g., marshy edges of Grass Lake (7700') in June.

yellowish-white • 3 petal-like sepals and 3 petals • June–July

BEAR BUCKWHEAT
Eriogonum ursinum • Buckwheat Family

Bear buckwheat is in many ways a typical buckwheat, with small, oval basal leaves and a leafless stem topped by an umbel of tiny, fuzzy flowers. However, it is unusual enough to easily distinguish it from its many close relatives in the eastern Sierra. First, its stem is unbranched. Second, its flowers are usually **pale, creamy yellow**. Third, **just beneath the 'spokes' of the umbel are narrow, green bracts that usually curve up or are nearly erect**. Fourth, the leaves tend to be light green on top and yellow-brown underneath. And fifth, you probably won't find it south of Carson Pass. The anthers are bright yellow and the stamens stick up out of the flowers, so the creamy umbels are dotted with yellow.

Names: *Eriogonum:* see p. 47. *Ursinum* means 'pertaining to bears.' **Where found:** northern Mixed Conifer Forest to 9000'; also in Sagebrush Steppe. Sandy or gravelly flats, rock ledges; e.g., along Route 88 just east of Carson Pass (8000') in July.

pale yellow • 6 tiny, petal-like sepals • June–August

LOBB'S BUCKWHEAT
Eriogonum lobbii • Buckwheat Family

Lobb's buckwheat looks like a typical buckwheat, but a tired one. Its distinguishing feature is that its **stems are usually prostrate, placing the fuzzy umbels of flowers right on the ground**. When you see a cluster of the basal leaves surrounded by a tight ring of these umbels, you may be reminded of a castle surrounded by a moat. The leaves are round or oval and gray-green, like those of many buckwheats, but they are larger than most (1" or so long). The flowers are pale yellow or creamy white, turning to rose late in the season. • Early or late in its blooming season, Lobb's buckwheat puts on quite a show in the high country, for it often snuggles into cracks in granite outcrops, splashing the granite with fuzzy spheres of cream or red.

Names: *Eriogonum:* see p. 47. William Lobb was a 19th-century British plant collector and explorer. **Where found:** also in Sagebrush Steppe. Gravelly or rocky slopes, rock ledges; e.g., along trail to Mono Pass (11,000') in July, and near summit of Freel Peak (10,600') in August.

yellow (or creamy white or rose) • 6 tiny petal-like sepals • July–September

SULFUR FLOWER
Eriogonum umbellatum • Buckwheat Family

Sulfur flower is common and widespread in the eastern Sierra—you can find it all the way from sandy sagebrush flats to wind-ravaged alpine ridges. Its growth form reflects its environment, ranging  from a shrub several feet tall (in the lower elevations) to a dwarf rising only a few inches above basal leaves (above timberline). All of the forms, however, have the same distinctive **umbels of tiny, sulfur yellow flowers rising on stems above small, round or spoon-shaped leaves**. The leaves (especially the undersides) are often covered with matted, gray hairs. There is a whorl of leafy bracts at the branching point of the stem. As the flowers mature, they become pink or red.

Names: *Eriogonum:* see p. 47. *Umbellatum* means 'in an umbel.' **Where found:** also in Sagebrush Steppe and in Alpine to 12,000'. Dry, rocky places; e.g., along Highway 395 on Sherwin Summit (7000') in June.

yellow • 6 tiny petal-like sepals • May–August

KELLEY'S TIGER LILY
Lilium kelleyanum • Lily Family

With their large, usually hanging, brightly colored flowers, *Lilium* species are certainly among the most spectacular plants of the Sierra. Kelley's tiger lily is no exception, for its 1¹/₂–2" flowers will catch your eye and your heart no matter how entangled they are in the thickets of flowers that thrive in Sierra seeps and streambanks. Like many lilies, Kelley's tiger lily is a tall plant (to 6') with whorls of grass-like leaves along the lower part of the stem. Higher on the stem the leaves alternate. A few or many (1–25) of the dazzling flowers hang from the ends of long pedicels. The flowers are distinguished from those of other *Lilium* species in the Sierra (e.g., see p. 180) by their color and shape. The flowers of Kelley's tiger lily are **yellow to yellow-orange with maroon dots, but they are the same yellowish base color throughout, i.e., not 2-toned.** The **tepals curve all the way back** with their tips touching or almost touching.

Names: *Lilium* is the Latin form of the original Greek name. *Kelleyanum* is of uncertain origin. **Where found:** southern and central Mixed Conifer Forest. Seeps, streambanks, often in thickets; e.g., above Onion Valley on trail to Kearsarge Pass (9500') in July, and along trail to Mono Pass (10,500') in July.

yellow or yellow-orange • 6 separate tepals • July–August

PRETTY FACE
Triteleia ixioides • Lily Family

Even when you're expecting it, finding pretty face still elicits a delighted 'Aha!' Its **straw yellow tepals with dark purple midveins** create a strikingly beautiful star. Because each plant has an umbel of several blooms, and because plants often gather together in large groups, you will frequently find what looks like an entire sky of pretty face stars lighting up their sandy or gravelly homes. Each flower has 6 stamens, 3 tall alternating with 3 short. Behind each stamen is an erect, forked appendage. The 6–18" plant stem is only a little taller than the grass-like leaves are long (8–16"), though the leaves usually arch out close to the ground. They wither early, so you may not see leaves when the flowers are in bloom.

Names: *Triteleia* means '3 complete,' in reference to the flower parts in 3s. *Ixioides* means 'resembling *Ixia*,' a genus in the iris family. Formerly called *Brodiaea lutea*. **Where found:** Mixed Conifer Forest to 10,000'; also in Sagebrush Steppe. Sandy or gravelly flats, open woods; e.g., sandy edges of Grass Lake (7700') in July.

yellow • 6 tepals • May–July

BUSH CHINQUAPIN
Chrysolepis sempervirens • Oak Family

There's no confusing chinquapin with any other shrub, for its leaves and fruits are unmistakable. The **leathery, elliptic leaves** are an undistinguished dull green on top, but their **undersides are a striking golden yellow** with minute scales. Since the 1–1$^{1}/_{2}$", **spherical, spiny burs (fruits) are this same gold color,** chinquapin's overall appearance, even from a distance, is unique—**an evergreen shrub with a decided bronze to gold tinge**. There are separate male and female flowers. The male flowers form erect, cylindrical clusters, while the female flowers form round clusters just beneath the males. • This shrub sometimes covers entire hillsides with a thicket so dense and forbidding, you will probably think twice about trying to penetrate it.

Names: *Chrysolepis* means 'golden scale,' in reference to the undersides of the leaves. *Sempervirens* means 'always green.' **Where found:** also in Sagebrush Steppe. Dry hillsides, rocky slopes, open woods; e.g., above Onion Valley on trail to Kearsarge Pass (9500') in July.

yellow • 6 tiny sepals • June–September

WOODY-FRUITED EVENING-PRIMROSE
Oenothera xylocarpa • Evening-Primrose Family

A number of flowers are a somewhat different color when they dry than when they first bloom, but many evening-primroses turn this process into a fine art. Woody-fruited evening-primrose may be the most spectacular example of this dramatic change, for the **fresh blooms are bright yellow and the drying ones (only 1 day later!) are deep red**. To make the drama even more vivid, the flowers are very large (2–3") and rest directly on a **basal rosette of round, red-spotted leaves**. Like most other *Oenothera* species, woody-fruited evening-primrose opens at dusk and withers by mid-morning of the following day, so if you come across this plant around dusk, you are likely to find bright yellow blossoms and drying red ones side by side. As with all *Oenothera* species, the anthers and lobed stigma are narrow and sticky and are often covered with pollen. • This stemless plant can spread out for a couple of feet, bringing stunning color to its frequently rather bare, sandy or gravelly habitat.

Names: *Oenothera:* see p. 84. *Xylocarpa* means 'woody-fruited.' **Where found:** Mixed Conifer Forest to 10,000'. Sandy or gravelly flats, open woods; e.g., east side of Mt. Rose (9500') in August.

yellow • 4 separate petals • July–September

TANSYLEAF SUN-CUP
Camissonia tanacetifolia • Evening-Primrose Family

Sun-cup is such an appropriate name for this plant, for its **1–2" cupped flowers warm you with their dazzling, bright yellow cheer**. They are all the more striking because they occur in **large clusters and they lie directly on a bed of gray-green leaves** (the plant is stemless, sending flower shoots up from lateral rhizomes). The **leaves are deeply and irregularly pinnately lobed**. The yellow flower cups cradle long, yellow stamens and an even longer yellow pistil with the globular stigma characteristic of the genus *Camissonia*.

Names: *Camissonia:* see p. 47. *Tanacetifolia* means 'tansy-leaved,' in reference to the deeply lobed leaves. **Where found:** Mixed Conifer Forest to 8000'; also in Sagebrush Steppe. Fields, open flats; e.g., along Mt. Rose Highway (7000') in May.

yellow • 4 separate petals • May–June

PRIMROSE MONKEYFLOWER
Mimulus primuloides • Snapdragon Family

Many species of monkeyflower inhabit the eastern Sierra, with flowers ranging from red to pink to purple to yellow. Primrose monkeyflower is a particularly charming yellow-flowered species. A **slender, leafless stem rises only a few inches above a rosette of hairy, basal leaves**. Often even in midday, these hairs hold drops of moisture that glisten in the sun. At the tip of the stem is one $1/2$" flower whose 5 shallowly lobed petals resemble little hearts. The 3 petals of the lower lip usually have a small, red dot toward each base.

Names: *Mimulus:* see p. 67. *Primuloides* translates as 'primrose-like,' in reference to the naked flower stem above basal leaves, reminiscent of some *Primula* species. **Where found:** Mixed Conifer Forest to 11,000'; also in Sagebrush Steppe. Wet meadows, bogs; e.g., along trail from Mosquito Flat to Morgan Pass (10,500') in July.

Related plant: Common monkeyflower (*M. guttatus,* inset photo) has similar, though larger, unlobed, yellow, red-speckled petals. It usually grows much taller (to $2^1/2$') and has clasping stem leaves. It grows in wet places over a remarkable range from Mojave Desert Scrub to 10,000', e.g., along creeks in the Alabama Hills (4000') in June and along trail to Winnemucca Lake (9500') in July. *Guttatus* means 'speckled.'

yellow • 5 petals united in 2-lipped tube • June–August

LARGE MONKEYFLOWER
Mimulus tilingii • Snapdragon Family

Although similar to common monkey-flower (p. 169) with its large (1–1½"), bright yellow flowers, large monkeyflower may be even more spectacular, for its **flowers appear huge on the relatively short (1–15") plant**. And though its individual blossoms are extremely showy, large monkeyflower also dazzles by its profusion—you will often find seep areas, especially in rocky places, swarming with hundreds or even thousands of these glorious flowers. When the plant goes to seed, **the often red-spotted calyx swells asymmetrically, the lower lip curving up and closing the tube.** The pairs of opposite leaves are usually slightly toothed, do not clasp the stem, and are **slimy to the touch.**

Names: *Mimulus:* see p. 67. Heinrich Tiling was a 19th-century Baltic physician and botanist. Also called mountain monkeyflower. **Where found:** streambanks, seep areas, wet meadows; e.g., along trail to Mono Pass (11,500') in August.

yellow • 5 petals in 2-lipped tube • July–August

YELLOW NAVARRETIA
Navarretia breweri • Phlox Family

Yellow navarretia is a very small plant to **only 3" tall;** nevertheless, it calls attention to itself with its **clumps of prickly, needle-like leaves and its bright yellow flowers**. Though the **tubular flowers are tiny** (¼" long and ⅛" wide) and are partly hidden by the protruding leaves, they are still quite noticeable, for their yellow petals provide a dramatic contrast to the green leaves and to the plant's bare clay or grassy meadow habitat. The leaves are often edged with fine hairs and their spiny tips are frequently reddish brown. The plant stem is white, brown, or red. A final dash of color is provided by the tiny white anthers.

Names: Francisco Navarrete was a Spanish physician of the 1700s. Brewer: see p. 140. **Where found:** Mixed Conifer Forest to 10,000'; also in Sagebrush Steppe. Wet meadows, streambanks, dried clay; e.g., along Route 89 west of Monitor Pass (7000') in June.

yellow • 5 petals united in tube • June–July

FIVE-FINGER CINQUEFOIL
Potentilla gracilis • Rose Family

Most cinquefoil flowers are bright yellow—so bright yellow that the glare is almost blinding. But squint a little and take a close look, for the colorful flowers display a beautiful, intricate structure. The usually heart-shaped petals provide a delicious background for the symmetrical cluster of reproductive parts. As its name suggests, five-finger cinquefoil has **palmately compound leaves with 5 (sometimes 6 or 7) toothed leaflets**. The plant grows to 3' tall.

Names: *Potentilla:* see p. 143. *Gracilis:* p. 149. **Where found:** also in Sagebrush Steppe. Meadows, open woods; e.g., Mosquito Flat (10,230') in July.

Related plant: Drummond's cinquefoil (*P. drummondii* var. *drummondii*, bottom photo) has very similar flowers but quite different leaves and a different growth form. The 3–10" leaves are pinnately compound with several opposite pairs of toothed leaflets. The ¹⁄₂–2' stems are usually prostrate. Drummond's cinquefoil grows in similar habitats and at similar elevations, e.g., Onion Valley (9200') in July. Thomas Drummond was a 19th-century Scottish naturalist.

yellow • 5 separate petals • June–August

LARGE-LEAF AVENS
Geum macrophyllum • Rose Family

With their 5 separate, yellow petals and their cluster of many reproductive parts, the flowers of large-leaf avens **resemble those of cinquefoils** (e.g., see above), which are also in the rose family. However, unlike cinquefoils, which usually have notched or heart-shaped petals, **large-leaf avens has rounded petals with 5 reflexed sepals underneath**. The 1–3' plant bears large leaves (to 15"), which consist of a broad terminal leaflet and 2–4 opposite pairs of smaller leaflets. All the leaflets are shallowly toothed and slightly lobed. Like its fellow *Geum* old man's whiskers (p. 196), large-leaf avens has conspicuous and dramatic fruits. They are **prickly ¹⁄₂" spheres, dense with slender, hooked styles**.

Names: *Geum* is the ancient Latin name for plants in this genus. *Macrophyllum* means 'large-leaved.' **Where found:** Mixed Conifer Forest to 10,000'; also in Sagebrush Steppe. Damp meadows, streambanks; e.g., along the Thomas Creek trail (8000') in June.

yellow • 5 separate petals • June–July

TINKER'S PENNY
Hypericum anagalloides • St. John's Wort Family

Tinker's penny is a small plant that often makes a big impression. Its stem rarely exceeds 10", and it is nowhere near that tall because the stem lies flat on the ground. Despite its lack of height, however, it can create quite a display because it spreads by runners that root and sprout. The resulting **dense mat of leaves often covers several square feet** and is liberally sprinkled with the intriguing flowers. The $^1/_4$–$^1/_2$" **flowers are an unusual and showy color—salmon to yellow-orange or golden**. The green sepals are about the same size as the petals and usually show through between them.

Names: *Hypericum* is the ancient Greek name for the genus. *Anagalloides* means 'resembling *Anagallis*,' a genus in the primrose family whose species have similar leaves. *Anagallis* means 'to delight.' **Where found:** Mixed Conifer Forest to 10,000'; also in Sagebrush Steppe. Seeps, streambanks; e.g., around Grass Lake (7700') in July.

yellow-orange or salmon • 5 separate petals • July–August

NARROW-LEAF STONECROP
Sedum lanceolatum • Stonecrop Family

Stonecrops are most distinctive for their leaves, though most spectacular for their flowers. When you see a **basal rosette of thick, fleshy leaves above which rises a short stem bearing numerous star-shaped, bright yellow flowers,** you can be certain you have come across a *Sedum*. Almost all *Sedum* species grow in the rocks, for their succulent leaves allow them to thrive in hot, dry habitats. • Narrow-leaf stonecrop has **narrow basal leaves and similar narrow leaves alternating up the 1–8" stem.** You may not see the stem leaves, however, since they **usually have shriveled up by the time the flowers bloom.** The inflorescence can have as few as 3 or as many as 24 of the $^1/_2$–$^3/_4$" flowers.

Names: Depending upon which botanist you consult, *Sedum* means either 'to assuage,' in reference to the healing properties of *Sedum* species, or 'to sit,' in reference to their rock-hugging growth. *Lanceolatum* means 'narrow-leaved.' **Where found:** rocky outcrops and ledges; e.g., near Frog Lake just off trail to Winnemucca Lake (9000') in July.

yellow • 5 petals united in tube at base • June–August

STREAM VIOLET
Viola glabella • Violet Family

The violets have a special place in many people's hearts, long being associated with romance in folklore and myth. They are delightful, cheery, open flowers with a touch of sensuousness and surprise. Hidden at the back of the flower behind its wide-flaring face is a narrow, curved nectar spur holding secret pleasures for nectar-loving pollinators. Also, many violets are *cleistogamous,* hedging their bets with those pollinators by producing a backup flower that never opens (it self-pollinates), just in case. Stream violet has **large, dramatic, heart-shaped leaves that are dark green and deeply veined. The** $^{1}/_{2}-^{3}/_{4}"$ **flowers are a rich yellow with purple veins** that are mostly on the lower, middle petal.

Names: *Viola:* see p. 125. *Glabella* means 'smooth,' probably in reference to the leaves. **Where found:** Mixed Conifer Forest to 8000'; also in Sagebrush Steppe. Streambanks, forest shade; e.g., east slope of Mt. Rose (7000') in June.

Related plant: Pine violet (*V. lobata,* bottom photo) has quite similar yellow, usually purple-veined flowers, but the leaves are vastly different, resembling moose antlers rather than hearts. It has a similar range to that of *V. glabella* but tends to grow in dry forest openings; e.g., Thomas Creek trail (7500') in June.

yellow • 5 irregular petals • May–July

MOUNTAIN VIOLET
Viola purpurea • Violet Family

The flowers of mountain violet are quite similar to those of stream violet (above), with their bright yellow, blunt-tipped petals and the purple veins on the lower middle petal. A distinguishing characteristic of mountain violet, however, is the **brown-purple coloring on the back of the upper 2 petals.** The leaves are somewhat different in the 2 species, too: those of stream violet tend to be darker green, glossier, and rounder. The **1–2" leaves of mountain violet tend to be more ovate and vary from smooth edged to wavy or slightly toothed.** Sometimes the plant can be quite leafy, partly hiding some of the flowers under the leaf canopy.

Names: *Viola:* see p. 125. *Purpurea* means 'purple,' in reference to the brown-purple coloring on the back of the upper petals. Also called pine woods violet. **Where found:** central and northern Mixed Conifer Forest; also in Sagebrush Steppe. Dry flats, open woods often with sagebrush; e.g., along the Thomas Creek trail (7000') in May.

yellow • 5 irregular petals • May–June

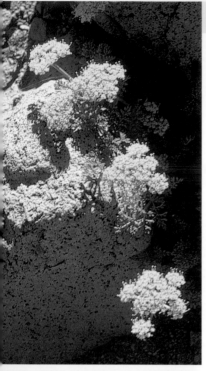

TEREBINTH PTERYXIA
Cymopterus terebinthinus • Carrot Family

Although its common and scientific names sound rather intimidating, evoking images of some kind of carnivorous dinosaur, terebinth pteryxia is really quite a gentle and delicate plant. Its **leaves are softly gray-green and deeply and intricately dissected,** looking like fine, lacy engraving on the rocks against which they often nestle. Rising above these leaves are 6–24" stems terminating in **umbels with 3–24 rays.** As with most members of the carrot family, the umbels are dense with scores of tiny flowers. However, unlike many of the carrot-family species in the eastern Sierra, which have white flowers (e.g., cow-parsnip, soda straw, ranger's buttons, yampah, poison hemlock), terebinth pteryxia has **yellow flowers.**

Names: *Cymopterus* means 'wave wing,' a description of the fruit. *Terebinthinus* means 'of turpentine,' a reference to the plant's pungent oil. Fomerly called *Pteryxia terebinthina.* **Where found:** central and northern Mixed Conifer Forest; also in Sagebrush Steppe. Sandy or rocky slopes, rock ledges; e.g., east side of Mt. Rose (9000') in July.

yellow • 5 tiny petals • July–August

FERN-LEAF LOMATIUM
Lomatium dissectum • Carrot Family

Despite its **fern-like leaves,** fern-leaf lomatium probably won't strike you as a very delicate plant. Its **stout, often reddish stem can extend up to 4' in height (though 1–2' is more common), and its umbel of yellow-green flowers can be 4" across.** (The variety of *L. dissectum* with red-purple flowers does not occur in the eastern Sierra.) And even though the leaves are deeply dissected, they are not soft but rather stiff and rough to the touch. When crushed they emit a sweet but medicinal smell. The umbel of flowers has 10–30 rays, each of which is tipped with a roundish cluster of tiny flowers. The reproductive parts stick out, creating a somewhat fuzzy look. The seeds resemble miniature pumpkin seeds.

Names: *Lomatium:* see p. 75. *Dissectum* means 'deeply divided,' in reference to the fern-like leaves. **Where found:** Mixed Conifer Forest to 10,000'; also in Sagebrush Steppe. Dry slopes often with sagebrush, open woods; e.g., along the Thomas Creek trail (7500') in May.

yellow • 5 tiny petals • May–June

WATER-PLANTAIN BUTTERCUP
Ranunculus alismifolius • Buttercup Family

Water-plantain buttercup is a spectacular herald of spring, often bringing the first floral color to cold, soggy meadows just emerging from winter's icy grip. And what color and warmth this buttercup brings— its brilliant yellow seems to thaw the ground all by itself! The 2–20" stems of the plant sometimes lie on the ground and sometimes stick up, so the $^1/_2$–1$^1/_2$" flowers may lie directly on the **long, narrow, undivided leaves** or rise well above them. The **petals are very shiny,** seeming to glisten with an inner light. Some flowers have only **5 petals, but most have 7 or 8 or more (sometimes as many as 15 or so).** The sepals underneath the petals are small and yellow or yellow-green and are usually reflexed.

Names: *Ranunculus* means 'little frog,' in reference to the wet habitat of most species. *Alismifolius* means 'leaves like *Alisma*,' a genus in the water-plantain family. **Where found:** also in Sagebrush Steppe. Wet meadows, streambanks, seeps; e.g., along Route 88 east of Carson Pass (8400') in June.

yellow • 5–15 separate petals • May–July

WOOLLY SUNFLOWER
Eriophyllum lanatum • Composite Family

Woolly sunflower is one of the brightest of the yellow composites, and since it usually grows in dense and extensive masses, it puts on quite a sunny show. The startling **contrast of the blazing, golden yellow rays with the white-hairy leaves** only adds to the drama. Each $^1/_2$" flowerhead consists of 7–13 (usually 8) broad, distinctly veined or grooved rays that radiate out from a raised central disk of scores of yellow disk flowers. There is usually only 1 flowerhead at the end of each leafless peduncle. Several recognized varieties of woolly sunflower differ in height, leaf shape, and number of rays.

Names: *Eriophyllum:* see p. 60. *Lanatum:* see p. 160. **Where found:** also in Sagebrush Steppe and in Alpine to 13,000'. Dry roadsides often with sagebrush, rocky places; e.g., along Route 89 near Markleeville (5700') in June, and along trail to Winnemucca Lake (9000') in July.

yellow • many ray and disk flowers • May–August

SOFT ARNICA
Arnica mollis • Composite Family

Soft arnica spreads by rhizomes, so it is not unusual to find great patches of these miniature suns lighting up meadows with their golden glow. Each 1/2–2' stem bears **several pairs of soft-hairy, tongue-like leaves beneath 1–3 of the bright yellow flowerheads,** making a field of soft arnica resemble a flotilla of golden ships floating on a soft green, furry sea. Each 1–2" flowerhead consists of 12–18 square-tipped rays radiating out from a raised central button of scores of yellow-orange disk flowers. *Arnica* species are among the easiest yellow-flowered composites to distinguish, for very few others have leaves in opposite pairs.

Names: *Arnica* means 'lamb's skin,' a description of the soft, hairy leaves. *Mollis:* see p. 100. **Where found:** moist, grassy meadows, streambanks, open woods; e.g., east side of Mt. Rose (9000') in August.

yellow • **many ray and disk flowers** • July–August

STREAMBANK ARNICA
Arnica amplexicaulis • Composite Family

A clump of streambank arnica along an aspen-lined creek is a dazzling sight, especially if the flowers are in the sun, for the 1–2", bright yellow flowerheads glow as if with their own light. Streambank arnica plants can grow to 3' and, sprouting from a rhizome, usually form large clusters. The **5–10 pairs of large, opposite, clasping leaves are narrower than those of most *Arnica* species, are slightly toothed, and are not hairy.** The flowerheads are made up of 8–14 rays surrounding a button of yellow disk flowers.

Names: *Arnica:* see above. *Amplexicaulis* means 'clasping leaves.' **Where found:** streambanks, moist open woods; e.g., along McGee Creek trail (9000') in July.

yellow • **many ray and disk flowers** • June–August

ARROW-LEAF SENECIO
Senecio triangularis • Composite Family

Many yellow-flowered composites have large and showy flowerheads, but with arrow-leaf senecio the plant and its leaves are much more conspicuous than the flowerheads. The **plant is 2–4' tall, with long (to 6"), broad, interesting leaves shaped much like arrowheads—complete with rough (toothed) edges**. Probably only after you notice the robust plant and its distinctive leaves will you notice the clusters of 10–30 small flowerheads. As in many *Senecio* species, the flowerheads look rather scraggly, with only a few (often 8) widely spaced rays surrounding a small button of disk flowers.

Names: *Senecio:* see p. 106. *Triangularis* means, not surprisingly, 'triangle-shaped,' in reference to the leaves. Also called arrow-leaf groundsel. **Where found:** also in Sagebrush Steppe. Wet meadows, streambanks, open woods; e.g., along Bishop Creek (8000') in July.

yellow • several ray flowers and many disk flowers • June–August

WHITESTEM GOLDENBUSH
Ericameria discoidea • Composite Family

Whitestem goldenbush is perfectly named, for its common name says it all about this plant's distinguishing characteristics. First, it grows as a **low sub shrub,** i.e., it has woody lower stems but non-woody upper stems that die back seasonally. The plant rarely exceeds 1½' in height but often exceeds this in diameter. Second, its **stems are bright white with felty, matted hairs**. And third, the **brushy flowerheads consist of golden yellow disk flowers** with protruding reproductive parts of the same color. The plant is thickly covered with small, oblong leaves that are glandular-sticky and exude a pleasant lemony fragrance.

Names: *Ericameria* refers to the narrow, heath-like leaves of some species (*Erica* is a genus in the heath family). *Discoidea* means 'disk-like,' in reference to the flowerheads with only disk flowers. **Where found:** Mixed Conifer Forest above 8500'. Rocky or sandy slopes; e.g., east side of Mt. Rose (9000') in August.

yellow • 10–25 disk flowers • July–September

COMMON DANDELION
Taraxacum officinale • Composite Family

Though you may think of dandelion as an ugly weed in your lawn, it really is a beautiful and interesting plant if you approach it with an open mind (it probably helps to approach it somewhere other than your lawn, too!). The flowerhead is large (to 1¹/₂") and fluffy-looking, full of bright yellow ray flowers (no disk flowers). One distinguishing characteristic is the **reflexed outer phyllaries under the flowerhead. The long leaves vary but almost always are at least somewhat lobed and/or toothed**. Dandelion may not always be welcome in lawns, but its bright burst of color can be a wonderful harbinger of spring, for it is one of the first flowers to bloom throughout its range.

Names: *Taraxacum* is the ancient Greek name. *Officinale* means 'medicinal.' **Where found:** Mixed Conifer Forest to 10,000'; also in Sagebrush Steppe. Meadows, roadsides; e.g., along Highway 395 near Bridgeport (6500') in April, and along Mt. Rose Highway (7500') in May. Alien.

yellow • many ray flowers • April–July

SHAGGY HAWKWEED
Hieracium horridum • Composite Family

As its common name suggests, the most noticeable aspect of shaggy hawkweed is its **densely hairy, 1–4", tongue-like leaves,** which attract much more attention than the small, yellow flowerheads. In the dry, rocky areas where this plant grows, it's not unusual to find plants with hairy leaves, but shaggy hawkweed has to be the hairy-leaf champion! The many stem leaves and the cluster of basal leaves are covered with soft but bristly, white or brownish hairs. The 4–15" branching stems bear several ¹/₂", **bright yellow flowerheads, each with 6–15 narrow rays**. There are no disk flowers.

Names: *Hieracium,* the ancient Latin name for the genus, means 'hawk.' *Horridum* means 'prickly,' in reference to the hairy leaves. **Where found:** also in Sagebrush Steppe. Rocky places; e.g., along trail to Mono Pass (11,000') in July.

yellow • 6–15 ray flowers • June–August

LEMMON'S ONION
Allium lemmonii • Lily Family

Many onions flourish in the eastern Sierra Nevada. Some love to have their feet wet in boggy meadows, and others choose to stay bone dry on sandy or gravelly flats. Lemmon's onion eschews both extremes, preferring instead a **habitat somewhere in between—damp clay that dries out as the flowers bloom**. Though only **4–8" tall,** this onion is a very showy plant with its many-flowered clusters of rich pink to rose flowers. Each cluster can contain as many as 40 of the ¹/₂" flowers. The **tepals are narrow and pointed and are usually only partly opened**. The **anthers are black-purple or yellow; the ovary is pink and bubbly-looking** down inside the flower. Under each umbel of flowers are 2 papery bracts with rose veins. The 2 grass-like leaves are about the same length as the flower stem.

Names: *Allium:* see p. 81. John and Sara Lemmon, a husband-and-wife team, collected plants in the 19th-century American West. **Where found:** northern Mixed Conifer Forest to 7000'; also in Sagebrush Steppe. Drying clay; e.g., along Route 89 east of Markleeville in forest openings (7000') in June.

pink to rose • 6 separate tepals • May–June

SIERRA ONION
Allium campanulatum • Lily Family

You will find Sierra onion **only in dry habitats,** usually on sandy flats or slopes among mule ears, pennyroyal, scarlet gilia, and various chaparral shrubs including sagebrush and manzanita. These hot, dry, open, often south-facing slopes can boast quite spectacular gardens! You may have to look close to the ground for Sierra onion (it grows only 4–12" tall), but you won't have any trouble finding it, for its loose umbels of 10–50 rose-purple, ¹/₄–¹/₂" flowers are quite showy. The shiny red-purple tepals often glisten in the sun. The **tepals are highlighted with dark rose veins and dark rose crescents at their bases**. The 2 grass-like leaves are about the same length as the plant stem.

Names: *Allium:* see p. 81. *Campanulatum* means 'bell-shaped,' in reference to the flowers. **Where found:** Mixed Conifer Forest to 9000'; also in Sagebrush Steppe. Dry flats and slopes; e.g., along Route 89 west of Monitor Pass (7500') in June, and along trail to Winnemucca Lake (8500') in July.

red-purple • 6 separate tepals • May–July

SWAMP ONION
Allium validum • Lily Family

You know that there must be something special about swamp onion, for it's one of the few wildflowers of the eastern Sierra that has a place named after it. If you go to Onion Valley (13 miles by a paved road west of Independence) in mid-summer, you will understand how that place got its name and what's so special about this stunning plant. The boggy meadows at road's end (9200') and along the lower parts of the trail to Kearsarge Pass are jungles of this robust plant with lush pink-purple flowers, and the air is thick with the strong, pleasant odor of onions. Because the **umbels of 15–40 flowers sit atop 3–4' stems,** swamp onion makes quite a statement in size, vitality, and beauty. The protruding, dark purple or black anthers contrast vividly with the **narrow, almost thread-like, pink-purple tepals**. The 3–6 grass-like leaves are much shorter than the plant stem.

Names: *Allium:* see p. 81. *Validum* means 'strong,' in reference to the powerful onion odor that often hangs like a cloud over these plants. **Where found:** also in Sagebrush Steppe. Wet meadows, streambanks; e.g., Onion Valley (9200') in July.

pink-purple • 6 separate tepals • June–September

TIGER LILY
Lilium parvum • Lily Family

The *Lilium* species of the eastern Sierra Nevada are imposing plants with dazzling flowers. Tiger lily is certainly no exception; its size (to 6') and its many (up to 40) spectacular, intensely colored flowers will catch your eye even when the plants are partly concealed in thickets of willow and alder along the edges of streams. Each bell-shaped flower has **6 tepals flared out,** not reflexed like those of *L. kelleyanum* (p. 167). The **center of the flower, i.e., the base of each tepal, is orange with maroon spots. The flaring tips of the tepals are sometimes orange but more frequently are a rich, bright red or red-orange**. In bud, the flowers are pendent (hanging), but in bloom, unlike those of most other lilies, the flowers are horizontal or erect. The lower leaves form beautiful whorls; some of the leaves higher on the stem are solitary and scattered.

Names: *Lilium:* see p. 167. *Parvum* means 'small'—a relative term, for tiger lily blossoms may be smaller than those of some other lilies, but they are anything but small compared to most wildflowers. **Where found:** also in Sagebrush Steppe. Wet meadows, streambanks, willow thickets; e.g., along Route 88 east of Carson Pass (8000') in July.

red-orange • 6 separate tepals • July–September

FIREWEED
Epilobium angustifolium • Evening-Primrose Family

Although fireweed is a **common plant,** often growing in large masses in burned or logged areas, it is uncommonly beautiful in summer and uniquely striking in fall. The stems are slender and tall (3–6') and bear many narrow, pointed, alternating leaves. Above the leaves, the top 1' or so of the plant is a spike of many 1–2", showy flowers. **From a distance the masses of flowers appear pastel pink or rose, but up close you can see** the striking color contrasts of pale rose petals, darker rose sepals, and white filaments and style. In fall the leaves turn a burnished red or bronze.

Names: *Epilobium* means 'upon pod,' in reference to the inferior ovary of these plants. *Angustifolium* means 'narrow-leaved.' **Where found:** Mixed Conifer Forest to 9000'; also in Sagebrush Steppe. Open woods, grassy fields, disturbed places; e.g., edges of Grass Lake (7700') in July.

rose-purple • 4 separate petals
• June–August

SMOOTHSTEM WILLOW-HERB
Epilobium glaberrimum • Evening-Primrose Family

With its 4 petals and long inferior ovary (especially noticeable late in the season when it swells to form the fruit), smoothstem willow-herb is easily recognized as a member of the evening-primrose family. However, unlike those of its relatives with many large, showy flowers, e.g., fireweed (above), rock fringe (p. 231), and California fuchsia (p. 182), this plant, despite its height (up to 3'), has only a few, relatively small flowers. Each ¼–½" flower, though, is quite striking—its **4 pink petals are 2-lobed** and have darker rose veins. The narrow, **squarish ovary under the petals can elongate to 3" in fruit**. The ½–3" clasping leaves come off the hairless stem in opposite pairs and are a distinctive waxy blue-green.

Names: *Epilobium:* see above. *Glaberrimum* means 'smooth,' in reference to the stems. **Where found:** also in Sagebrush Steppe and in Alpine to 12,000'. Seeps, rocky places, gravel bars; e.g., along the Tioga Pass road (8500') in August.

pink or rose-purple • 4 separate petals
• June–September

CALIFORNIA FUCHSIA
Epilobium canum • Evening-Primrose Family

As the flowers of summertime fade away with the season, a few special floral treats get ready to take center stage. California fuchsia, with its dazzling scarlet flower tubes, is certainly one of the most spectacular autumn bloomers, enticing not only hummingbirds on their southern migration but also human flower lovers on their last wildflower expeditions of the season. California fuchsia is a **subshrub to 2' tall** that is dense with grayish-green, ovate leaves. Rising out of the leaf axils are the **incredibly red, 1–2", tubular flowers**. The **4 petals are deeply 2-lobed**. The red stamens and the red, 4-lobed pistil protrude from the flower tube. To watch a brightly colored hummingbird reach deep into the red flower tubes for nectar is an unforgettable Technicolor treat.

Names: *Epilobium:* see p. 181. *Canum* means 'straight rod,' perhaps in reference to the tubular flowers or perhaps to the protruding stamens. The name fuchsia honors Leonard Fuchs, a 16th-century German physician and botanist. **Where found:** rock ledges, around boulders; e.g., along Route 88 east of Carson Pass (8000') in August.

red • 4 separate petals • August–September

JEFFREY'S SHOOTING STAR
Dodecatheon jeffreyi • Primrose Family

You're looking out over a wet mountain meadow in early spring. It's been a long, snowy winter and you're hungry for color and for flowers. Off in the distance, there appears to be a delicate pink ribbon snaking its way across the field. As you approach the ribbon, your spirits lift, for you have come across a line of Jeffrey's shooting star marking the sinuous path of a tiny creek. • This early bloomer is one of the loveliest of all eastern Sierra flowers. Hanging from their gracefully arching pedicels, the delicate ¹/₂–1" blossoms dance lightly in the slightest breeze. The **4 (sometimes 5) separate, pink petals are bent all the way back, fully exposing the black-purple 'nose' enfolding the reproductive parts. Above this nose, at the base of the petals, are bands of yellow and white**. It is not uncommon to find albinos mixed in with their pink siblings. The basal oval leaves are 3–20" long.

Names: *Dodecatheon* means '12 gods,' perhaps suggesting that this beautiful flower was worthy of protection by the Greek pantheon of Olympus. John Jeffrey was a 19th-century gardener at the Edinburgh Botanic Gardens. **Where found:** also in Sagebrush Steppe. Wet meadows, streambanks; e.g., around Grass Lake (7700') in June, and along trail to Morgan Pass (10,500') in July.

pink or rose • 4 (5) separate petals • June–July

BOG SHOOTING STAR
Dodecatheon redolens • Primrose Family

Bog shooting star is very similar to Jeffrey's shooting star (p. 182), with pink, inside-out flowers hanging from arching pedicels. In both plants the tall (to 2') plant stem rises above large basal leaves over 1' long and terminates in an umbel of several flowers on long pedicels. The most noticeable differences between these shooting stars are the color, the number of flowers in an umbel, and the number of petals and stamens. The flowers of bog shooting star have **5 stamens and 5 petals that tend to be pale pink. The umbels have 5–10 flowers**. Jeffrey's shooting star flowers have 4 stamens and usually 4 petals that tend to be a darker magenta or rose. Its umbels have 3–18 flowers. In both shooting stars, the flowers hang upside down until they've been pollinated, at which time they rise up to an erect position with their 'noses' heading skyward.

Names: *Dodecatheon:* see p. 182. *Redolens* means 'fragrant.' **Where found:** southern Mixed Conifer Forest. Wet meadows, streambanks; e.g., above Onion Valley on the trail to Kearsarge Pass (9500') in July.

pink to lavender • 5 separate petals • July–August

SNOWPLANT
Sarcodes sanguinea • Heath Family

When the **thick, fleshy, asparagus-like stems** of snowplant begin to power their way through the snow-compressed dirt and duff of the forest floor, you know spring is on its way. The growing tip of this remarkable plant is amazingly strong, sometimes piercing through asphalt! Growing in the dark of the forest, snowplant has **no green leaves**, getting its nutrients instead from the roots of neighboring plants with the help of mycorrhizal fungi. The only 'leaves' are strap-like bracts that cover the blooms when the plant first emerges. The **bracts, stem, and even flowers are all the same rich, red color. Most of the plant is cold, clammy, and sticky, being covered with tiny glands.** The black anthers are the only part of the urn-shaped flowers (and of the entire plant) that is not red. Snowplant is **protected under California law** by threat of fine.

Names: *Sarcodes* means 'flesh-like.' *Sanguinea* means 'blood red.' **Where found:** northern Mixed Conifer Forest to 10,000'. Forest shade; e.g., along the Thomas Creek road (7000') in May.

red • 5 petals united in urn • May–June

ALPINE LAUREL
Kalmia polifolia • Heath Family

The pink-saucer flowers of alpine laurel would be delightful in any setting, but they are especially cheering in their oozy, boggy habitat, and all the more so on a cold, drizzly day. Alpine laurel is a **4–12", evergreen shrub adorned with ¹/₂" pink flowers whose 5 petals form a shallow bowl or saucer. The 10 filaments splay out inside the saucer, laying the black anthers against the petals.** The anthers are held firmly in place by tiny pockets in the petals. Insects are in for a big surprise when they land on this flower, for their weight triggers the anthers to pop up and shake pollen over the unsuspecting visitors. The narrow, evergreen leaves have their edges rolled under.

Names: Peter Kalm was a student of Carolus Linnaeus (of binomial nomenclature fame) in the 1700s. *Polifolia* means 'white-leaved,' in reference to the white hairs on the undersides of the leaves. **Where found:** bogs, wet meadows, around lakes; e.g., around Frog Lake along trail to Winnemucca Lake (9000') in August.

pink or rose-purple • 5 petals united in a bowl • June–August

BOG WINTERGREEN
Pyrola asarifolia • Heath Family

As with all *Pyrola* species, bog wintergreen has numerous flowers along a leafless stem that rises above basal leaves. In bog wintergreen, the slender, **1–1¹/₂' stem bears 5–25 pink to red, ¹/₂" flowers hanging on short pedicels.** As with many other wintergreens, the style sticks way out of the flower and is usually somewhat curved. The **leathery basal leaves are large (to 3") and roundish with conspicuous veins.** • The leaves of many *Pyrola* species, including bog wintergreen, were used historically to treat bruises, and so these plants were sometimes called 'shinleaf.' Bog wintergreen is one of the few wintergreens that likes to grow in **wet areas.**

Names: *Pyrola* means 'little pear,' in reference to the leaf shape of many species. *Asarifolia* means 'leaves like *Asarum*,' the wild ginger genus, plants of which have large, round, glossy leaves. **Where found:** northern Mixed Conifer Forest to 10,000'. Streambanks, wet places in woods; e.g., along the Thomas Creek trail (7000') in June.

pink (red) • 5 petals united in urn • June–July

RED HEATHER
Phyllodoce breweri • Heath Family

Without flowers, red heather might be mistaken for the ground-hugging new growth of some evergreen tree, for it is an **evergreen shrub whose thin 6–12" stems are thickly covered with short, needle-like leaves**. But when it is blooming, red heather is unlikely to be confused with any plant except alpine laurel (p. 184). Like alpine laurel, red heather has 1/2" pink or **red-purple, bowl-shaped or saucer-shaped flowers with 10 stamens and 1 pistil**. The anthers of both plants shake pollen on visiting insects. Unlike alpine laurel, though, red heather does not have pockets in the petals to keep the anthers spring-loaded, **so the stamens of red heather stick up out of the flower bowl, giving the clusters of flowers a fuzzy look**.

Names: *Phyllodoce* was a sea nymph in Greek mythology. Brewer: see p. 140. **Where found:** rocky places, around lakes, meadows, open woods; e.g., around Heart Lake on the trail from Mosquito Flat to Morgan Pass (10,500') in July.

pink to rose-purple • 5 petals united in a bowl • June–August

BULL ELEPHANT'S HEAD
Pedicularis groenlandica • Snapdragon Family

A herd of pink elephants on a stick—you might not believe it until you see bull elephant's head, but then there's no denying it! The top several inches (to 12") of the 1/2–2 1/2' stem is packed with scores of the 1/2" flowers, each complete with broad, floppy 'ears' and a long, up-curving 'trunk'. The slender trunk usually curls at the tip, holding the tiny pistil like Dumbo hanging on to his feather. This trunk is actually the 2 petals of the upper lip of the flower, while the ears are the outer 2 petals of the 3 petals of the lower lip. Every now and then you will find an albino 'herd' (bottom photo). The 1–10" leaves are basal and fern-like, i.e., deeply divided.

Names: *Pedicularis* means 'lousewort,' referring to an old superstition that animals that eat some species of *Pedicularis* become susceptible to lice infestation. *Groenlandica* means 'of Greenland,' in reference to the circumboreal distribution of this species, though it does not actually occur in Greenland. **Where found:** wet meadows, streambanks, bogs; e.g., along trail to Winnemucca Lake (9000') in July, and around Gardisky Lake (10,500') in July.

pink to rose-purple • 5 petals united in 2-lipped tube • June–August

LITTLE ELEPHANT'S HEAD
Pedicularis attollens • Snapdragon Family

Little elephant's head is quite similar to its close relative bull elephant's head (p. 185), but as you would expect it is smaller—**only 4–18" tall with ¼–½" flowers. Also, its blossoms do not look quite as elephant-like; the floppy 'ears' are a good replica, but the 'trunk' is smaller and curves a bit sideways.** The inflorescence is covered with dense, soft, white hairs. • The 2 elephant's head species are often pollinated by the same bees on the same days, but they apparently avoid crossbreeding by means of the different orientation and shape of the 'trunks.' Each species uses a different part of the bee's body for depositing and picking up pollen, ensuring that their pollen is kept separate and the 2 *Pedicularis* species maintain distinct identities.

Names: *Pedicularis:* see p. 185. *Attollens* means 'upraised,' in reference to the trunk-like petals. **Where found:** wet meadows, streambanks, bogs; e.g., near Heart Lake on trail from Mosquito Flat to Morgan Pass (10,500') in July.

pink to rose-purple • 5 petals united in 2-lipped tube • July–August

MOUNTAIN PRIDE
Penstemon newberryi • Snapdragon Family

The mountains must be delighted with all their wildflowers, for each plant has some special quality or attribute—color, form, size, growth habit, fruits. Although all flowers are wonderful, mountain pride is exceptional. It is easy to understand how this plant got its name, and it's tempting to believe that the mountains themselves did the naming! Mountain pride is a low **(6–12") subshrub that frequently cascades down rocky slopes, bringing bright, cherry red color** to the white or gray of the granite. The flowers are 1–1½" tubes that flare only slightly at the mouth. The **stiff, leathery, roundish leaves are mostly basal,** so the flowers are on full and glorious display.

Names: *Penstemon:* see p. 71. John Newberry was a 19th-century naturalist in the American West. **Where found:** also in Sagebrush Steppe. Rock ledges, talus slopes; e.g., along Route 88 west of Woodfords (6000') in June, and near Kearsarge Pass along trail from Onion Valley (11,000') in July.

red • 5 petals united in 2-lipped tube • June–August

BRIDGE'S PENSTEMON
Penstemon rostriflorus • Snapdragon Family

The 1–3', slender stems of Bridge's penstemon are often **so thick with the 1–1½", scarlet, bugle-like blossoms that you can barely see the stems**. And who would be looking at the stems or the opposite pairs of small, narrow leaves, anyway, for the flowers' spectacular color and intriguing form monopolize all the attention. **In bud the flowers are tight, scarlet torpedos; in bloom they look like seals swimming through the air**. The 3 petals of the lower lip bend out and back, resembling flippers in action. The 2 petals of the upper lip form a sort of snout that sticks straight out. The red-purple calyx is glandular-sticky.

Names: *Penstemon:* see p. 71. *Rostriflorus* means 'beaked flower,' in reference to the snout-like projection formed by the upper 2 petals. **Where found:** southern and central Mixed Conifer Forest to 10,000'; also in Sagebrush Steppe. Dry hillsides (often with sagebrush), open woods; e.g., near South Lake along the road from Bishop (9500') in July, and along the Tioga Pass road (9500') in July.

red • 5 petals united in 2-lipped tube • May–September

LEMMON'S PAINTBRUSH
Castilleja lemmonii • Snapdragon Family

Like magenta beacons rising above a green sea, the **6–12" spikes of Lemmon's paintbrush stick up above the surrounding grass** of their meadow habitat. Even if the grass outgrows it, this paintbrush refuses to be hidden; its vivid and intense color announces its presence in no uncertain terms. As with all paintbrushes, most of the color of Lemmon's paintbrush comes not from the flowers but from the bracts (modified leaves). The true flowers, with their yellow beaks and 3 yellow-green sacs (formed from the lower 3 petals), are almost completely concealed by the showy magenta bracts. Unlike many paintbrushes whose colorful bracts extend far down the stem, Lemmon's paintbrush has a relatively **short (1–4") 'brush.'** The leaves on the upper stem have 3 lobes, while those lower down are usually unlobed. All the leaves tend to be pressed against the stem, not protruding as much as the leaves of most paintbrushes.

Names: *Castilleja:* see p. 67. Lemmon: see p. 179. **Where found:** moist meadows; e.g., along trail from Mosquito Flat to Morgan Pass (10,500') in July.

magenta to rose-purple bracts • 5 petals united in 2-lipped tube • June–August

GREAT RED PAINTBRUSH
Castilleja miniata • Snapdragon Family

Great red paintbrush, as its name suggests, is one of the largest and most robust of the paintbrushes. It can grow **almost 3' tall,** it often grows in large clumps, and its 'brush' is long and broad. As with all paintbrushes, most of the color of great red paintbrush comes from its bracts, but unlike most paintbrushes, its flowers *do* contribute to the color of the plant. The **beaks, formed by the 2 petals of the upper lip, are yellow-green and stick out conspicuously beyond the bracts**. The 3 petals of the lower lip of the flower have atrophied to tiny, green, leaf-like structures. Unlike most paintbrushes, the leaves of great red paintbrush (even those on the upper stem) are unlobed. The inflorescence is often white-hairy, and the stems are often reddish.

Names: *Castilleja:* see p. 67. *Miniata* means 'cinnabar red.' Also called streamside paintbrush. **Where found:** also in Sagebrush Steppe. Moist meadows, streambanks; e.g., along the trail to Winnemucca Lake (9000') in July, and east of Saddlebag Lake (10,500') in September.

red bracts • 5 petals united in 2-lipped tube • July–September

LEWIS' MONKEYFLOWER
Mimulus lewisii • Snapdragon Family

If you are a monkeyflower aficionado, or if you simply take a look at all the monkeyflowers in this book, you will probably appreciate their perky charm and their remarkable diversity in color, size, and form. All *Mimulus* flowers have 5 petals united into a 2-lipped tube that flares into a wide 'face,' but the flowers can range from 1/8" to 2" and from yellow to orange to pink or red to purple. • Lewis' monkeyflower is one of the largest *Mimulus* species, in terms of both the plant and the flowers. Its **1–3' stems bear many 1–2" flowers,** which range from pale **pink to darker rose**. The **petals are squarish** and are usually marked with vertical rose-purple streaks. The bases of the lower petals have clumps of yellow or white hairs.

Names: *Mimulus:* see p. 67. Lewis: see p. 129. **Where found:** streambanks, seeps; e.g., along the Tioga Pass road (9000') in July.

pink to rose-purple • 5 petals united in 2-lipped tube • June–September

SCARLET MONKEYFLOWER
Mimulus cardinalis • Snapdragon Family

Although you may think 'yellow' when you think of monkeyflowers, many *Mimulus* species in the eastern Sierra are some shade of red. It's amazing how many such shades there are in monkeyflowers—from pink to rose to magenta to fuchsia to rose-purple. But even when you think you've seen all the shades, you haven't really seen red at all until you've seen *M. cardinalis*. The 1¹/₂–2" **flowers have velvety, flaming scarlet petals that bend back, giving the flowers a rather puffy look**. The stamens are tall and erect, bearing white, hairy anthers. The flowers are borne at the tips of long pedicels that rise out of the leaf axils. The 2–4' plant stem bears many pairs of broad, fleshy leaves 1–3" long.

Names: *Mimulus:* see p. 67. *Cardinalis* means 'red.' **Where found:** Mixed Conifer Forest to 9000'; also in Sagebrush Steppe. Seeps, streambanks; e.g., Alabama Hills (4500') in July, along trail to Baxter Pass (7000') in July, and along Mt. Whitney trail (9000') in September.

red • 5 petals united in 2-lipped tube • June–September

TORREY'S MONKEYFLOWER
Mimulus torreyi • Snapdragon Family

Some *Mimulus* species dazzle you with a few large, colorful flowers; others amaze you with solid carpets of small or even tiny, colorful flowers. The blooms of Torrey's monkeyflower are only moderately large (¹/₂"), but they may be the **largest *Mimulus* flowers that consistently form extensive carpets**. Each 2–8" stem bears several pink to magenta flowers, and the plants usually mass together. This combination creates a glorious magenta spread on the usually rather bare, sandy ground where these monkeyflowers grow. The **inside of the magenta flower tube is marked with 2 parallel gold stripes, each bordered by dark rose margins**. Only a few opposite pairs of small, oval leaves are scattered along the stem. Often these green leaves have red-purple margins.

Names: *Mimulus:* see p. 67. John Torrey was a 19th-century professor of botany and collector of California plants. **Where found:** Mixed Conifer Forest to 7500'; also in Sagebrush Steppe. Sandy or gravelly flats, open woods; e.g., Hope Valley (6500') in June.

pink or magenta • 5 petals united in 2-lipped tube • June–August

BRIDGE'S GILIA
Gilia leptalea • Phlox Family

Although it hugs the ground (the plant stems are 1–10" tall) and has small (¹⁄₄") flowers, Bridge's gilia can dazzle you with a carpet of color, for it **often covers several square yards with hundreds of its pink to purple flowers**. From a distance these gilia carpets appear to be solid pink, but close examination of a flower reveals a remarkable range of colors. The **narrow flower tube is pale yellow, the flaring petal lobes are pink or lavender, and the protruding anthers are turquoise or blue-purple**. The leaves, like everything else about this plant, are narrow and delicate.

Names: Gil: see p. 63. *Leptalea* means 'slender,' perhaps in reference to the very narrow flower tubes or to the leaves. **Where found:** Mixed Conifer Forest to 10,000'; also in Sagebrush Steppe. Sandy or gravelly flats, open woods; e.g., around Frog Lake along trail to Winnemucca Lake (9000') in July.

pink or lavender • 5 petals united in tube • June–August

SCARLET GILIA
Ipomopsis aggregata • Phlox Family

You might think that dry, scrubby sagebrush openings in the Mixed Conifer Forest zone wouldn't have much color, but in many such areas of the eastern Sierra you'd be very wrong. On sandy or gravelly patches between various shrubs, you will often find an amazing array of intense colors including blues and purples (larkspur, phacelia, penstemon), yellows (mule ears, pretty face, wallflower), whites (yampah, mariposa lily, pennyroyal), pinks (Bridge's gilia, horse-mint, Sierra onion, checkermallow), and reds (Anderson's thistle, scarlet gilia). Of all these colorful wildflowers of the dry slopes, the flowers of scarlet gilia are certainly among the fieriest. The **1–1¹⁄₂" trumpets are usually an intense scarlet, though they are sometimes pale pink or even white** (some botanists consider the pink- or white-flowered plants a separate species, *I. tenuituba*). The upper parts of the 1–3' stems bear many flowers. The needle-lobed leaves are mostly basal.

Names: *Ipomopsis* means 'striking appearance.' *Aggregata* means 'clustered.' Formerly called *Gilia aggregata*. **Where found:** also in Sagebrush Steppe. Dry flats often with sagebrush, open woods; e.g., along the Thomas Creek trail (7500') in June, and along Horseshoe Meadow Road (9500') in July.

red • 5 petals united in tube • June–August

TINY TRUMPET
Collomia linearis • Phlox Family

Although the flowers of tiny trumpet are indeed tiny (¹/₄" across), especially for such a relatively large plant (to 2'), they are nonetheless quite showy in a diminutive sort of way. At first glance the plant may seem all leaves, for the **narrow, 2–3" leaves cover the plant from bottom to top, threatening to completely overwhelm the flowers.** But the **flowers make up for their small size by forming clusters of 7–20 and by being bright pink** (sometimes white). These splotches of color draw your eye despite the proliferation of leaves. The 5 stamens with their sticky, white pollen protrude slightly from the flower tubes.

Names: *Collomia:* see p. 86. *Linearis* means 'narrow,' in reference to the leaves. **Where found:** Mixed Conifer Forest to 8500'; also in Sagebrush Steppe. Sandy flats, open woods, grassy meadows; e.g., Hope Valley (6500') in July.

pink (white) • 5 petals united in tube • June–August

CHECKERMALLOW
Sidalcea glaucescens • Mallow Family

Checkermallow is a common resident of dry slopes, bringing cheery patches of rosy pink to these hillsides. The ¹/₂–2' stems bear a few of the 1–1¹/₂" flowers scattered along their length. The **5 separate, pink petals have white veins and overlap to form a bowl.** The reproductive parts are unusual in that the stamens and the pistil are all part of the same column-like structure in the center of the bowl. The **many white, bubbly-looking stamens ripen first** (top photo); **later the red, thread-like stigmas** (bottom photo) **emerge above the male parts.** The leaves are hollyhock-like with 5–7 lobes. The lobes of the leaves near the base of the plant are further divided.

Names: *Sidalcea* is a combination of 2 Greek names, *Sida* and *Alcea,* which are both genera in the mallow family. *Glaucescens* means 'glaucous,' in reference to the whitish, waxy film covering the stem. **Where found:** Mixed Conifer Forest to 10,000'; also in Sagebrush Steppe. Dry slopes, meadows; e.g., near Monitor Pass (8300') in July.

pink to rose-purple • 5 separate petals • June–August

BOG MALLOW
Sidalcea oregana • Mallow Family

The flowers of bog mallow (or, if you have a sweet tooth, marsh mallow) are quite similar to those of its dry-habitat relative, checkermallow (p. 191). Both have a bowl shape, pink color, and central column of male and female reproductive parts. Bog mallow, however, is a taller plant (1–5') with many more flowers packed onto its spike inflorescence. **Although the flowers are somewhat smaller (¹/₂–1") than those of checkermallow, their numbers and their density make the plant extremely showy.** The mostly basal leaves are hollyhock-like, with 5–7 lobes.

Names: *Sidalcea:* see p. 191. *Oregana:* see p. 153. Also called marsh mallow, Oregon mallow. **Where found:** Mixed Conifer Forest to 10,000'; also in Sagebrush Steppe. Wet meadows, seeps, bogs; e.g., Hope Valley (6500') in July.

pink to rose • 5 separate petals • June–August

PURSH'S MILKVETCH
Astragalus purshii • Pea Family

There are over 2000 species of *Astragalus* worldwide, of which at least 70 species occur in the Sierra Nevada, the Great Basin, and the California–Nevada deserts. Most of these species are ideally suited for dry, sandy, or gravelly habitats, for they are dwarfed, ground-hugging plants with tiny, hairy leaflets. Pursh's milkvetch is a perfect illustration of such a dry-adapted plant; it forms ground-hugging mats, it has pinnately compound leaves with tiny leaflets, and the stems and leaves are covered with silky hairs. In fact it is so well adapted to dry environments that it occurs all the way from the Mojave Desert to near timberline in the Sierra. The **1" flowers are a beautiful pink-purple with a purple-streaked white patch on the banner. The fuzzy, white seedpods resemble cotton balls.**

Names: *Astragalus:* see p. 66. Pursh: see p. 98. **Where found:** also in Mojave Desert Scrub and in Sagebrush Steppe. Dry flats and slopes; e.g., along Bishop Creek (6000') in June, and east side of Mt. Rose (9500') in July.

pink-purple • 5 irregular petals • June–August

NEVADA PEA
Lathyrus lanszwertii • Pea Family

The ¹/₂" flowers of Nevada pea are easily recognizable as pea flowers, with the erect, showy banner and 'cupped-hands' wings. The *Lathyrus* genus has ladder-like, pinnately compound leaves whose main axis ends in a **tendril** or bristle. Nevada pea is generally a sprawling plant (though the tendrils can hold it up if there's something tall nearby to grab on to) with a cluster of 2–10 flowers on each stem. The flowers are a **delicate pink or rose (sometimes lavender) with darker rose or purple veins**. The sharply pointed calyx teeth are noticeably unequal. The **2–5 opposite or nearly opposite pairs of leaflets are long (to 3"), narrow, and pointed.**

Names: *Lathyrus* is the ancient Greek name for the genus. Dr. L. Lanszweert was a 19th-century Belgian physician who collected plants in the American West and was a member of the California Academy of Science. **Where found:** northern Mixed Conifer Forest to 7500'; also in Sagebrush Steppe. Dry slopes, open woods; e.g., along the Thomas Creek trail (7500') in May.

pink to rose (lavender) • 5 irregular petals • May–June

HORSE-MINT
Agastache urticifolia • Mint Family

Horse-mint usually grows in great masses, so when you see one spike of its pink to rose flowers, you usually see what looks like a forest of them. Because the plants **are tall (3–5') and leafy and the 2–7" flower spikes are crammed with scores of the ¹/₂" flowers,** this sight is impressive indeed. The flower spikes have a **brushy appearance because the 2 pairs of long, slender stamens protrude well out of the flower tube.** The petals are pink or pale rose, but the spikes have a somewhat darker appearance because the sepals tend to be dark rose. Many opposite pairs of 1–3", triangular, serrated leaves branch off the square stem. When crushed, they exude a pungent aroma. Where horse-mint grows with its fellow mint pennyroyal (p. 208), the cloud of mint fragrance can be almost overwhelming.

Names: *Agastache* means 'many spikes.' *Urticifolia* means 'nettle-leaved,' referring to the similarity of the leaves to those of stinging nettle (p. 210). Also called giant hyssop. **Where found:** Mixed Conifer Forest to 10,000'; also in Sagebrush Steppe. Dry slopes, open woods; e.g., along trail to Winnemucca Lake (9000') in July.

pink to rose or white • 5 petals united in 2-lipped tube • June–August

CRIMSON COLUMBINE
Aquilegia formosa • Buttercup Family

If you are a hummingbird, you must have visions of crimson columbine in your dreams. Its **bright red to orange** color is extremely visible and alluring to you (whereas it is outside the spectrum of visible light for most insects); its upside-down orientation is easily handled by your hovering skill; its **1–1½" tubular petals ending in nectar spurs** are a perfect fit for your long bill and tongue; and the nectar is plentiful and delicious. You couldn't have come up with a more perfect flower if you'd designed it yourself! The 1–4' plant stem has only a few of these gorgeous flowers hanging at the ends of long, arching pedicels. Contrasting with the red of the tubular petals and flaring sepals is the bright yellow at the mouth of the petals and the yellow anthers at the tips of long, protruding stamens. As with shooting stars (pp. 182, 183), the hanging flowers of crimson columbine celebrate being pollinated by rising up to an erect position.

Names: *Aquilegia* comes from the Latin *aquila,* 'eagle,' probably in reference to the talon-like nectar spurs. *Formosa* means 'beautiful' or 'graceful.' **Where found:** also in Sagebrush Steppe. Streambanks, open woods; e.g., along the Thomas Creek trail (7000') in June, and along the trail to Morgan Pass (10,500') in July.

red or orange • 5 irregular petals • June–August

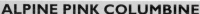

ALPINE PINK COLUMBINE
Aquilegia formosa/A. pubescens hybrid • Buttercup Family

Within only a narrow elevational range (9000–10,500') and in only a few places (Yosemite and south) do both crimson columbine (above) and alpine columbine (p. 222) grow. If you find one of these places, you may be fortunate enough to see one of the eastern Sierra's greatest wildflower wonders—a hybrid between these very different columbines. The flowers of the hybrid are typically as large as those of alpine columbine (1½–2"), but other characteristics, such as color and orientation of the flowers, are a blend of both species. The result is truly spectacular—flowers with **pale pink petals and sepals (often with white at the base of the petals), hanging at some intermediate angle from the plant stem.** Adding to the drama

and poignancy of seeing these rare and gorgeous flowers is the knowledge that they can't reproduce; you are looking at the 'end of the line' until a bee happens to carry pollen from one species to the other again.

Names: *Aquilegia:* see above. *Formosa:* see above. *Pubescens:* see p. 222. **Where found:** southern and central Mixed Conifer Forest from 9000' to 10,500'. Rock ledges, talus slopes; e.g., along trail to Morgan Pass (10,500') in July, and above Saddlebag Lake (10,500') in August.

pink • 5 irregular petals • July–August

WAX CURRANT
Ribes cereum • Gooseberry Family

Wax currant is a **shrub that can reach 6' tall** in the relatively favorable environment below timberline. In the more difficult conditions of the alpine environment it stays closer to the ground, rarely exceeding 1–2'. In either environment you'll probably be happy to encounter it, for its flowers are lovely, its fruits are tangy and tasty, and its leaves exude a pleasant, spicy fragrance when crushed. The plant is extremely leafy—the small, round, shallowly lobed leaves are dense all the way to the ends of the stems. They have a noticeable waxy sheen on the upper surface and are usually slightly sticky to the touch. The ¹/₂" pink or white flowers are narrow tubes flaring slightly at the tips like **tiny trumpets**. They occur in **clusters of 3–7 that hang downward or lie horizontally**. The **fruits are ¹/₄–¹/₂" red spheres**.

Names: *Ribes* is the ancient Arabic name for these plants. *Cereum* means 'waxy glands,' in reference to the glandular-sticky leaves. **Where found:** also in Sagebrush Steppe and in Alpine to 13,000'. Open woods, rocky slopes; e.g., along trail to Baxter Pass (9000') in June.

pink or white • 5 petals united in tube • May–July

MOUNTAIN SPIRAEA
Spiraea densiflora • Rose Family

Although the individual flowers of mountain spiraea are tiny (¹/₈"), they cram together by the scores into **flat-topped clusters that can be up to 5" across**. These dense, rosy clusters of flowers are always a delight to discover, for their **soft pink color** is soothing and their gentle **rose fragrance** is intoxicating. The scent is not quite as strong as that of wild rose (p. 115), but on a warm summer day it is just as sweet and caressing. Like other members of the rose family, mountain spiraea has 5 separate petals, but you have to look closely to see them for they are nearly concealed by the clusters of protruding reproductive parts. Mountain spiraea is a **shrub up to 3' tall** whose reddish new stems and dark green, toothed, ¹/₂–1¹/₂" leaves create a striking background for its pink, fuzzy-looking clusters of flowers.

Names: *Spiraea* comes from a word for 'coil' or 'wreath.' *Densiflora* means 'densely flowered.' **Where found:** also in Sagebrush Steppe. Moist and rocky places, open woods; e.g., along Bishop Creek (7000') in July, and along trail to Morgan Pass (10,500') in August.

pink or rose • 5 separate petals • July–August

OLD MAN'S WHISKERS
Geum triflorum • Rose Family

Old man's whiskers is one of those unusual flowers that is just as intricate and showy in fruit as it is in bloom. In flower, the **5 pink or cream petals and 5 similar sepals form a puckered kiss** that hangs at the end of a long, arching pedicel. At the base of the flower are 5 narrow, pink bracts. The $^1/_2$–2' stem sometimes bears only a single flower, but more often bears 2 or 3. In fruit, the pedicels straighten, lifting the flowers to an erect position. The petals and sepals shrivel but stay at the base of the flower, while the many styles (so small and inconspicuous before) elongate into long, slender, sinuous, red threads covered with short, white hairs. These **scores of styles, which may grow 1$^1/_2$" long, form an astonishing, soft, wavy, feathered brush**. The 2–8" leaves are pinnately compound with 1 leaflet at the end.

Names: *Geum*: see p. 171. *Triflorum* means '3-flowered,' in reference to this plant's tendency to bear flowers in clusters of 3. The common name refers to the dense cluster of feathery styles in fruit. Also called prairie smoke and downy avens. **Where found:** northern Mixed Conifer Forest to 10,000'; also in Sagebrush Steppe. Dry slopes, meadows; e.g., around Frog Lake along trail to Winnemucca Lake (9000') in July.

pink or white • 5 separate petals • June–August

PURPLE CINQUEFOIL
Potentilla palustris • Rose Family

You probably expect cinquefoils to have bright yellow flowers, and most of the time you'd be right. Sometimes, however, the flowers are pale yellow or even white (e.g., sticky cinquefoil, p. 143), while in purple cinquefoil the flowers are an amazing wine purple. The color of the flower is not the only surprising aspect of this plant, for its habitat is also unusual for cinquefoils: **bogs and marshes**. The 8–20" stems rise above spreading (and often floating) runners. The upper part of the stem supports several $^1/_2$–$^3/_4$" flowers, while the lower part of the stem bears a few 2–8" compound leaves. The leaflets are narrow and toothed and are often purple tinged. The **petals and sepals and central cluster of many reproductive parts are usually all the same red-purple color, though the sepals are sometimes yellowish green**.

Names: *Potentilla*: see p. 143. *Palustris* means 'of the marsh.' **Where found:** northern Mixed Conifer Forest. Bogs, marshes; e.g., swampy edges of Grass Lake (7700') in July.

red-purple • 5 separate petals • July–August

CORYMB BROOMRAPE
Orobanche corymbosa • Broomrape Family

Corymb broomrape lives up to its ominous name—it does 'rape' and 'strangle' by **parasitizing** neighbors (often sagebrush or buckwheat; you can see buckwheat in the photo). The 1–6" plant consists of many **(frequently more than 20) tubular flowers clustered on or near the ground**. The 2-lipped tubes tend to be pale **pink-salmon**, while their 'faces' are often darker pink-purple. The middle petal of the lower lip is noticeably narrower than the other 4 petals. Being a parasite, corymb broomrape has no need for leaves, so the entire plant is the same rather fungal-looking pink or pink-purple color.

Names: *Orobanche* means 'vetch strangler,' in reference to the parasitic habit. *Corymbosa* means 'corymbose,' in reference to the branching inflorescence. **Where found:** Mixed Conifer Forest to 9500'; also in Sagebrush Steppe. Sandy or gravelly slopes often with sagebrush, ridges, open woods; e.g., above Winnemucca Lake (9000') in August.

pink-purple • 5 petals united in tube
• July–September

WANDERING DAISY
Erigeron peregrinus • Composite Family

Wandering daisy is similar in many respects to several other *Erigeron* species of the eastern Sierra. It has a large (to 1¹/₂") flowerhead composed of a central disk of scores of yellow disk flowers surrounded by many radiating ray flowers, and each plant stem usually bears only 1 flowerhead (though there can be as many as 4). Some characteristics of wandering daisy, however, do help distinguish it from some of its close relatives. Unlike Coulter's daisy (p. 162), whose rays are always white, and unlike Eaton's daisy (p. 162), whose white rays can be pink tinged at the tips, wandering daisy has **rays that can be white but are usually pale pink, lavender, or purple throughout**. Also, wandering daisy looks messier than those other 2 daisies, for its **30–100 rays are crowded and overlapping**. The 2–8" leaves are mostly basal but there are a few clasping stem leaves.

Names: *Erigeron*: see p. 106. *Peregrinus* means 'exotic' or 'wanderer,' in reference to this plant's wide distribution that includes Asia. Also called subalpine daisy. **Where found:** meadows, rocky places; e.g., above Onion Valley along the trail to Kearsarge Pass (9500') in July.

pink, white, lavender or purple • many ray and disk flowers • June–August

ANDERSON'S THISTLE
Cirsium andersonii • Composite Family

If you have any doubt about what kinds of flowers humming-birds are attracted to, just tail some of these darting birds for a while—if you can keep up—and you will quickly notice a pattern emerge. After you've seen them hover persistently around California fuchsia, crimson columbine, mountain pride, great red paintbrush, and Anderson's thistle, you will probably conclude (correctly) that they favor **red, tubular flowers**. Although the spiny disk flowers of Anderson's thistle do not have large tubes, there are certainly many of them in each flowerhead. Since most plants have several flowerheads, hummingbirds are kept busy for several minutes probing all the flower tubes for nectar. The **1–3' plants bear numerous large, deeply lobed, spiny leaves**. The phyllaries under the flowerheads are also spiny. Often the leaves and stems are covered with white hairs.

Names: *Cirsium:* see p. 70. Nils Anderson was a 19th-century Swedish botanist who collected plants in California. **Where found:** Mixed Conifer Forest to 10,000'; also in Sagebrush Steppe. Dry slopes, open woods; e.g., along Thomas Creek (7000') in July.

red • many disk flowers • July–September

WESTERN EUPATORIUM
Ageratina occidentalis • Composite Family

As summer slowly fades to fall, most wildflowers fade from the flamboyance of their youth to the subtlety of their old age. The bright colors drop with the petals, and browns take center stage. But in the midst of this muted world, a few colorful wildflower glories are just reaching their peak. Sierra primrose and California fuchsia dazzle the landscape with bright red, while explorer's gentian intensifies it with rich blue, and rabbitbrush brightens it with sparkling yellow. **Cascading down talus slopes and over rock ledges, western eupatorium tempers the intensity of these colors with soft blankets of pink or lavender**. Each flowerhead consists of **clusters of long, slender, tubular disk flowers atop ¹/₂–2¹/₂' stems**. The leaves are broadly triangular and toothed. When hundreds of eupatorium flowerheads mass together, the landscape seems to soften, perhaps in sweet acceptance of the end of another cycle.

Names: *Ageratina* means 'resembling *Ageratum*,' another genus in the composite family. *Occidentalis:* see p. 102. Formerly called *Eupatorium occidentale*. **Where found:** also in Sagebrush Steppe. Rocky areas; e.g., along Bishop Creek (8000') in September.

pink, lavender, or white • many disk flowers • July–September

BLUE-EYED GRASS
Sisyrinchium idahoense • Iris Family

As you are walking through what you think is a damp field of knee-deep grass, you are surprised to see flashes of blue-purple and yellow among the flat, green grass blades. You've come across the stunning color contrasts of blue-eyed grass. The 1/2–1" flowers have **deep blue-purple (sometimes paler blue) tepals with darker purple veins**. The tepals are either round tipped or notched with 1 tiny point. Contrasting with the blue-purple is the **bright yellow of the protruding reproductive parts and of the inside of the flower tube**. Insects probably expect nectar glands, but in the case of blue-eyed grass, the bright yellow is a ruse—no nectar, just a patch of pigment. You might wonder whether that insect will ever fall for this trick again! The unbranched 4–16" stem rises well above the grass-like leaves and bears 1 or a few flowers.

Names: *Sisyrinchium* was the ancient Greek name for an iris-like plant. *Idahoense* means 'of Idaho.' **Where found:** Mixed Conifer Forest to 10,000'; also in Sagebrush Steppe. Moist meadows, streambanks; e.g., along the Tioga Pass road (8500') in July, and along the trail to Kearsarge Pass (10,000') in August.

blue or blue-purple • 6 tepals • June–August

ALPINE VERONICA
Veronica wormskjoldii • Snapdragon Family

Despite their small size, the 1/4" blossoms of alpine veronica dazzle with their intense blue or blue-purple petals. They also reveal unsuspected subtlety and range of color, from the **bright green ovary and the white flower center to the delicate, red-purple streaks on the petals**. Unlike almost all members of the snapdragon family, which have 5 petals, the veronicas have only **4 petals,** though the 1 petal of the upper lip is larger than the 3 petals of the lower lip and is actually 2 petals that have fused. The stamens are also unusual, only 2 instead of the normal 5, and they along with the long pistil stick out of the flower. Alpine veronica's **leaves are small and elliptic** and occur in several opposite pairs along the stem.

Names: *Veronica* probably honors Saint Veronica. Morton Wormskjold was a 19th-century Danish plant collector. Formerly called *V. alpina.* **Where found:** moist meadows, streambanks, seeps; e.g., along the Tioga Pass road (9000') in July.

Related plant: American brooklime (*V. americana*, bottom photo) has very similar flowers but shiny, much larger leaves. It usually grows in great masses on decumbent stems, frequenting wet areas throughout the Sagebrush Steppe and Mixed Conifer Forest zones; e.g., along Bishop Creek (6000') in July.

blue or blue-purple • 4 petals united in 2-lipped tube • June–August

HIKER'S GENTIAN
Gentianopsis simplex • Gentian Family

Growing only **4–12" tall, hiker's gentian is often overgrown by the lush grass of its wet-meadow habitat.** Overgrown— but certainly not concealed, for the remarkable color and form of its flowers give them an eye-catching presence that belies their short stature. Each stem bears only 1 flower. The narrow flower tubes, cradled by finger-like, green sepals, can be up to 2" long and (as with most gentians) flare out into showy petal lobes. It is these **petal lobes that are so distinctive. They are long and oddly twisted, they are ragged on the edges,** and they are an amazingly saturated blue.

Names: *Gentianopsis* means 'resembling *Gentiana*,' another genus in the gentian family (see pp. 201 and 219). *Simplex* means 'simple.'
Where found: wet meadows; e.g., around Grass Lake (7700') in August.

Related plant: Sierra gentian (*G. holopetala*, bottom photo) is another late-blooming, 4-petaled, tubular gentian but without the twisted and ragged petals. It tends to be more shiny purple than rich blue. It occurs in wet meadows throughout the Mixed Conifer Forest zone and up into the Alpine zone, e.g., at the north end of Saddlebag Lake (10,100') in September.

blue • 4 petals united in tube • July–September

FELWORT
Gentianella amarella • Gentian Family

Fall is such a glorious time in the eastern Sierra. Aspens and willows and a few other deciduous trees celebrate another year's leaving with magnificent bursts of gold, bronze, and sometimes burgundy. The sky is Caribbean blue, the sun is bright but muted, the air is crisp and full of earthy smells, and the ground is thick and mulchy with fallen leaves and drying plants. But if you look closely, you can find a few flowers, such as felwort, still in bloom down in the grass. Felwort can be difficult to find, for it is **only 4–20" tall and has small (¹⁄₄") blooms that barely stick up above their green sepals.** It's worth trying to find them, though, for they are little floral treasures, their slender tubes flaring into **delicately fringed, violet or blue (sometimes red-purple) petal lobes.** Many of the small flowers cluster along the plant stem among the pairs of small, ovate leaves.

Names: *Gentianella* means 'little *Gentiana*' (see above). *Amarella* means 'bitter.' Also called northern gentian.
Where found: wet meadows, bogs, seeps; e.g., east of Saddlebag Lake (10,500') in September.

blue to rose-violet or red-purple • 5 (or 4) petals united in tube • July–September

STAR FELWORT
Swertia perennis • Gentian Family

In a group of plants (gentian family) known for deep blue or purple, tubular flowers, star felwort is a bit unusual. Its flowers are much more 'face' than tube and the color is much paler, tending **toward light violet with narrow, darker purple veins.** Whereas most gentians have prominent, sometimes very large tubes out of which flare the petal lobes, star felwort is a 1/2" flat **star with hardly any tube at all.** Also unusual is the growth form. The 4–12" stem bears clusters of flowers, each on a long pedicel that rises out of a leaf axil. (In many members of the gentian family, the flowers are solitary or grow in small clusters on short, often concealed, pedicels.) The elliptic stem leaves occur in opposite pairs; the basal leaves are spoon shaped.

Names: Sweert: see p. 141. *Perennis* means 'perennial,' distinguishing this species from the many of the genus that die after flowering. **Where found:** southern Mixed Conifer Forest. Wet meadows, bogs; e.g., above Onion Valley on trail to Kearsarge Pass (9500') in July.

violet or pale blue • 5 (or 4) united petals • July–September

EXPLORER'S GENTIAN
Gentiana calycosa • Gentian Family

Several members of the closely related genera *Gentiana*, *Gentianella* (p. 200), and *Gentianopsis* (p. 200) grow in the eastern Sierra, all of which have gorgeous tubular flowers. Most of them are richly colored (usually some shade of blue or blue-purple), but explorer's gentian may be the *crème de la crème* with its incredibly deep blue, satiny petals. The **tips of the petals are decorated with greenish spots and flare slightly, creating a voluptuous 2" floral vase.** This vase contrasts deliciously with the narrow, black-purple sepals and the deep green, fleshy leaves. Between the petal lobes are delicate fringes. Explorer's gentian is a late bloomer, usually not reaching full splendor until fall. If you want to see bumblebees in pure bliss, spend some time in fall watching bees dive headlong into this flower and then back out several minutes later covered with pollen and a wide, silly grin!

Names: *Gentiana* honors King Gentius of ancient Illyria, who purportedly discovered the medicinal qualities of gentian roots. *Calycosa* means 'full calyx.' Also called bog gentian. **Where found:** also in Alpine to 12,500'. Wet meadows, rocky seeps, open slopes; e.g., around Heart Lake along trail from Mosquito Flat to Morgan Pass (10,500') in August.

blue • 5 petals united in tube • July–September

BROAD-LEAF LUPINE
Lupinus polyphyllus • Pea Family

Of all the lupines that frequent the eastern Sierra, broad-leaf lupine is certainly one of the showiest, both for its size and for the extensive thickets it forms. The stout stem **can reach 5' tall** and is usually at least 3'. The **spike-like inflorescence, which is dense with whorls of** $^1/_2$–$^3/_4$**" flowers, can be up to 18" long**. The flowers are the usual color for lupines: blue to violet, often with a yellow or white patch on the banner that turns red-purple with age. As its names suggest, the plants bear many large leaves, each of which has 5–17 broad leaflets. Broad-leaf lupine often forms thickets covering many square yards. All the spikes of blue flowers rising above a dense jungle of bright green leaves is an amazing and exhilarating sight.

Names: *Lupinus:* see p. 74. *Polyphyllus* means 'many-leaved.' **Where found:** also in Sagebrush Steppe. Wet meadows, streambanks, bogs; e.g., along trail to Winnemucca Lake (9000') in July.

blue • 5 irregular petals • May–July

BREWER'S LUPINE
Lupinus breweri • Pea Family

If you've done any exploring in the eastern Sierra, you will probably be very familiar with the blue flowers of lupine. No matter what habitat or elevation you're in, it seems that some species of *Lupinus* will be with you. Desert flats, sagebrush steppe, streambanks, rock ledges, subalpine meadows, rocky alpine ridges and flats—you will find at least 1 species of lupine in all these environments, often forming large patches to the virtual exclusion of other species. • Although Brewer's lupine is a **dwarfed plant only 1–8" tall,** it can still put on quite a show, covering large areas of sandy hillsides with its striking and fragrant $^1/_4$–$^1/_2$" flowers. Though the flowers of Brewer's lupine are the typical blue, they have a larger and **brighter patch of white on their banner than do most lupines, so the patch of flowers will usually look a bit like a blue-and-white checkered tablecloth. The** stems and leaves are covered with silky, silvery hairs.

Names: *Lupinus:* see p. 74. Brewer: see p. 140. **Where found:** also in Alpine to 12,000'. Dry slopes and flats, open woods; e.g., along June Lake Loop Road (7700') in June; east side of Sonora Peak (10,000') in July.

blue • 5 irregular petals • June–August

TORREY'S LUPINE
Lupinus lepidus • Pea Family

Although Torrey's lupine is another of the many blue-flowered lupines in the eastern Sierra, it is distinctive enough to make identification relatively easy. Most noticeably, it is a **short (4–12") plant with very tight, 2–4", cylindrical clusters of flowers rising cleanly above basal leaves.** The ¹/₂" blossoms are so densely packed on the stem that the flower clusters look a bit like pipe cleaners. The petals are generally blue (with a white or yellow banner), though this blue often **tends toward violet or even slightly pinkish.** The 5–8 leaflets are ¹/₂–1" long and are soft-hairy, as is the short stem.

Names: *Lupinus:* see p. 74. *Lepidus* means 'scaly.' Torrey: see p. 189. This particular variety (var. *sellulus*) was formerly called *L. sellulus.* Also called dwarf lupine. **Where found:** Mixed Conifer Forest to 10,000'; also in Sagebrush Steppe. Rocky or gravelly places, open woods; e.g., along Route 89 near Markleeville (5600') in June, and along Route 88 east of Carson Pass (7500') in July.

blue • 5 irregular petals • June–August

SHOWY PENSTEMON
Penstemon speciosus • Snapdragon Family

On practically any dry, sandy slope or flat in the eastern Sierra you can find some species of *Penstemon.* They are not only trusty companions, but gorgeous ones as well, sometimes cheering you with bright red flowers (e.g., pp. 116, 186, 187), sometimes surprising you with white ones (e.g., p. 91), and sometimes soothing you with sky blue ones (e.g., p. 204). Showy penstemon is **one of the bluest of the blue, its dense clusters of 1–1³/₄", tubular flowers** looking like pieces of sky fallen to earth. The **outside of the tube can be tinged with red-purple, but the flaring petal lobes are an amazingly rich blue. The throat of the flower is splotched with white and marked with purple.** The 2"–2' stem is covered with narrow, in-folded, 1–3" leaves. The clusters of large, thick flowers extend beyond the leaves.

Names: *Penstemon:* see p. 71. *Speciosus* means 'showy.' **Where found:** also in Sagebrush Steppe. Dry flats and slopes often with sagebrush, open woods; e.g., along Route 89 near Markleeville (5500') in June, and along trail to Winnemucca Lake (8800') in July.

blue • 5 petals united in 2-lipped tube • June–August

SLENDER PENSTEMON
Penstemon gracilentus • Snapdragon Family

Most of the many penstemons in the eastern Sierra are anything but subtle. Their tubular flowers are large and robust and intensely colored, so they paint the hillsides with broad and spectacular brush strokes. Slender penstemon is one of only a few species of *Penstemon* that has small, subtle flowers. Although they are a beautiful blue or purple, you might overlook them because they are **only ¹/₂–³/₄" long, very slender, and scattered loosely on the 1–2¹/₂' stem. The flower tubes are often red-purple, while the small 'faces' tend more to blue.** The pedicels and sepals are usually glandular-sticky.

Names: *Penstemon:* see p. 71. *Gracilentus* means 'slender and flexible.' **Where found:** Mixed Conifer Forest to 10,000'; also in Sagebrush Steppe. Open woods; e.g., openings in woods with sagebrush along Highway 50 near Spooner Summit (7000') in July.

blue • 5 petals united in 2-lipped tube • July–August

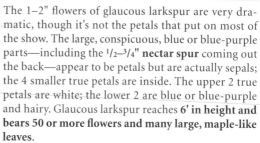

GLAUCOUS LARKSPUR
Delphinium glaucum • Buttercup Family

The 1–2" flowers of glaucous larkspur are very dramatic, though it's not the petals that put on most of the show. The large, conspicuous, blue or blue-purple parts—including the ¹/₂–³/₄" **nectar spur** coming out the back—appear to be petals but are actually sepals; the 4 smaller true petals are inside. The upper 2 true petals are white; the lower 2 are blue or blue-purple and hairy. Glaucous larkspur reaches **6' in height and bears 50 or more flowers and many large, maple-like leaves.**

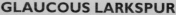

Names: *Delphinium:* see p. 71. *Glaucum* means 'glaucous,' in reference to the whitish film on the lower part of the stem. Also called towering larkspur. **Where found:** Mixed Conifer Forest to 10,000'. Streambanks, seeps; e.g., along trail to Winnemucca Lake (9000') in July, and Onion Valley (9200') in July.

Related plant: Mountain marsh larkspur (*D. polycladon,* inset photo) tends to be a shorter plant (1–3'), though it also grows in wet areas and so is quite robust. Its deep blue-purple sepals fold forward, forming a bit of a funnel around the petals and reproductive parts. It occurs along streams and seeps throughout the Mixed Conifer Forest zone, e.g., along the trail to Mono Pass (11,000') in July. *Polycladon* means 'with many branches,' in reference to the several stems per root system.

blue or blue-purple • 5 petal-like sepals (4 true petals) • July–August

ANDERSON'S LARKSPUR
Delphinium andersonii • Buttercup Family

The flowers of Anderson's larkspur are quite similar to those of glaucous larkspur (p. 204), but Anderson's larkspur is a much shorter plant ($^1/_2$–2' tall) of much drier environments. The 1" flowers have broad, blue sepals with a $^1/_2$–$^3/_4$" **spur that is often curved down at the tip.** The upper 2 petals are white with tinges of blue, and the lower 2 petals are blue and rounded. The sepals and lower petals are somewhat hairy. There are usually 5–12 flowers branching up off the **smooth, reddish stem**. The narrowly divided leaves have long petioles, most of which branch off the lower part of the plant stem.

Names: *Delphinium:* see p. 71. C.L. Anderson: see p. 116. **Where found:** central and northern Mixed Conifer Forest to 9000'; also in Sagebrush Steppe. Dry slopes often with sagebrush, open woods; e.g., along the Thomas Creek trail (7500') in May.

blue • 5 petal-like sepals (4 true petals)
• May–July

MONKSHOOD
Aconitum columbianum • Buttercup Family

At first glance you might mistake monkshood for glaucous larkspur (p. 204), for both **are enormous plants (to 6') with 1–2" blue flowers and large, maple-like leaves**. Because both love wet habitats, you will often find them growing together, frequently with corn lily and swamp onion along streambanks and in seep areas. As in larkspur, the showy parts of monkshood flowers are the sepals. The **upper sepal forms the 'hood' that gave rise to the common name**. The 2 lateral sepals make up the monk's body, and the lower 2 sepals form downward-pointing feet. If you gently pull the hood and the body a little apart, you can see the **2 small blue or white petals** (as opposed to 4 small petals in glaucous larkspur) and a large cluster of yellowish-green reproductive parts. • Like many members of the buttercup family, monkshood is **very poisonous**.

Names: *Aconitum* is the ancient Greek name for this genus. *Columbianum* means 'of western North America.' **Where found:** Mixed Conifer Forest to 10,500'. Streambanks, wet meadows, open woods; e.g., along the Tioga Pass road (8500') in July, and on the east side of Saddlebag Lake (10,100') in September.

blue • 5 petal-like sepals (2 true petals)
• July–September

LOW POLEMONIUM
Polemonium californicum • Phlox Family

You have a good chance of seeing most Sierra flowers in bright sunlight. A few, however, prefer the shade of deep forests, so you may have to wait awhile to get a shaft of sun to illuminate them. Low polemonium is one such **shade-loving plant**—you will frequently find tangles of its **distinctive ladder-rung leaves** around the trunks of pines and firs in the deep forest. The plant grows to only about 1' tall, so the leaves are almost a groundcover. Even in the shade, the flowers of low polemonium are lovely and cheery. The **5 blue to violet petals form a shallow bowl with a yellow center surrounded by a white ring**. The slender filaments with tiny, round, white or yellowish anthers gracefully protrude. The leaves have 5–12 pairs of opposite leaflets and 1 terminal leaflet.

Names: *Polemonium* probably honors Polemon, the Greek philosopher. *Californicum:* see p. 137. Also called California Jacob's ladder. **Where found:** Mixed Conifer Forest to 10,000'. Shade around trees; e.g., around edges of Grass Lake (7700') in June, and along trail to Winnemucca Lake (8600') in July.

blue to violet • 5 petals united in bowl • June–August

GREAT POLEMONIUM
Polemonium occidentale • Phlox Family

The flowers of great polemonium are quite similar to those of low polemonium (above), with delicately blue to violet petals forming a shallow bowl from which protrude graceful reproductive parts. The most noticeable difference in the flowers is that those of great polemonium have **white centers rather than yellow ones**. Both polemoniums have the ladder-like pinnately compound leaves that inspired the alternative common name Jacob's ladder. However, great polemonium, as its name suggests, is a much **taller plant (to 3') that grows only in wet habitats**. You might find it interesting to return to these flowers several times during their blooming period. At first the stamens are erect, their anthers ripe with pollen, while the pistils lie flat against the petals with stigmas closed. Several days later you will find the anthers drying up, while (you guessed it) only now do the pistils rise up and the stigmas open for action.

Names: *Polemonium:* see above. *Occidentale:* see p. 121. Also called great Jacob's ladder. **Where found:** wet meadows, seeps; e.g., along the Tioga Pass road (8500') in July.

blue to violet • 5 petals united in bowl • June–August

ROTHROCK'S NAMA
Nama rothrockii • Waterleaf Family

Each ¹/₂" flower of Rothrock's nama is a lovely **violet or blue (or sometimes pink) bowl**. Multiply this loveliness by 30 or 40, for the flowers form **dense, spherical heads packed tight with flowers**. Then multiply again by at least another 30 or 40 or even 100 or more, for the **plants spread by rhizomes, forming extensive colonies covering several square yards of ground**. After all this multiplying, you have quite a dazzling product! The leaves add greatly to this plant's appeal, for they are crinkly and serrated and have a dramatic deep midvein. The stems, leaves, and sepals are all sticky-hairy and strongly aromatic. To come across a great colony of Rothrock's nama spreading out over an otherwise bare patch of sand or gravel is a treat for the eye and for the nose.

Names: *Nama:* see p. 68. Rothrock: see p. 91. **Where found:** also in southern and central Alpine to 13,000'. Sandy or gravelly flats and slopes, rock ledges; e.g., along Horseshoe Meadow Road (8000') in July, and at end of the Onion Valley road (9200') in July.

blue to violet (pink) • 5 petals united in bowl • June–August

MOUNTAIN BLUEBELLS
Mertensia ciliata • Borage Family

Despite its stout stem, large leaves, and considerable height (**to 5'**), mountain bluebells presents a picture of grace. The flowers start pink in bud and transform to baby blue in bloom. They are **narrow, ¹/₂" bells that hang in dainty clusters at the ends of long, arching stems**. These bells are noticeably **2-tiered with a constricted tube and a slightly wider limb toward the tip**. The clapper-like style sticks slightly out of the bell. It's easy to imagine a gentle breeze stirring the bells to play some sweet melody. You will often find mountain bluebells joining the botanical chorus in seep-area thickets with such other robust plants as willows, corn lily, glaucous larkspur, monkshood, and Lewis' monkeyflower.

Names: Mertens: see p. 149. *Ciliata* means 'having fine hairs,' in reference to the tiny hairs often found on the edges of the sepals. Also called streamside bluebells. **Where found:** northern Mixed Conifer Forest. Wet meadows, streambanks, seeps; e.g., along the trail to Winnemucca Lake (9000') in July.

blue • 5 petals united in bell • June–August

VELVETY STICKSEED
Hackelia velutina • Borage Family

As you're laboriously picking the prickly burrs (i.e., seedpods) out of your socks and off your legs, it may be difficult to recall the delicate beauty of these flowers. But beautiful they are! The ¹/₂" **pinwheels are sky blue with bright white, raised tooth-like appendages in the center.** As with many members of the borage family, the flowers of velvety stickseed start pink in bud. Sometimes the mature blossoms will be tinged with pink, and occasionally a mature flower will be mostly pink. The lower parts of the 1–3' stem and the narrow, clasping, 2–6" leaves are covered with soft, white hairs. The **round nutlets are armed with radiating, barb-tipped prickles that stick tenaciously to practically anything they touch.**

Names: Joseph Hackel was a 19th-century Czech botanist. *Velutina* means 'velvety,' in reference to the velvety hairs on the lower stem. **Where found:** Mixed Conifer Forest to 8000'; also in Sagebrush Steppe. Dry slopes, disturbed areas, open woods; e.g., around Grass Lake (7700') in July.

blue • 5 petals united in shallow bowl • June–August

PENNYROYAL
Monardella odoratissima • Mint Family

If you walk off trail across almost any vegetated, dry slope (especially a south-facing slope) in the eastern Sierra, you will soon smell strong, sweet fragrances. As you step on or brush against various leaves, clouds of aroma are released and cling to you as you continue. Perhaps the strongest of these fragrances will be pennyroyal. Its opposite pairs of narrow leaves are the main source of the fragrance, but even the flowers have a strong enough mintiness to make a tasty tea. (As with all wild herbs, drink this tea in moderation.) Each **square ¹/₂–1' stem is topped by a ¹/₂–1", flat-topped flowerhead that is crammed with scores of the narrow-petaled flowers.** The dense flowers and the protruding reproductive parts create quite a fuzzy appearance. The **flowers are sometimes white but are usually at least tinged with pink, rose, or lavender. Sometimes they are quite intensely blue-purple or rose-purple.**

Names: *Monardella:* see p. 120. *Odoratissima* means 'very fragrant.' **Where found:** Mixed Conifer Forest to 10,000'; also in Sagebrush Steppe. Dry slopes and flats, open woods, rocky places; e.g., along trail to Winnemucca Lake (8800') in July, and along the Tioga Pass road (9000') in July.

blue-purple, red-purple, pink, or white • 5 petals united in 2-lipped tube • June–August

WESTERN DOG VIOLET
Viola adunca • Violet Family

Although leaves are not usually the best way to identify plants, because they can vary in size and shape depending on the environment, the leaves of violets are often quite diagnostic. When you see a large, thick, heart-shaped or kidney-shaped, glossy-green leaf, you can be pretty certain that it belongs  to some species of violet—though not all *Viola* species have such leaves (e.g., see p. 173). Western dog violet leaves are typical: large, thick, and heart shaped or round. Each plant has several leaves, a 2–6" stem, and 1 or 2 flowers at the ends of slender 1–4" peduncles. The ½" **flower is a soothing violet or blue-purple with a violet-veined white patch at its center. The 2 lateral petals are white-bearded.** The short nectar spur at the back of the flower is often red tinged.

Names: *Viola:* see p. 125. *Adunca* means 'hooked,' in reference to the 2 lateral petals, which are often curved or hooked at the tip. **Where found:** also in Sagebrush Steppe. Moist meadows, open woods; e.g., Hope Valley (6500') in June.

**violet or blue-purple • 5 irregular petals
• May–July**

HOARY ASTER
Machaeranthera canescens • Composite Family

Hoary aster is very much like members of the genera *Aster* and *Erigeron* (daisies), with its central button of yellow disk flowers and its many radiating ray flowers. It does, however, have some characteristics that will help you distinguish it. First, the **stems, leaves, and phyllaries are glandular-sticky.** Second, the phyllaries are not neatly arranged in 1 or 2 rows but come off rather haphazardly in as many as 10 messy series. Third, these **phyllaries stick out and taper to a fine point.** Fourth, there are **only 8–13 rays.** The narrow, 1–4" leaves are often in-folded and clasp the stem. Clusters of this 1–3' plant can add delicious intensity to otherwise bare patches of sand or gravel.

Names: *Machaeranthera* means 'sword-like anthers.' *Canescens:* see p. 110. **Where found:** Mixed Conifer Forest to 10,000'; also in Sagebrush Steppe. Dry slopes, open woods; e.g., along trail to Winnemucca Lake (9000') in July.

blue-purple • several ray flowers (8–13) and many disk flowers • June–September

BROAD-LEAVED TWAYBLADE
Listera convallarioides • Orchid Family

You could spend years in the Sierra without ever seeing broad-leaved twayblade. Not only is it uncommon (it is more frequent in the Cascades of the Pacific Northwest), it can be difficult to find even when present. Only 4–12" tall, it tends to hide under the much larger, leafy plants that share its wet habitats. Even when it's visible, it is by no means conspicuous because the small ($^1/_4$–$^1/_2$"), **green flowers** tend to blend right in with their sur-

roundings. Being an orchid, broad-leaved twayblade has flowers with 3 sepals and 3 petals, all but one of which are nearly identical. In this twayblade, the **5 identical parts are all narrow, pointed, and swept back. The 1 different part is the lower petal that is much broader, heart shaped, and projecting.** The 1 pair of 1–3", broadly ovate leaves cling to the stem about halfway up, like a pair of unfolded wings.

Names: Martin Lister was an English naturalist of the late 1600s and early 1700s. *Convallarioides* means 'resembling *Convallaria*,' the lily-of-the-valley genus. **Where found:** Mixed Conifer Forest to 8000'. Moist openings in woods, streambanks; e.g., edges of Grass Lake (7700') in July.

greenish • 3 petal-like sepals and 3 petals • July–September

STINGING NETTLE
Urtica dioica • Nettle Family

Whenever you see a tall (3–7'), **slender plant thick with opposite pairs of large, serrated, ovate or heart-shaped, velvety, crinkly leaves,** be on your guard. If it has several **stringy plumes of tiny, brownish-green flowers coming out of the leaf axils,** run the other way! You have come across stinging nettle, with the emphasis on the participle. The finely pointed hairs covering the plant can pierce your skin and inject formic acid, causing an **intense burning sensation** that can last for several hours. Unless you're trying to distract yourself from some other pain, you will probably want to avoid touching any part of this plant. • As the species name indicates, plants have either male or female flowers. None of the flowers has actual petals.

Names: *Urtica* means 'to burn,' in reference to the stinging hairs. *Dioica* means 'dioecious,' i.e., having separate male and female plants. **Where found:** Mixed Conifer Forest to 10,000'; also in Sagebrush Steppe. Streambanks, open woods, seeps, disturbed places; e.g., along the Tioga Pass road (8500') in July.

brownish-green • 4 or 5 tiny sepals • June–August

FENDLER'S MEADOW RUE
Thalictrum fendleri • Buttercup Family

For a 2–5' tall plant with leaves up to 1' wide, meadow rue is remarkably delicate-looking. Its leaves are very thin and are divided into rounded, scalloped lobes. These leaves are clustered at the base of the plant and are gracefully scattered on short branches well up the plant stem. Also on short, slender branches are many tiny (¹⁄₄") flowers, which dangle and shimmer in even the faintest of breezes. The shimmering is caused by clusters of brownish-yellow stamens, each hanging from a tiny, greenish 'cap.' This cap turns out to be the sepals—there are no petals at all. When you realize that there are no pistils with the stamens, you may suspect (correctly) that Fendler's meadow rue is dioecious. With a little scouting, you'll probably find a female plant (bottom photo) nearby bearing flowers with erect, white pistils instead of the dangling stamens.

Names: *Thalictrum* means 'plant with divided leaves.' Augustus Fendler was a plant collector in the American West in the mid-1800s. The 'rue' in the common name does not here mean regret but rather derives from a word for a bitter herb. **Where found:** Mixed Conifer Forest to 10,500'; also in Sagebrush Steppe. Open woods; e.g., along trail to Winnemucca Lake (8800') in July, and along trail to Gardisky Lake (10,000') in July.

greenish-white • 5 (4) petal-like sepals • May–August

BREWER'S MITREWORT
Mitella breweri • Saxifrage Family

You might think that Brewer's mitrewort would be difficult to spot. It grows in seeps and other wet areas that are usually thick with greenery, and it has small (¹⁄₄") greenish flowers that cling to green, leafless stems rarely more than 1' tall. However, despite its green camouflage, this plant always seems to stand out. It's the flowers that grab your attention—they're peculiar, even bizarre. Each **petal consists of 2–5 pairs of thread-like segments that radiate out from the tiny (¹⁄₈") flower cup, creating a feathery flower that resembles a group of television antennae or perhaps a delicate, green spider.** The stem teems with up to 60 of these strange flowers. The leaves are typical of the saxifrage family—broad, round, toothed, and basal.

Names: *Mitella* means 'small cap,' in reference to the fruit. Brewer: see p. 140. Also called bishop's cap. **Where found:** seeps, streambanks; e.g., along trail to Winnemucca Lake (9000') in July.

greenish (yellowish) • 5 separate petals • June–August

Alpine
above 11,500'

mountains as fountains

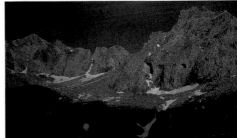

last light

The intensely blue skies call you; the clean, crisp, thin air exhilarates you; the blocks and slabs and soaring peaks of fractured rock seem to speak to you of worlds beyond time. Even the light seems purer up here, as if you have penetrated to its very beginnings. Sometimes it seems that if you kept on climbing you would just disappear into the ether.

Paradoxically, as you struggle higher and higher, laboring over every breath and every step, your spirits soar and your heart lightens. You are now in the alpine world and in the alpine state of mind, perfectly prepared to meet the flowers of this world, which weave their spell over you with their rugged beauty and fragile charm.

At about 11,000–11,500' in the south and at about 10,500' in the north, you reach that elevation where the total heat during the growing season is insufficient for tree growth. For several hundred feet below this elevation, the forests have been thinning and the trees have been getting shorter. Clumps of the highest-elevation Sierra trees—whitebark pine in the north, joined by foxtail pine and limber pine in the south—have been replacing the evergreens of the subalpine: lodgepole pine, western white pine, red fir, juniper, hemlock. And now, near timberline, even the whitebarks are struggling. In this *krummholz* ('crooked wood') zone, the whitebarks are battered and sheared and shaped by the wind and the cold until they are just thick, gnarled trunks a few feet off the ground with only a few scraggly, needled branches reaching tentatively

whitebark pine near the Minarets
opposite: alpine gold at Mono Pass

tundra near timberline on Mt. Rose

into the cold wind. And higher still, even these shadows of trees fade out, leaving alpine willow as the only woody plant that can survive—a miniature tree whose 2–3" catkins stick up farther off the ground than does its ground-hugging 'trunk,' stems, and leaves!

Up here in the alpine world the sun beats unmercifully and the cold winds howl unabated. You might wish you were as small as the plants up here, for they often hide behind rocks or huddle together in dense mats or cushions. Despite the obstacles, however (or perhaps because of them), you will find some places where the ground is covered nearly solid with flowers, and much of the alpine tundra has at least scattered clumps and clusters of gorgeous blossoms. Up here, the whites seem brighter, the yellows cheerier, the reds hotter, and the blues richer. The flowers seem to glow with a rugged vitality unmatched by their larger and more comfortable relatives of the lower elevations. As beautiful as are the flowers of the subalpine meadows and the sagebrush plains, perhaps only the flowers of the harsh desert can rival the alpine flowers for intensity and exuberance.

alpine garden (left), alpine willow

Perhaps some of their extraordinary appeal relates to *our* struggle to reach them and to *our* sheer exuberance at sharing their home here on top of the world. As your gaze reaches out over miles and miles of rugged Sierra terrain, it's comforting to look down and see all the flowers at your feet—fellow journeyers and kindred souls.

Where and When to See the Flowers

To enter this alpine world you'll have to do some hiking. A few roads in the eastern Sierra will get you close, but none extends up above timberline. The highest trailhead in the eastern Sierra is Mosquito Flat (10,230') at the end of the Rock Creek road south of Mammoth (see map on p. 29).

From here you can reach the Alpine zone by hiking 3–4 miles toward Mono Pass (12,000') or Morgan Pass (11,100').

Gardisky Lake

For the most part, alpine flowers bloom later than lower-elevation flowers, because it takes a while for the alpine environment to warm up enough to melt off the snow and provide conditions conducive to growing and blooming. With some exceptions, the alpine gardens usually won't be in full bloom until July or August. Although many of the flowers have very short blooming seasons, you can find some flowers still in bloom in September and maybe even in October (depending on fall temperatures and snow).

Because much of the Sierra crest is above 11,000', many trails and non-trail routes will take you into the alpine environment. Most require more than a leisurely stroll, but not all of them are grueling hikes. The following are some of the easier ones (still strenuous), all of which are north of Yosemite (all distances are one way):

- from Tioga Pass (9941') on Route 120 to the summit of Mt. Dana (13,053')—3 miles

- from along the road to Saddlebag Lake (10,100') to Gardisky Lake (10,800')—a very steep 1-mile hike

- from Saddlebag Lake (10,100') east to Tioga Crest (11,000–12,000')—a scramble of a couple of miles and then wandering to your heart's content

- from Sonora Pass (9620') on Route 108 to the summit of Sonora Peak (11,462')—a trail and then a scramble of about 3 miles

- from the Mt. Rose trailhead (8840') just west of the Mt. Rose Highway summit to the summit of Mt. Rose (10,778')—5 miles.

All of these climbs are steep but will take you into the alpine world in only a few miles and only a few hours.

South of Yosemite—with the exception of the roads to Mosquito Flat at 10,230' and to Horseshoe Meadow at 10,040'—the roads don't take you as high as the roads mentioned above. Also, in the south, timberline is higher (11,000–11,500'), so getting to the Alpine zone will take considerably more time and effort.

Kearsarge Pass

alpine garden

Many trails between Mt. Whitney and Bishop reach the alpine environment. Some are long and strenuous; some are longer and more strenuous (distances are one way):

- from Onion Valley (9200') to Kearsarge Pass (11,823')—5 miles

- from the Bishop Creek area (9300–9700') to Bishop Pass (11,972') or Piute Pass (11,423')—5 miles

- from Taboose Creek (5400') to Taboose Pass (11,400')—8 miles

- from Oak Creek (6000') to Baxter Pass (12,320')—8 miles

- from Division Creek (4640') to Sawmill Pass (11,347')—11 miles

- from Whitney Portal (8365') at the upper end of Whitney Portal Road to the summit of Mt. Whitney (14,496')—almost 11 miles.

If you are unable to hike, you can still find some of the flowers in the Alpine section of this book along the upper parts of the highest Sierra roads. If you can hike at least a little at high altitude and can take your time, you will find many places in the eastern Sierra where you can reach the awesome flower world above timberline. If you are a strong high-elevation hiker, there are miles and miles of alpine flowers available to you; just find a place where the Sierra escarpment towers above you and start climbing—with adequate safety precautions, of course.

On any visit to the Alpine zone, take plenty of water and food, sunscreen, a hat, a sweater, rain gear, a first-aid kit, maybe a hiking stick, and (of course) this book, and wander among the sky gardens of the high Sierra. If you choose not to come back any time soon, we won't be too surprised!

alpine columbine on Tioga Crest

PRICKLY PHLOX
Leptodactylon pungens • Phlox Family

The same characteristics that enable prickly phlox to thrive in the rocks far above timberline also enable it to grow in difficult, dry habitats at much lower elevations. You will find it throughout the eastern Sierra and Great Basin, even reaching the edges of the Mojave Desert. Take a look at the leaves and you will understand its adaptability, for they are divided into needle-like lobes with minimal surface area. They are also tipped with spines, as you will find out if you grab the plant. **In the alpine environment, prickly phlox may be a scraggly, ground-hugging shrub, but at lower elevations it can form showy, densely flowered mounds to 3' tall** (top photo). The 1/2" flowers look much like those of spreading phlox (p. 148), but they **rarely fully open during the day because they open at night to be pollinated by moths**. During the day you are likely to see them rolled into narrow funnels.

Names: *Leptodactylon* means 'narrow-fingered,' in reference to the leaves. *Pungens* means 'sharp-pointed.' Also called granite gilia. **Where found:** Alpine to 13,000'; also in Sagebrush Steppe and in Mixed Conifer Forest. Rocky or gravelly flats, rock ledges; e.g., the Alabama Hills (4500') in May, and above Ellery Lake (10,500') in August.

white (sometimes pink-tinged) • 5 petals united in tube • May–September

COVILLE'S PHLOX
Phlox condensata • Phlox Family

It's hard to imagine a plant more suited to the harsh conditions above timberline than Coville's phlox. **It forms such dense, rounded cushions with such tiny leaves that you would have difficulty penetrating them with your finger.** Just imagine, then, how well protected they are against the wind. On a typical summer night such a cushion plant can be up to 20 degrees warmer inside the cushion than outside. As amazing as the leaves are, the 1/2" flowers may be even more so. Often, they are so numerous and so dense on the plant that they form a **nearly solid floral blanket almost completely concealing the cushion underneath.** The bright white of the petals (sometimes pink or lavender) is highlighted by the tiny, yellow anthers nestled in the flower tube. The flowers often have a deliciously sweet fragrance.

Names: *Phlox:* see p. 113. *Condensata* means 'condensed.' Dr. Frederick Coville was the botanist on the 1891 Death Valley Expedition. **Where found:** Alpine to 13,000'; also in Mixed Conifer Forest. Rocky or gravelly flats and ridges, rock ledges; e.g., near summit of Job's Sister Peak (10,800') in July.

white (pink or lavender) • 5 petals united in tube • July–August

BALLHEAD GILIA
Ipomopsis congesta • Phlox Family

Above timberline in the eastern Sierra you will find lots of granite. Some of the rocky ridges and talus slopes seem almost pure white or silver as the intense sunlight becomes even brighter in reflecting off the rock. Often snuggling in the rocks and hiding in the brightness are the white to gray, spherical clusters of ballhead gilia. **Scores of the tiny ($1/8$–$1/4$"), tubular blooms are clustered together in 1" balls atop 1–10" stems.** Whether the balls rest right on the ground or are elevated slightly above it, the color of the flowers is such a perfect match for the granite that ballhead gilia often seems to disappear right in front of your eyes. The balls have a fuzzy look to them because of the protruding stamens and the hairy sepals. The 1–$1^1/2$" leaves are hairy and deeply lobed into 3–5 narrow segments.

Names: *Ipomopsis:* p. 190. *Congesta* means 'crowded,' in reference to the dense flowerheads. **Where found:** central and northern Alpine to 12,000'; also in Mixed Conifer Forest. Sandy or rocky slopes, rocky ridges; e.g., near summit of Mt. Rose (10,600') in July.

white to gray (pale lavender) • 5 petals united in tube • July–August

TIMBERLINE PHACELIA
Phacelia hastata • Waterleaf Family

Find a colony of timberline phacelia in bloom and you may think you've strayed into a **nest of creamy white, furry caterpillars.** The 2–8" stem ends in a coiled inflorescence of scores of $1/2$", white (sometimes lavender) flowers packed tightly together. The **long-protruding reproductive parts and the dense fuzz on the darker sepals give these coils a decidedly hairy look.** The stems and the mostly basal, elliptic, 1–4" leaves are covered with stiff, bristly, white hairs, further enhancing the plant's shaggy appearance. As it gets late in the day and the sun begins to abandon you, this phacelia's furry-looking coat may start to look more and more appealing!

Names: *Phacelia:* see p. 72. *Hastata* means 'spear-shaped,' in reference to the pointed leaves. Also called silverleaf phacelia. **Where found:** Alpine to 13,000'; also in Mixed Conifer Forest. Sandy or rocky slopes and flats, talus; e.g., near Kearsarge Pass on trail from Onion Valley (11,500') in July, and along trail to Mono Pass near pass (12,000') in July.

white (lavender) • 5 petals united in bowl • July–August

ALPINE GENTIAN
Gentiana newberryi • Gentian Family

Many of the gentians are late bloomers, holding off their blossoms until late summer or early fall when most other flowers have already had their days in the sun. And what incredible parting gifts the gentians are—large and showy blossoms of stunning color and fascinating detail. In a family  with many intensely blue and blue-purple flowers (e.g., see hiker's gentian and Sierra gentian, p. 200, and explorer's gentian, p. 201), alpine gentian is a bit of a surprise. With its very long (to 2"), broad tubes and its fringes between the petals, alpine gentian greatly resembles explorer's gentian but is **bright white instead of deep blue.** Adding to the color are the **green freckles all over the inner surfaces of the petals.** The **large flowers grow on very short (1–4") stems,** so despite the size of the flowers, they can often be hidden in the grass of their meadow habitat.

Names: *Gentiana:* see p. 201. Newberry: see p. 186. **Where found:** Alpine to 13,000'; also in Mixed Conifer Forest. Moist meadows; e.g., Tioga Crest east of Saddlebag Lake (11,500') in September.

white • 5 petals united in tube • July–September

SIERRA FORGET-ME-NOT
Cryptantha nubigena • Borage Family

Now this is one plant that appears to be taking no chances! It has **armed its stems and leaves against the rigors of its dry, windy environment with long, stiff, bristly hairs.** Its tongue-like, gray-green, 1–2" leaves are mostly basal, though a few leaves branch off the 1–12" stem. The stem ends in a **cylindrical inflorescence packed with white, ¹/₈–¹/₄" flowers.** As with many members of the borage family, there is a slightly **raised ring in the center of the flower,** delineating the tiny flower tube. In Sierra forget-me-not this ring is yellow, creating a tiny yellow eye in the middle of the white flower. • Despite its hairy protection against the wind and intense radiation, this plant frequently grows behind the shelter of rocks.

Names: *Cryptantha* means 'hidden flower,' probably in reference to the typically small (even tiny) flowers of members of this genus, though it could also refer to the cleistogamous flowers of some species. *Nubigena* means 'born of the clouds,' a poetic reference to this species' high mountain habitat. **Where found:** southern and central Alpine to 12,500'; also in Mixed Conifer Forest. Gravelly flats, talus; e.g., near Kearsarge Pass on trail from Onion Valley (11,500') in July.

white • 5 petals united in bowl • July–August

ALPINE SAXIFRAGE
Saxifraga aprica • Saxifrage Family

Finding alpine saxifrage in the difficult environment above timberline may surprise you, because it is such a delicate-looking plant. Its **single, round flowerhead of tiny 1/8–1/4" flowers sits atop a slender, red-purple, leafless 1–5" stem**. It looks as if it would be blown away in the first wind or burned up by the searing alpine sun. But look where it grows—in wet meadows or near melting snowbanks where it gets plenty of water and some shelter. Though the tiny, shovel-shaped petals are bright white, the flowerheads have greenish and reddish tints too, for the **large, green ovary and the many reddish anthers are almost as conspicuous as the petals**. The basal leaves are round and fleshy.

Names: *Saxifraga:* see p. 153. *Aprica* means 'exposed to the sun.' **Where found:** Alpine to 11,500'; also in Mixed Conifer Forest. Wet, rocky flats, grassy meadows, rock ledges, often near snowbanks; e.g., Tioga Crest east of Saddlebag Lake (11,500') in July.

white • 5 separate petals • May–August

SARGENT'S CAMPION
Silene sargentii • Pink Family

As is characteristic of the genus *Silene,* Sargent's campion has flowers whose calyx tube is as noticeable and beautiful as its petals. The **1/2" long calyx is a swollen, beige vase lined with 10 brown-purple, vertical veins. Its entire surface and the upper part of the 4–8" plant stem are glandular-sticky**. True to its family, Sargent's campion has 'pinked' petals, and like Maguire's catchfly (see p. 154), each of its 5 petals is divided into 4 lobes. However, in Maguire's catchfly the 4 petal lobes are equal; in Sargent's campion the **2 inner petal lobes are much broader and longer than the 2 outer lobes**. The basal leaves are fleshy, while the few opposite pairs of stem leaves are narrow, pointed, and white-hairy.

Names: *Silene:* see p. 154. Charles Sargent, an American professor of horticulture and arboriculture, wrote the *Manual of the Trees of North America* (1905). **Where found:** Alpine to 12,500'; also in Mixed Conifer Forest. Rocky flats, grassy slopes; e.g., Tioga Crest east of Saddlebag Lake (11,500') in July.

white (sometimes pink-tinged) • 5 separate petals • July–August

NUTTALL'S SANDWORT
Minuartia nuttallii • Pink Family

As the name sandwort suggests (wort means 'plant'), you can expect to find *Minuartia* (and *Arenaria*) species on sandy and rocky flats throughout the Sierra Nevada and Great Basin. Several quite similar species extend well up into the Alpine zone in the eastern Sierra.  Atypical of the pink family, sandwort petals are not pinked (lobed). The sandworts of the high elevations all have small, white, star-shaped flowers and needle-like leaves that form low mats. Nuttall's sandwort differs from its close relatives by having **pointed sepals that are visible between the petals**. Its 5 petals, 5 sepals, and 10 flaring stamens create a series of nested stars. The **short, needle-like leaves, in addition to forming a ground-hugging mat, extend well up the stems**. The leaves and stems are glandular-hairy.

Names: Juan Minuart was an 18th-century Spanish botanist and pharmacist. Nuttall: see p. 148. Formerly called *Arenaria nuttallii*. **Where found:** Alpine to 12,500'; also in Mixed Conifer Forest. Sandy or rocky slopes, talus, rock ledges; e.g., Tioga Crest east of Saddlebag Lake (11,500') in July.

white • 5 separate petals • July–August

CREAMBUSH
Holodiscus microphyllus • Rose Family

Creambush is a **low 1–3' shrub whose reddish stems, crinkly green leaves, and plumes of creamy white flowers** brighten up rocky slopes below and above timberline. The young, reddish stems make quite a contrast to the old, gray ones. The new stems bear many obovate leaves, which are distinctly veined and scalloped. Mixed in with the leaves are numerous 2–10" panicles packed with scores of the 1/4", white flowers. The many protruding reproductive parts, typical of the rose family, give the plumes a soft, fuzzy look. The flower centers often have a pink to rose tinge. The crinkly leaves can be smooth but often are covered with fine hairs.

Names: *Holodiscus* means 'entire disk.' *Microphyllus* means 'small-leaved' (in comparison to the leaves of some other *Holodiscus* species). Also called rock spiraea. **Where found:** Alpine to 13,000'; also in Mixed Conifer Forest. Rocky slopes, rock outcrops; e.g., east of Saddlebag Lake (10,500') in August, and along trail to Mono Pass (11,500') in August.

white • 5 separate petals
• July–September

ALPINE COLUMBINE
Aquilegia pubescens • Buttercup Family

Alpine columbine is among the most spectacular eastern Sierra flowers, all the more remarkable for its harsh, wind-exposed, high-elevation habitat. The 6–20" stems rise above mostly basal, round, lobed leaves. The few stem leaves are narrower. At the ends of the branching stems are the incredible 1¹/₂–2" **flowers**. Like all columbines, their 5 petals are long tubes ending in nectar spurs, while their 5 sepals flare out between the petals. Unlike the lower-elevation, hummingbird-pollinated crimson columbine (see p. 194), alpine columbine blooms are **upright and bright white throughout**. They are pollinated by moths attracted by the ultraviolet light reflected off the white petals and sepals. Sometimes bees cross-pollinate alpine columbine and crimson columbine, with remarkable results (see p. 194).

Names: *Aquilegia:* see p. 194. *Pubescens* means 'hairy.' Also called Coville's columbine. **Where found:** southern and central Alpine to 12,000'; also in Mixed Conifer Forest from 9000'. Rocky slopes, talus, rock ledges; e.g., around Box Lake on trail from Mosquito Flat to Morgan Pass (10,500') in July, and along trail to Mono Pass near the pass (12,000') in July.

white • 5 irregular petals • July–September

ALPINE PAINTBRUSH
Castilleja nana • Snapdragon Family

Although most paintbrushes have inconspicuous, largely atrophied flowers, these plants are still very flashy because of their colorful, showy bracts. Most paintbrushes light up their environment with intense, bright colors ranging from red (see pp. 67, 188) or red-purple (see p. 187) to orange or yellow (see p. 117). Alpine paintbrush, however, is much more subtle and muted, blending into its environment instead of dazzling it. You could easily overlook it, for it **rarely exceeds 6" in height** and its bracts are anything but bright. The **bracts vary from gray to pale purple to light yellow and are covered with soft hairs.** As with most paintbrushes, the bracts have 3–5 lobes. The flowers are mostly concealed by the bracts, though often the black tip of the corolla is visible.

Names: *Castilleja:* see p. 67. *Nana:* see p. 158. **Where found:** Alpine to 12,000'; also in Mixed Conifer Forest. Rocky flats and ridges; e.g., Tioga Crest east of Saddlebag Lake (11,500') in July.

white (pale purple or pale yellow) bracts • 5 petals united in 2-lipped tube • July–August

DWARF LEWISIA
Lewisia pygmaea • Purslane Family

The alpine environment offers many splendid floral treats; dwarf lewisia is one of the most beautiful and intriguing. Even without its flowers, it is a fascinating plant, for its **basal leaves form amazing patterns on the ground like many-armed starfish reaching for the sky.** Each leaf rosette is composed of scores of narrow, fleshy, overlapping 'arms' curving up from their gravel home. Set in among the leaves are many short (1–2") radiating stems mimicking the angles of the leaves. Each stem typically bears only 1 small flower. The **6–9 petals are white (sometimes pink) and translucent. The calyx is deep maroon with distinctive, jagged edges** like the profile of a miniature mountain range. This is a plant that begs for a long look and a close examination regardless of where it happens to be in its blooming cycle.

Names: Lewis: see p. 129. *Pygmaea* means 'pygmy,' in reference to the plant's diminutive size. **Where found:** Alpine to 14,000'; also in Mixed Conifer Forest. Wet, rocky flats, along streams; e.g., Tioga Crest east of Saddlebag Lake (12,000') in August.

white (pink) • 6–9 petals • July–September

CUT-LEAF DAISY
Erigeron compositus • Composite Family

Daisies are bright and cheery wherever they grow, but when you find them on wind-battered, rocky ridges high above timberline, they seem especially exuberant and charming. Cut-leaf daisy is a typical dwarfed alpine plant with its small, basal leaves and short (1–6") stems. The **hairy, lobed, mitten-like leaves form a loose mat** above which the hairy stems rise. Though the **1–1¹/₂" flowerhead of 30–60 rays** surrounding the button of yellow disk flowers is typical of daisies, it is a bit surprising on this plant, for it looks huge on such a short stem. Just imagine how big the flowerhead of a typical 3' tall, low-elevation daisy would be if the width of its flowerhead were a quarter to half the length of its stem! The rays are usually white, though they can be pale pink or blue. There is a rayless variety (*E. compositus* var. *discoidea,* bottom photo).

Names: *Erigeron:* see p. 106. *Compositus* means 'compound,' in reference to the deeply divided leaves. **Where found:** Alpine to 14,000'. Rocky slopes and flats, talus, rock ledges; e.g., near summit of Mt. Rose (10,600') in July.

white • many disk and ray flowers (or ray flowers absent) • July–August

BUTTERBALLS
Eriogonum ovalifolium • Buckwheat Family

Just take a look at butterballs' leaves, and you won't be surprised to see the plant growing on the highest alpine ridges where the summer sun beats unmercifully, the winds howl incessantly, and the temperatures at night drop 40 or 50 degrees. Butterballs has tiny, **fleshy, egg-shaped leaves** that are covered with matted hairs, giving them a distinctive gray-green appearance. These leaves **cluster very tightly, forming almost impenetrable mats or cushions that can be 1–2' wide**. Rising above these leaves are slender, 2–10" stems, each with a **round umbel of many tiny (¹/₈–¹/₄"), papery flowers**. The flowers are usually creamy yellow or white early in their blooming, turning pink or rose as they age, though sometimes even the early flowers are a rich rose. As with all buckwheats, the papery 'petals' are actually sepals—there are no true petals.

Names: *Eriogonum:* see p. 47. *Ovalifolium* means 'oval-leaved.' **Where found:** Alpine to 13,000'; also in Mixed Conifer Forest. Sandy or gravelly flats, rocks; e.g., Tioga Crest east of Saddlebag Lake (11,500') in August.

creamy yellow (white or rose) • 6 tiny petal-like sepals • July–September

LEMMON'S DRABA
Draba lemmonii • Mustard Family

Although Lemmon's draba was named for John and Sara Lemmon (see p. 179), it could just as well have been called lemon's draba after the **intense lemon color of the flowers**. From a distance a cluster of these bright yellow flowers can look like a patch of lichen on the rock, for the plant forms mats that tend to grow in rock crevices or on rock ledges. The tiny, oval leaves are hairy but are greener than the gray-woolly leaves of many alpine plants. Above the leaves rise 1–5" stems bearing at their tips **showy clusters of 3–30 of the 4-petaled, ¹/₄–¹/₂" flowers**. Distinguishing this draba from the several others that frequent the Alpine zone in the eastern Sierra are its **strangely twisted seedpods** (top photo).

Names: *Draba* means 'acrid,' in reference to the taste of the leaves. Lemmon: see p. 179. **Where found:** Alpine to 14,000'; also in Mixed Conifer Forest above 8500'. Rock ledges, talus slopes, ridges; e.g., near summit of Mt. Dana (12,500') in July.

yellow • 4 petals in cross • July–August

ALPINE BUTTERCUP
Ranunculus eschscholtzii • Buttercup Family

Many buttercups are early bloomers, ushering in spring with their shiny yellow flowers as if to symbolize the sun melting away the cold and dark of winter. In mid-elevations in the eastern Sierra Nevada in May and June, buttercups are among the first flowers to appear in cold and soggy meadows just out from under the snow. Alpine buttercup is one such spring blossom, but, of course, spring may not arrive above timberline until much later—perhaps not until July or even August, depending on the amount of snow. If you're up near timberline in the alpine spring, you have a good chance of seeing alpine buttercup. The **bright yellow, 1" flowers** are such a vivid contrast to their rock environment that they're difficult to miss. The **5 broad petals curl up slightly at the tips to form a shallow bowl around the central clump of green pistils and the ring of yellow stamens.**

Names: *Ranunculus:* see p. 175. Eschscholtz: see p. 55. **Where found:** Alpine to 13,000'; also in Mixed Conifer Forest. Rocky slopes, rock ledges; e.g., near summit of Mt. Rose (10,700') in June.

yellow • 5 separate petals • June–August

BUSH CINQUEFOIL
Potentilla fruticosa • Rose Family

If you're at all familiar with the *Potentilla* species that frequent the lower elevations (e.g., p. 171), you probably will recognize the flower of bush cinquefoil as a *Potentilla* flower immediately. It has the 5 separate, rounded, bright yellow petals and the 5 green, triangular sepals as well as the many pistils and stamens that you would expect. The big surprise, though, is the growth form—bush cinquefoil is the **only *Potentilla* shrub in the Sierra Nevada** (or in all of California, for that matter). It is a soft and leafy shrub that can reach 3' in height. Its many pinnate leaflets provide a lush, green backdrop for its many yellow, ³/₄–1¹/₂" flowers. What a joy it is to see so many cinquefoil flowers together in one place at one time! Bush cinquefoil is a circumboreal species, which means you can find it all around the world in the northern latitudes.

Names: *Potentilla:* see p. 143. *Fruticosa* means 'shrubby.' Also called shrubby cinquefoil. **Where found:** Alpine to 12,500'; also in Mixed Conifer Forest. Rocky slopes, meadows; e.g., along trail to Mono Pass (11,000') in July, and Tioga Crest above Gardisky Lake (12,000') in July.

yellow • 5 separate petals • July–August

ALPINE DRUMMOND'S CINQUEFOIL
Potentilla drummondii var. *breweri* • Rose Family

If you were to look at only the flowers, you would see very little difference between alpine Drummond's cinquefoil and the lower-elevation Drummond's cinquefoil (*P. drummondii* var. *drummondii*, p. 171), for they have almost identical bright yellow, ¹/₂–1" flowers with heart-shaped petals. This similarity isn't surprising: these plants are considered 2 varieties of the same species. So what are the differences that led botanists to distinguish separate varieties? Look at the leaves, and you will have your answer. On both plants the leaves are pinnately compound, but in var. *drummondii* the leaflets are larger, fewer, and pinnately toothed, while in var. *breweri* the **leaflets are smaller, more numerous, and palmately lobed**. As well, the **leaves of var. *breweri* are very noticeably white-hairy**, while those of var. *drummondii* are green. It probably won't surprise you, then, that var. *breweri* (with its densely hairy leaves) is the only one of the two that extends up into the Alpine zone.

Names: *Potentilla:* see p. 143. Drummond: see p. 171. Brewer: see p. 140. **Where found:** Alpine to 12,000'; also in Mixed Conifer Forest from 9000'. Meadows, rocky slopes; e.g., Tioga Crest east of Saddlebag Lake (11,500') in September.

yellow • 5 separate petals • July–September

GORDON'S IVESIA
Ivesia gordonii • Rose Family

Gordon's ivesia is a fascinating plant, for both its intricate flowers and its even more intricate leaves. You'll probably notice the leaves first, for they form basal clusters that look a bit like nests of green centipedes. **Each 1–3" leaf is pinnately divided into 10–25 opposite pairs of tiny, lobed leaflets.** The flowers appear at first to have 10 petals, but close examination will show that **5 narrow, rounded, yellow petals alternate with 5 slightly broader, pointed, yellow-green sepals.** Each 2–10" stem ends in a cluster of 10–20 of the ¹/₂" flowers.

Names: Ives: see p. 144. George Gordon was a 19th-century London horticulturist. **Where found:** Alpine to 12,000'; also in Mixed Conifer Forest. Rocky slopes and ridges; e.g., Tioga Crest east of Saddlebag Lake (11,500') in September.

Related plant: Club-moss ivesia (*I. lycopodioides*, bottom photo) has yellow flowers with broader, rounded petals and has braided-looking basal leaves with up to 70 tiny leaflets. It grows in similar habitats and elevations including on the Tioga Crest (11,500') in September. *Lycopodioides* means 'resembling *Lycopodium*,' a genus of club-moss.

yellow • 5 separate petals • July–September

SIBBALDIA
Sibbaldia procumbens • Rose Family

The flowers of *Sibbaldia* are similar to those of some species of *Ivesia*, a fellow genus in the rose family. Although the flowers of both genera share rose-family characteristics (e.g., 5 separate petals and lots of reproductive parts), their resemblance goes beyond this. If you compare Gordon's ivesia (p. 226), for example, with sibbaldia, you will see that in both flowers the sepals seem to compete with the petals for center stage. In both cases, the **sepals show through between the wide-spread petals** and are at least as large as the petals. In sibbaldia, this 'sepal-icity' is more pronounced than in ivesia, for in sibbaldia the **narrow, yellow petals** seem almost an afterthought placed on the **much larger, green sepals** as frivolous decoration. The strawberry-like, wedge-shaped, 3-lobed leaves form mats that can carpet several square yards and, with the sepals, provide a green canvas for the small dabs of yellow petals.

Names: Robert Sibbald was a Scottish naturalist and physician of the late 17th and early 18th centuries. *Procumbens* means 'procumbent.' **Where found:** Alpine to 12,000'; also in Mixed Conifer Forest. Moist, rocky areas; e.g., Tioga Crest east of Saddlebag Lake (11,500') in July.

yellow • 5 separate petals • July–August

SIERRA PODISTERA
Podistera nevadensis • Carrot Family

In a family with many tall plants—some of which reach 6' or more—bearing large leaves and umbels up to 1' or more across (e.g., cow-parsnip, ranger's buttons, poison hemlock, soda straw), Sierra podistera is certainly unusual. Its **stems are only a couple of inches tall, its leaves are tiny and form dense mats, and its umbels of flowers are rarely over 1" across**. Though in most ways, Sierra podistera is a miniaturized plant, its **dense mat of leaves can completely cover several square yards of rocky terrain like a gently rolling blanket.** Each tiny leaf is pinnately compound. Scattered over the blanket are the small, rounded umbels of tiny, yellow (sometimes creamy white) flowers. The flowers fade brown.

Names: *Podistera* means 'solid foot,' in reference to the compact, ground-hugging growth form. *Nevadensis:* see p. 150. **Where found:** Alpine to 13,000'. Rocky flats, crevices in rocks; e.g., near summit of Freel Peak in the Tahoe Basin (10,500') in August.

**yellow • 5 tiny petals
• August–September**

ALPINE GOLD
Hulsea algida • Composite Family

The Alpine zone above the trees is a world of miniature plants only a few inches high whose flowers are small and whose leaves huddle near the ground or contour it with mats or cushions. Typically, the leaves of these plants are waxy or densely hairy—anything to help protect them from the wind and intense solar radiation. Alpine gold certainly has the hair, but otherwise it is very unusual for an alpine plant. Its **stems reach 1¹/₂'** and though it has a cluster of basal leaves, it also has narrow, toothed leaves over halfway up the stem. The **flowerheads are up to 1" across and are packed with 25–60 bright yellow rays around a central button of scores and scores of yellow-orange disk flowers**. There is nothing subtle or miniaturized about this plant! The **leaves, stems, and phyllaries are white-hairy and glandularsticky**. If you rub a leaf, you will smell an almost overpowering, sticky-sweet fragrance.

Names: G.W. Hulse was a 19th-century U.S. Army surgeon and botanist. *Algida* means 'of the cold.' **Where found:** Alpine to 13,000'. Rocky slopes, talus; e.g., on Starr Peak just above Mono Pass (12,300') in July, and near the summit of Mt. Dana (12,500') in August.

yellow • many ray and disk flowers • July–September

GOLDEN-ASTER
Pyrrocoma apargioides • Composite Family

Although golden-aster occurs commonly above timberline, don't expect to find it in the really rugged habitats such as open, exposed ridges or talus slopes. You'll often find it growing in the more protected sites, such as grassy meadows. This restricted distribution probably won't surprise you when you observe its **leaves, for they are relatively large (to 4") and mostly hairless**—not well suited to the harshest, windiest conditions. The reddish, 2–12" stems are sometimes prostrate but usually curve up to an almost erect posture. At the tip of each stem is 1 flowerhead (to 1" across) of 11–40 yellow rays surrounding a yellow-orange button of 45–90 disk flowers. The **phyllaries are distinctive—broad and fleshy and arranged in 3–4 series**. The leaves are often somewhat in-folded.

Names: *Pyrrocoma* means 'reddish pappus.' *Apargioides* means 'resembling *Apargia*,' a former genus in the composite family now merged with *Leontodon*. **Where found:** Alpine to 12,000'; also in Mixed Conifer Forest. Rocky slopes, open woods; e.g., east of Saddlebag Lake (10,500') in September.

yellow • many ray and disk flowers • July–September

SILKY RAILLARDELLA
Raillardella argentea · Composite Family

If you didn't know you were above timberline, you might guess it when you saw silky raillardella, for it has many features you would expect of a plant adapted to a harsh, windy environment. Its **narrow basal leaves are thickly covered with silky, silvery hairs**. Its stem is glandular-sticky and rises only 1–7" above these leaves. Atop its stem, this dwarfed plant has only 1 small flowerhead that consists of 7–25 **bright yellow disk flowers** and **no showy ray flowers**. The 2-parted yellow stigmas sticking out of the flower tubes do add some pizzazz to the otherwise restrained flowers.

Names: *Raillardella* means 'small *Raillardia*.' *Argentea* means 'silvery,' in reference to the leaves. **Where found:** Alpine to 13,000'; also in Mixed Conifer Forest. Gravelly or rocky slopes and ridges; e.g., Mt. Dana (12,000') in August.

Related plant: Green-leaf raillardella (*R. scaposa*, bottom photo) resembles silky raillardella, but it can be a bit taller (to 20"), its leaves are not silky-hairy, and its yellow flowerhead sometimes has a few rays radiating from the 9–40 disk flowers. It grows in more protected places throughout the Mixed Conifer Forest zone and into the lower Alpine zone, e.g., along the trail to Mono Pass (11,000') in July. *Scaposa* means 'with scapes,' i.e., long, leafless flower stalks.

yellow · many disk flowers · July–August

ALPINE GOLDENROD
Solidago multiradiata · Composite Family

Goldenrod species, with their plumes of yellow-orange flowerheads, are cheery members of the fall flora across much of the U.S., but they have a bad reputation among allergy sufferers. Ironically, not only are they innocent of the charges (ragweed usually being the guilty party), but they have many medicinal uses. · Alpine goldenrod, which grows in meadows below timberline and on alpine slopes, is a short version **(to 16" tall)** with less elongated inflorescences than those of most low-elevation species. Several to many of the ½–¾" flowerheads congregate toward the tips of the branched stems. Each flowerhead consists of **many disk flowers and 12–18 (often 13) ray flowers**. Unlike those of many yellow composites, the **ray and disk flowers of alpine goldenrod are hard to distinguish**. They are all the same yellow color and seem to mix together to form a rather chaotic flowerhead. The 2–5" leaves are narrow (sometimes spoon-shaped). The upper stem leaves clasp the stem.

Names: *Solidago* means 'make well,' in reference to the medicinal uses. *Multiradiata* means 'with numerous rays.' **Where found:** Alpine to 12,000'; also in Mixed Conifer Forest above 8500'. Meadows, rocky slopes, flats; e.g., along the Tioga Pass road (9500') in July, and the Tioga Crest east of Saddlebag Lake (11,500') in August.

yellow · 12–18 ray flowers and many disk flowers
· July–September

MOUNTAIN SORREL
Oxyria digyna • Buckwheat Family

Most plants of the alpine environment adapt to the drying conditions by having specialized leaves with very little surface area or very protected surfaces. Some of these alpine leaves are narrow and needle-like (e.g., p. 217), some are deeply lobed (e.g., p. 226), some form mats or cushions (e.g., pp. 217, 227), and some are thickly covered with hair (e.g., pp. 219, 226). Mountain sorrel adopts different strategies. Its **kidney-shaped leaves are surprisingly large and broad,** with lots of surface area, and they are hairless. They are, however, fleshy and juicy and manage to stay out of most of the wind by staying close to the ground and by hiding behind rocks. The leaves are deliciously tangy to the taste, but don't be greedy—the plants need them more than you do! The 2–15" stem has a **panicle of tiny red or greenish flowers.** The tiny seedpods are red.

Names: *Oxyria* means 'sour,' in reference to the tart taste of the leaves. *Digyna* means 'with 2 pistils.' **Where found:** Alpine to 13,000'; also in Mixed Conifer Forest. Rock ledges, talus; e.g., along trail to Mono Pass near pass (12,000') in July, and near summit of Mt. Dana (12,500') in July.

red or yellow-green • 4 tiny petal-like sepals • July–September

ROSY SEDUM
Sedum rosea • Stonecrop Family

Despite growing in the high mountains, rosy sedum radiates lushness and luxuriance. Though technically not a shrub (it doesn't have a woody base), its **2–12" stems grow in such profusion and in such dense clusters that they form what appears to be a shrub that can be several feet long and just as wide.** This mass of plants is amazingly dense with thousands of small but thick, succulent leaves. And seeming to float on this sea of leaves are **hundreds of clusters of tiny, 4-petaled, wine red flowers.** The brown-purple anthers protrude, giving the flower clusters a fuzzy look. Even before the flowers bloom, the 'shrub' is spectacular, for the buds are a deep, sensuous red-purple.

Names: *Sedum:* see p. 172. *Rosea* means 'rosy,' probably in reference to the color of the flowers or perhaps to the fragrance of the roots. Also called western roseroot. **Where found:** Alpine to 13,000'; also in Mixed Conifer Forest. Rocky ridges, talus; e.g., Tioga Crest above Gardisky Lake (11,500') in July.

red • 4 petals united at base • July–August

ROCK FRINGE
Epilobium obcordatum • Evening-Primrose Family

Although the common name rock fringe gives you a good idea of where this plant grows, it does nothing to prepare you for how truly spectacular the flowers are. The small, round leaves form **low mats that sprawl across rocky flats and the edges of boulders, but the** flowers are so large (1–1¹/₂") and bloom in such profusion that they almost completely hide the leaves. Even if there were only 1 flower per mat, you still might not notice the leaves, for the flowers rivet your attention with their **gorgeous rose color, their large, heart-shaped petals, and their velvety, 4-parted, deep rose stigma**. If you were to forget for a moment where you were, you might imagine that these incredible flowers were tropical birds or butterflies that have come to roost.

Names: *Epilobium:* see p. 181. *Obcordatum* means 'inversely heart-shaped,' in reference to the petals. **Where found:** Alpine to 12,000; also in Mixed Conifer Forest. Around rocks; e.g., near Kearsarge Pass along trail from Onion Valley (11,500') in July, and along trail to Mono Pass (11,500') in July.

rose • 4 separate petals • July–September

PUSSYPAWS
Calyptridium umbellatum • Purslane Family

Hike sandy or rocky slopes or flats practically anywhere in the eastern Sierra, and you will probably have pussypaws as a companion—and it is as charming and endearing as it is constant. The long, often **shiny, spoon-shaped leaves form an intricate rosette** with the leaves tiered, so that each leaf is fully exposed to the sun while lying as low as possible. Mimicking the radiating leaves are the 1–6" stems bearing the ¹/₂–1¹/₂", fuzzy 'pussypaws.' **When the ground is cold, the stems radiate nearly flat on the ground, but when the ground heats up, they rise to a steep angle, lifting the umbels of flowers several inches off the ground**. Each pussypaw consists of scores of tiny flowers, each with 2 sepals and 4 petals. The sepals and petals are very difficult to tell apart, for both are papery and scale-like. Although the flowers can be white, they are usually pink tinged if not intensely rose or red-purple.

Names: *Calyptridium* means 'cap,' in reference to the uniting of the petals in fruit into a cap-like structure. *Umbellatum:* see p. 166. **Where found:** Alpine to 14,000'; also in Sagebrush Steppe and in Mixed Conifer Forest. Sandy or rocky flats and slopes, open woods, ridges; e.g., east side of Sonora Peak (11,000') in July.

pink or white • 4 tiny petals • June–September

SIERRA PRIMROSE
Primula suffretescens • Primrose Family

At first glance you might mistake Sierra primrose for rock fringe (p. 231). Both plants have large flowers with **gorgeous, pink to rose petals,** and both form large mats around rocks in high elevations. A closer look, however, will reveal very noticeable differences. Sierra primrose has 5 petals rather than the 4 of rock fringe, and its flowers have what looks like a **yellow bull's-eye in the center** surrounding the flower tube. Out of this tube projects a round, unbranched stigma atop a slender style. The ovary of Sierra primrose is superior, unlike the inferior ovary of rock fringe, so you won't find a swelling beneath its petals. The **leaves are wedge shaped and toothed** and crowd around the base of the stem. Sierra primrose tends to grow on north-facing slopes where it can receive some moisture from late-melting snow.

Names: *Primula* means 'first,' in reference to the early blooming of some species. *Suffretescens* means 'somewhat shrubby.' **Where found:** Alpine to 13,000'. Rock crevices, rock ledges; e.g., near Kearsarge Pass along trail from Onion Valley (11,600') in July.

pink to rose • 5 separate petals • July–August

WHITNEY'S LOCOWEED
Astragalus whitneyi • Pea Family

Astragalus is a large genus worldwide, so it probably won't surprise you to keep meeting *Astragalus* species in the eastern Sierra. From the fiery blooms of scarlet locoweed in the Mojave Desert Scrub, to the strange, nearly circular seedpods of Humboldt River milkvetch in the Sagebrush Steppe, to the pink-purple flowers and cottonball seedpods of Pursh's milkvetch in the Mixed Conifer Forest, these plants intrigue us. And to top it off, Whitney's locoweed sprawls its 4–10" stems across rocky or gravelly places above timberline. It has the typical pinnately compound leaves and the small (¹/₄–¹/₂"), pea-type flowers that can be shades of pink or purple or creamy white. The real attraction of this *Astragalus* is its amazing **seedpods—yellow-green or gold or pink, inflated, papery bladders with splotches of rust-red or brown.** Shake them late in the fall, and you will hear an ominous sound like a death rattle.

Names: *Astragalus:* see p. 66. J.D. Whitney was the 19th-century geologist and explorer after whom Mt. Whitney was named. **Where found:** Alpine to 12,500'; also in Mixed Conifer Forest. Sandy or gravelly flats, talus; e.g., Tioga Crest east of Saddlebag Lake (11,500') in July.

pink-purple to blue-purple or white • 5 irregular petals • July–August

ALPINE DOUGLAS' PINCUSHION
Chaenactis douglasii var. *alpina* • Composite Family

When you see this plant in the rocks above timberline and admire its cylindrical flowerheads crowded with showy disk flowers, you may recognize an old friend from lower elevations—dusty maidens (p. 108). Alpine Douglas' pincushion seems to have the same **tiny, exquisite disk flowers with the long-protruding, 2-branched stigmas** and the same **feathery, pinnately compound, gray-green leaves**. But you will soon realize that this isn't quite the same plant, for it differs in several ways. First, like many high-elevation plants, it is miniaturized, with stems that rarely exceed 10". Second, the leaves, though similar, are much smaller and tighter. And third, the **flowers are usually deep pink or rose** rather than yellow or white with pink tinges.

Names: *Chaenactis:* see p. 52. Douglas: see p. 95. **Where found:** northern Alpine to 11,500'. Rocky or gravelly slopes and ridges, rock crevices; e.g., near summit of Freel Peak (10,700') in July.

pink to rose • many disk flowers
• July–September

SHOWY POLEMONIUM
Polemonium pulcherrimum • Phlox Family

We are blessed in the eastern Sierra to have the cheery blue flowers of *Polemonium* smiling at us in just about every habitat. From wet meadows (great polemonium, p. 206) to shady woods (low polemonium, p. 206), and from rocky slopes near timberline (showy polemonium) to rock ledges and talus slopes near the summit of the highest peaks (sky pilot, p. 234), you will meet a variety of these species, all with the familiar 5-petaled, blue to violet faces and the distinctive, pinnately compound leaves. • Showy polemonium forms **shrub-like mounds to about 1' high** that seem to be swarming with tightly pinnate leaves. Each leaf is composed of 9–21 oval, $^{1}/_{4}$–$^{1}/_{2}$" leaflets that overlap, creating a **leaf that looks a little like the armored, scaly tail of a stegosaurus.** Scattered on this leafy canvas are many small ($^{1}/_{2}$"), blue to violet flowers with yellow centers. The reproductive parts stick way out of the flower tubes.

Names: *Polemonium:* see p. 206. *Pulcherrimum* means 'beautiful.' **Where found:** central and northern Alpine to 12,500'; also in Mixed Conifer Forest above 8000'. Rocky slopes, talus; e.g., near summit of Mt. Rose (10,500') in July.

blue to violet • 5 petals united in bowl • July–August

SKY PILOT
Polemonium eximium • Phlox Family

Of the 4 gorgeous species of *Polemonium* that grace the eastern Sierra (see also pp. 206, 233), sky pilot soars above all the rest, for it grows near the summit of many of the highest peaks, including Mt. Whitney. Sometimes it really seems that if the plant moved any higher, it would leave earth once and for all and become a creature of the sky. Sky pilot also soars with its dramatic beauty. **Atop its 4–12" stems are dense, spherical heads of deep blue to purple flowers.** Unlike most *Polemonium* species, the flowers do not have a yellow or white 'bull's-eye' at the center. Instead, the petals slope down into a dark, mysterious tube. The **stems and the tightly pinnately compound, mousetail-like leaves are glandular-sticky.**

Names: *Polemonium:* see p. 206. *Eximium* means 'distinguished.' **Where found:** southern and central Alpine to 14,000'. Rocky slopes, rock ledges, talus; e.g., near summit of Mt. Dana (13,000') in August, and near summit of Mt. Whitney (14,000') in August.

blue to blue-purple • 5 petals united in bowl • July–August

DAVIDSON'S PENSTEMON
Penstemon davidsonii • Snapdragon Family

As with the alpine species of many genera, *Penstemon davidsonii* seems to have grafted large, low-elevation flowers onto dwarfed, alpine plants. The result is startling and spectacular and maybe even a little unsettling! **On some Davidson's penstemon plants the 1–1¹/₂" tubular blossoms are actually longer than the plant stems.** These miniature stems trying to support the large, robust flowers look a bit like Atlas struggling to support the globe. Since Davidson's penstemon usually forms mats with numerous flowers, you have a whole pantheon of gods and demigods trying to hold up a whole solar system of planets! The **small, oval leaves are smooth and fleshy.** The blossoms range from violet to blue-purple to pink-purple.

Names: *Penstemon:* see p. 71. George Davidson was the first botanist to collect this plant in California. Also called alpine penstemon. **Where found:** Alpine to 12,000'; also in Mixed Conifer Forest. Rocky slopes and flats, rock ledges, talus; e.g., above Ellery Lake (10,500') in July, and along trail to Mono Pass near pass (12,000') in July.

violet to pink-purple • 5 petals united in tube • July–August

WHORLED PENSTEMON
Penstemon heterodoxus • Snapdragon Family

Whorled penstemon has the typical tubular *Penstemon* flowers and opposite pairs of narrow leaves, but its flowers have an unusual arrangement on the plant stem. While many *Penstemon* species have clusters of flowers along the stem, whorled penstemon is one of the few to have **wheel-like clusters (whorls) of flowers encircling the stem**. In whorled penstemon the 2–8" stem usually has only 1 whorl at its tip, though it may have a second whorl beneath the first. Each whorl consists of 10–30 flowers pointing in all directions around the stem. The blue or blue-purple, tubular flowers are slender and short (½") and often have a reddish tinge along the tube. Whorled penstemon's **glandular inflorescence** distinguishes it from a lower-elevation relative that also has whorls of flowers (meadow penstemon, *P. rydbergii*).

Names: *Penstemon:* see p. 71. *Heterodoxus* means 'unique glory,' perhaps in reference to the whorled beauty of the flowers. **Where found:** Alpine to 13,000'; also in Mixed Conifer Forest. Meadows, rocky slopes; e.g., Tioga Crest east of Saddlebag Lake (11,500') in July, and along trail to Mono Pass (11,500') in July.

blue-purple or pink-purple • 5 petals united in tube
• July–September

DWARF ALPINE DAISY
Erigeron pygmaeus • Composite Family

When you put a ¾–1" flowerhead crammed with showy ray and disk flowers atop a **1–3" stem,** you get a stunning, flamboyant flower show almost as wide as tall, and you get dwarf alpine daisy. The **narrow, glandular-sticky leaves** form thick, basal clusters above which rise (slightly) the stems bearing their striking flowerheads. Each flowerhead consists of 15–35 narrow rays surrounding a raised central button of scores and scores of yellow disk flowers. The **rays are usually some shade of violet or blue-purple but sometimes range all the way to pink-purple**. Whatever the color, dwarf alpine daisy can provide some of the most vivid patches of color in the rocks above timberline, for the flowers often bloom in such profusion and so close together that they almost completely conceal the leaves and rocks beneath.

Names: *Erigeron:* see p. 106. *Pygmaeus* means 'pygmy,' in reference to the dwarfed growth form. **Where found:** Alpine to 13,000'. Rocky or gravelly flats, talus; e.g., near Kearsarge Pass along trail from Onion Valley (11,200') in July.

blue-purple or pink-purple • many disk and
ray flowers • July–August

Glossary

anther: the pollen-producing tip of the male sex part of the flower (e.g., camas lily, p. 123)

appressed: pressed against, such as hairs appressed against the stem (e.g., flax-leaved monardella, p. 120)

axil: the angle between the leaf and the stem (e.g., cotton-thorn, p. 61)

banner: the upper petal in flowers of the pea family (e.g., wild licorice, p. 50)

basal leaves: leaves located at the base of a plant as opposed to up the plant stem (e.g., nude buckwheat, p. 139)

bracts: leaf-like structures performing a different function from a leaf, such as the colorful bracts in the inflorescence of paintbrushes that attract pollinators (e.g., great red paintbrush, p. 188)

bulbil: a small, bulb-like structure of asexual reproduction, usually attached to a plant stem, that falls to the ground and sprouts to become a clone of the parent plant (e.g., rock star, p. 151)

calyx (pl. calyces): collective term for the sepals (e.g., purple sage, p. 125)

clasping: holding or surrounding tightly, such as a leaf clasping the stem (e.g., stream orchid, p. 62)

cleistogamous: having bud-like, non-opening flowers that self-pollinate as a sort of backup for the regular, blooming flowers (e.g., stream violet, p. 173)

cross-pollination: the transfer of pollen from the anthers of a flower on one plant to the stigma of a flower on another plant of the same species (e.g., blue flax, p. 129)

cushion plant: an herbaceous perennial plant forming a dense, rounded mass of short stems and many leaves (e.g., Coville's phlox, p. 217)

cyme: a flat-topped or round-topped flower cluster in which the flowers on the inner (upper) branches bloom first (e.g., fiddleneck, p. 56)

dioecious: describes species in which male flowers and female flowers are borne on separate plants (e.g., stinging nettle, p. 210)

disk flowers: in the composite family, the small, tubular flowers that make up the 'button' in the center of the flowerhead (e.g., Rocky Mountain aster, p. 130); some composites have only disk flowers (e.g., desert pincushion, p. 52)

elliptic: in the shape of an ellipse, i.e., a flattened circle (e.g., the elliptic leaves of bush chinquapin, p. 168)

filament: in the male reproductive part of the flower, the stalk that bears the anther at its tip (e.g., alpine laurel, p. 184)

flowerhead: a dense cluster of several flowers often appearing to be a single blossom, such as the clustered ray and/or disk flowers in the composite family (e.g., Anderson's thistle, p. 198)

glandular: bearing glands that usually secrete a sticky liquid (e.g., Labrador tea, p. 150)

heterostyly: a reproductive system in which a species has different kinds of flowers with different style lengths, in order to prevent self-pollination (e.g., blue flax, p. 129)

inferior ovary: an ovary situated beneath the point where the petals attach (e.g., smoothstem willow-herb, p. 181)

inflorescence: an entire cluster of flowers and associated structures such as bracts and pedicels (e.g., death camas, p. 82)

involucre: a set of bracts beneath an inflorescence, as in the set of phyllaries under the flowerhead in the composite family (e.g., cobweb thistle, p. 121)

keel: the inner two petals cradling the reproductive parts in flowers of the pea family, somewhat resembling the keel of a boat (e.g., wild licorice, p. 50)

leaf axil: *see* axil

leaflet: one leaf-like unit of a compound leaf (e.g., mountain strawberry, p. 143)

limb: in calyces or corollas with fused parts, the expanded, outer portion (e.g., mountain bluebells, p. 207)

mat: a plant with densely interwoven and ground-hugging growth (e.g., yellow peppergrass, p. 54)

naturalized: not native but adapted to the new environment, reproducing without human aid (e.g., black locust, p. 90)

nectary: a gland that secretes nectar, usually associated with a flower (e.g., sego lily, p. 83)

node: the place on a stem where a leaf or branch is attached (e.g., desert trumpet, p. 53)

nutlet: a small, dry fruit that does not split to release its (usually single) seed at maturity (e.g., velvety stickseed, p. 208)

oblanceolate: lance-shaped with the widest part near the tip, usually referring to a leaf (e.g., desert ceanothus, p. 87)

oblong: elongate with parallel sides, usually referring to a leaf (e.g., whitestem goldenbush, p. 177)

obovate: egg-shaped with the widest part near the tip, usually referring to a leaf (e.g., creambush, p. 221)

ovary: the hollow base of a pistil that contains the young, undeveloped seeds and that ripens to form all or part of a fruit (e.g., northern sun-cup, p. 97)

ovate: egg-shaped with the widest part near the base, usually referring to a leaf (e.g., stinging nettle, p. 210)

ovoid: egg-shaped, in reference to 3-dimensional parts (e.g., red clover, p. 114)

pad: the succulent, broad, flat stem of a cactus (e.g., beavertail cactus, p. 69)

palmately compound: describes a compound structure in which the parts (often leaflets of a leaf) radiate from a common point, rather like the fingers of a hand (e.g., five-finger cinquefoil, p. 171)

panicle: an inflorescence in which the pedicels are attached to a branching plant stem (e.g., brook saxifrage, p. 153)

pappus: a modified calyx of bristles or scales, borne at the tip of a dry, 1-seeded fruit; usually associated with members of the composite family (e.g., yellow salsify, p. 109)

pedicel: the stalk of an individual flower (e.g., Jeffrey's shooting star, p. 182)

peduncle: the stalk of an entire inflorescence (e.g., big sagebrush, p. 107)

perianth: the sepals and the petals collectively (e.g., stream orchid, p. 62)

petiole: a leaf stalk (e.g., yellow bee plant, p. 55)

phyllaries: the narrow, usually green bracts forming the cup under the flowerhead in the composite family (e.g., curly gumweed, p. 107)

pinnately compound: describes a compound structure in which the parts (often leaflets of a leaf) branch off the main axis, rather feather-like (e.g., great polemonium, p. 206)

pistil: the female reproductive structure consisting of ovary, style, and stigma (e.g., Brown's peony, p. 131)

raceme: an inflorescence in which the pedicels are attached to an unbranched plant stem (e.g., red elderberry, p. 157)

ray flowers (rays): in the composite family, the wide-flaring flowers that radiate from the central 'button' (e.g., Parry's rock pink, p. 51); some composites have only ray flowers (e.g., desert dandelion, p. 59)

reflexed: abruptly bent or curved downward or backward (e.g., Dedecker's clover, p. 113)

rhizome: underground, often elongated, horizontal stem connecting numerous plant stems (e.g., Rothrock's nama, p. 207)

rosette: a crowded whorl of basal leaves (e.g., dwarf lewisia, p. 223)

runner: a slender, horizontally spreading stem on the ground that usually roots at its nodes or tips (e.g., tinker's penny, p. 172)

self-pollination: the transfer of pollen from the anthers to the stigma of the same flower, or to a flower on the same plant (e.g., blue flax, p. 129)

sepal: the usually green, but sometimes showy, flower parts beneath the petals, forming the outer protective layer in the bud (e.g., chia, p. 74)

silicle: a short silique, not much longer than wide (e.g., bush peppergrass, p. 48)

silique: a long, thin seedpod with two valves (e.g., prince's rock-cress, p. 62)

spike: an unbranched inflorescence with the flowers attached directly to the stem (e.g., yellow ladies' tresses, p. 165)

stamen: the male reproductive part of the flower, composed of the filament and the anther (e.g., alpine veronica, p. 199)

stigma: the pollen-receiving tip of the female reproductive part (e.g., checker-mallow, p. 191)

style: the stalk of the female reproductive part, connecting the ovary and the stigma (e.g., old man's whiskers, p. 196)

subshrub: a plant that has woody lower stems and non-woody upper stems, and that dies back seasonally (e.g., whitestem goldenbush, p. 177)

superior ovary: an ovary that is situated above the point where the petals attach (e.g., shieldleaf, p. 140)

tepal: one of the petals or sepals in flowers whose sepals look just like its petals (e.g., Lemmon's onion, p. 179)

twice pinnate (bipinnate): usually in reference to a pinnately compound leaf in which the pinnate leaflets are further divided into smaller, pinnate leaflets (e.g., desert sweet, p. 145)

umbel: an inflorescence in which all of the pedicels radiate from a common point on the plant stem (e.g., Mojave desert-parsley, p. 75)

whorl: a group of three or more structures of the same kind (often leaves or flowers) that radiate, ring-like, from the same point on the stem (e.g., whorled penstemon, p. 235)

wings: the two lateral petals in flowers of the pea family, usually cradling the keel (e.g., wild licorice, p. 50)

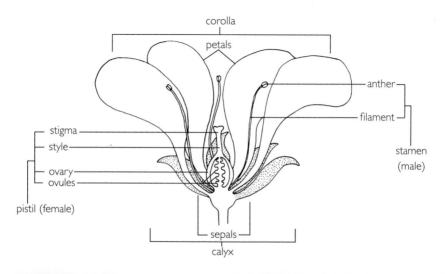

References

Austin, Mary. *The Land of Little Rain*, Penguin, New York, 1988.

Barbour, Michael and Jack Major, eds. *Terrestrial Vegetation of California*, John Wiley and Sons, New York, 1977.

Blackwell, Laird. *Wildflowers of the Sierra Nevada and the Central Valley*, Lone Pine Publishing, Edmonton, Alberta, Canada, 1999.

Blackwell, Laird. *Wildflowers of the Tahoe Sierra*, Lone Pine Publishing, Edmonton, Alberta, Canada, 1997.

Bowers, Janice. *Shrubs and Trees of the Southwest Deserts*, Southwest Parks and Monuments Association, Tucson, Arizona, 1993.

Coombes, Allen J. *Dictionary of Plant Names*, Timber Press, Portland, Oregon, 1994.

Cronquist, Arthur, Arthur Holmgren, Noel Holmgren, Pat Holmgren, James Reveal. *Intermountain Flora: Vascular Plants of the Intermountain West*, New York Botanical Gardens, New York.

Vol. I: *Geological and Botanical History*, 1972.

Vol. IIIa: *Subclass Rosidae (except Fabales)*, 1977.

Vol. IIIb: *Fabales*, 1989.

Vol. IV: *Subclass Asteridae*, 1984.

Vol. V: *Asterales*, 1994.

Vol. VI: *The Monocotyledons*, 1977.

Crowther, Jack and Pat. *A Bishop Creek Plant List*, Bristlecone Chapter of California Native Plant Society, n.d.

Dodge, Natt. *Mojave Desert Wildflowers*, Southwestern Parks and Monuments Association, Tucson, Arizona, 1985.

Hall, Clarence, ed. *Natural History of the White-Inyo Range of Eastern California*, University of California Press, Berkeley, 1991.

Hart, John. *Hiking the Great Basin*, Sierra Club Books, San Francisco, 1991.

Hickman, James, ed. *The Jepson Manual: Higher Plants of California*, University of California Press, Berkeley, 1993.

Irwin, Sue. *California's Eastern Sierra*, Cachuma Press, Los Olivos, California, 1997.

Jaeger, Edmund. *Desert Wild Flowers*, Stanford University Press, Stanford, California, 1941.

Morey, Kathy. *Hot Showers, Soft Beds, and Dayhikes in the Sierra*, Wilderness Press, Berkeley, California, 1996.

Munz, Philip. *California Desert Wildflowers*, University of California Press, Berkeley, 1962.

Niehaus, Theodore. *Pacific States Wildflowers*, Houghton Mifflin, Boston, 1976.

Secor, R.J. *The High Sierra*, The Mountaineers, Seattle, 1992.

Shreve, F. and I.L. Wiggins. *Vegetation and Flora of the Sonoran Desert*, 2 vols., Stanford University Press, Stanford, California, 1964.

Smith, Genny, ed. *Deepest Valley: Guide to Owens Valley*, Genny Smith Books, Mammoth Lakes, California, 1995.

Smith, Genny, ed. *Mammoth Lakes Sierra*, Genny Smith Books, Mammoth Lakes, California, 1993.

Stearn, William. *Botanical Latin*, Fitzhenry and Whiteside, Toronto, Ontario, Canada, 1983.

Stewart, Jon. *Mojave Desert Wildflowers*, Jon Stewart Photography, Albuquerque, New Mexico, 1998.

Taylor, Ronald. *Desert Wildflowers of North America*, Mountain Press, Missoula, Montana, 1998.

Taylor, Ronald. *Sagebrush Country: A Wildflower Sanctuary*, Mountain Press, Missoula, Montana, 1992.

Trimble, Stephen. *The Sagebrush Ocean*, University of Nevada Press, Reno, Nevada, 1989.

Ward, Grace and Onas. *190 Wild Flowers of the Southwest Deserts*, Best-West, Palm Desert, California, n.d.

Whitson, Tom, ed. *Weeds of the West*, Western Society of Weed Science, Newark, California, 1996.

Yoder, Vincent. *An Alabama Hills Plant List*, Bristlecone Chapter of California Native Plant Society, 1996.

Places Mentioned

requires hiking; distances indicated are one way

Aberdeen (4000'): tiny settlement just west of Highway 395, 14 miles south of Big Pine

Agnew Lake trailhead (7240'): off June Lake Loop Road just north of Silver Lake Resort

Alabama Hills (4000–5000'): miles of volcanic and granitic rock just west of Lone Pine, reached by Whitney Portal Road in Lone Pine, then right on Movie Road

*Baxter Pass (12,320'): very strenuous 8-mile hike from the north fork of Oak Creek (6000'); trailhead 6 miles west on Hatchery Road off Highway 395, 2 miles north of Independence

Big Pine Creek: along much of the 13-mile Crocker Road west from center of Big Pine

Bishop Creek (9300'): several drainages of Bishop Creek reached 14 miles west on West Line Street (Route 168) from center of Bishop, then choice of branch roads

Bridgeport (6465'): town along Highway 395, 25 miles north of Lee Vining

Carson Pass (8573'): along Route 88, 20 miles west of Minden

Clear Creek road (5000'): parallels Highway 50 between Carson City and Spooner Summit, reached along Old Spooner Summit Road, west off Highway 395 just south of junction of Highway 395 and Highway 50

Coleville (5400'): town along Highway 395, 5 miles north of Walker

Division Creek: *see* Sawmill Pass

Ellery Lake (9538'): along the Tioga Pass road just east of turnoff to Saddlebag Lake

Fish Slough (4000'): just northeast of Bishop on Highway 6, then Five Bridges Road

*Freel Peak (10,881'): highest peak in the Tahoe Basin, located at south end of Lake Tahoe; strenuous 7-mile hike from trailhead (7840') at end of dirt road off Oneidas Street in South Lake Tahoe (get directions locally)

*Frog Lake (8860'): easy 0.5-mile hike from Carson Pass trailhead (8573')

*Gardisky Lake (10,800'): steep though short 1-mile hike from trailhead (9800'), which is along dirt road to Saddlebag Lake north off the Tioga Pass road a few miles east of Tioga Pass

Genoa (4750'): town along the eastern base of the Sierra 8 miles northwest of Minden along Jack's Valley Road (Route 206), west off Highway 395 just south of its intersection with Highway 50

Goodale Creek road (4000'): dirt road west off old Highway 395 about 0.25 miles south of Aberdeen (old Highway 395 parallels new Highway 395 less than 1 mile to the west)

Grant Lake (7130'): along June Lake Loop Road just south of the northern intersection of that road with Highway 395

Grass Lake (7700'): shallow, swampy lake with many aquatic plants, just west of Luther Pass

*Heart Lake (10,420'): easy 1.25-mile hike from Mosquito Flat (10,230')

Hope Valley (6500'): large, open meadow along Route 88, 10 miles east of Carson Pass

Horseshoe Meadow Road (to 10,040'): 20-mile paved road south off Whitney Portal Road, 3 miles west of Lone Pine; marks south end of region covered in this book

*Job's Sister Peak (10,823'): short scramble northeast from Freel Peak

June Lake Loop Road (about 7000'): Route 158 passing Grant Lake, Silver Lake, and June Lake, west off Highway 395, 6 miles south of Lee Vining

*Kearsarge Pass (11,823'): strenuous 5-mile hike from Onion Valley (9200'); trailhead 15 miles west on Market Street from Independence

Kingsbury Grade: Route 207 from Minden (4720') to South Lake Tahoe (6300'), west off Highway 395 just north of Minden

Lundy Canyon (7800'): reached by 4 miles of paved road west off Highway 395 about 5 miles north of Lee Vining

Luther Pass (7740'): along Route 89 about 16 miles south of South Lake Tahoe

Mammoth (Lakes) (7800'): town along Route 203 just west off Highway 395, 38 miles north of Bishop

Markleeville (5500'): town along Route 89, 12.5 miles northwest of Monitor Pass

*McGee Creek trail (8100'): 6.5-mile hike along McGee Creek to Big McGee Lake (10,480'); trailhead at end of the McGee Canyon road (8100'), west off Highway 395, 28.5 miles north of Bishop

Mill Canyon (5400'): along dirt road (Mill Canyon Road) west off Highway 395, 2 miles north of Walker

Minden (4720'): town along Highway 395, 15 miles south of Carson City

Monitor Pass (8314'): 9.3 miles west along Route 89 from Highway 395, just south of Topaz Lake

*Mono Pass (12,000'): moderate 3-mile hike from Mosquito Flat

*Morgan Pass (11,100'): easy 3-mile hike from Mosquito Flat

Mosquito Flat (10,230'): highest trailhead in the Sierra Nevada, at end of 11-mile paved Rock Creek road, west off Highway 395 at Tom's Place (22 miles north of Bishop)

*Mt. Dana (13,053'): strenuous 3-mile hike from Tioga Pass (9945')

*Mt. Rose (10,778'): strenuous 5-mile hike from trailhead (8840') along Route 431 (Mt. Rose Highway), 17 miles west of Highway 395; marks north end of region covered in this book

*Mt. Whitney (14,496'): strenuous 10.7-mile hike from Whitney Portal trailhead (8365') at end of Whitney Portal Road

Onion Valley (9200'): at end of 15-mile paved road west off Highway 395 in Independence

Red Lake (8300'): along Route 88 just east of Carson Pass

Rock Creek road: *see* Mosquito Flat

Saddlebag Lake (10,100'): at end of 2-mile paved and dirt road north off the Tioga Pass road (Route 120) 10 miles west of Highway 395

*Sawmill Pass (11,347'): strenuous 10.5-mile hike from trailhead (4660') along Division Creek Powerhouse road, west off old Highway 395 a couple of miles south of Aberdeen

Sherwin Summit (7000'): along Highway 395, 20 miles north of Bishop

Silver Lake (7223'): along June Lake Loop Road

*Sonora Peak (11,462'): moderately strenuous 3-mile scramble from Sonora Pass (9628'); trailhead along Route 108 west off Highway 395, 17 miles north of Bridgeport

South Lake (9768'): reached by 14-mile paved road west off Highway 395 in Bishop, then 7 miles south on the South Lake road

Spooner Summit (7146'): on Highway 50, 9 miles west from Highway 395 in Carson City; Spooner Lake is just north of summit

*Taboose Pass (11,400'): very strenuous 8-mile hike from trailhead (5400') along Taboose Creek Road west off Highway 395, 14 miles north of Independence

*Thomas Creek: runs off northeast side of Mt. Rose, reached by a 4.5-mile dirt road (Timberline Road) north off Mt. Rose Highway at base of Mt. Rose; the Thomas Creek trail is a moderately strenuous 5-mile hike and scramble from end of dirt road (7000') to summit of Mt. Rose (10,778') (you may have to walk the last 0.5 miles of the road because of temporary road closure for meadow restoration)

*Tioga Crest (11,000–12,000'): ridge directly to east of Saddlebag Lake with wonderful displays of alpine plants

Tioga Pass road (to 9945'): Route 120 west off Highway 395 just south of Lee Vining; 12 miles to Tioga Pass and entrance to Yosemite National Park

Topaz Lake (5050'): along Highway 395, 23 miles south of Minden

Walker (5400'): town along Highway 395, 56 miles north of Lee Vining

Washoe Lake (5100'): along Highway 395 just north of Carson City

Whitney Portal Road (to 8365'): 13-mile paved road west off Highway 395 in Lone Pine; leads to trailhead for hike to summit of Mt. Whitney

*Winnemucca Lake (8980'): moderately easy 2-mile hike from Carson Pass trailhead (8573')

Woodfords (5630'): town at intersection of Route 88 and Route 89, 15 miles southwest of Minden

Index to Families and Genera

Index to Scientific Names

Index to Common Names

About the Author

Laird R. Blackwell, who received his Ph.D. from Stanford University, has taught field wildflower classes in the American West for over 25 years. He lives with his wife, Melinda, in Tahoe, where he is professor and department chairman of Humanities at Sierra Nevada College. His first three wildflower books were *Wildflowers of the Tahoe Sierra* (1997), *Wildflowers of the Sierra Nevada and the Central Valley* (1999), and *Wildflowers of Mount Rainier* (2000). In this book, he expands his coverage to the incredible eastern escarpment of the Sierra Nevada and the high deserts (Mojave and Great Basin) adjoining it.

Laird has spent more than 10 years exploring the eastern Sierra and hopes that this book will help you deepen your knowledge and love of this remarkable part of the world. He also hopes that everyone will be fortunate enough to see the high desert in a wet year, for he believes it is one of the most glorious of wildflower treats.

California Wild

EXPLORE THE WORLD OUTSIDE YOUR DOOR WITH LONE PINE'S ACCLAIMED FIELD GUIDES

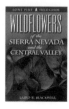     

WILDFLOWERS OF THE SIERRA NEVADA AND THE CENTRAL VALLEY
by Laird R. Blackwell

A photographic guide to 200 wildflower species from the Central Valley near Sacramento, west up to the peaks of the Sierra Nevada mountains. Each species has a photograph, description and notes on its distribution, native and modern uses, and similar species.

$15.95 • ISBN 10: 1-55105-226-1 • ISBN 13: 978-1-55105-226-7 • 5.5" x 8.5" • 288 pages

WILDFLOWERS OF THE TAHOE SIERRA
by Laird R. Blackwell

In this pocket-sized book, the author combines his poetic appreciation for nature with his superb photographs to produce a guide to more than 100 of Tahoe's most common wildflowers.

$9.95 • ISBN 10: 1-55105-085-4 • ISBN 13: 978-1-55105-085-0 • 4" x 6.25" • 144 pages

BIRDS OF NORTHERN CALIFORNIA
by David Fix and Andy Bezener

Learn in fascinating detail about 320 species of northern California birds. Descriptions, illustrations and range maps help you identify birds and understand their habits. Perfect for both novice and experienced birders. According to the *San Francisco Chronicle*, "this is one book you can judge by its cover...a beautiful and cleverly designed guide."

$21.95 • ISBN 10: 1-55105-227-X • ISBN 13: 978-1-55105-227-4 • 5.5" x 8.5" • 384 pages

WHALES AND OTHER MARINE MAMMALS OF CALIFORNIA AND BAJA
by Tamara Eder; illustrated by Ian Sheldon

Whether you venture out on the high seas or observe nature from the shore, you'll enjoy this full-color guide to the whales, dolphins, seals, sea-lions and other aquatic mammals that populate the coastal waters of California and Baja. Designed to enhance your whale-watching experience, the book includes a quick reference guide, tips for spotting whales and illustrated dive sequences. You'll also find information on myths surrounding whales, the history of human interaction with whales and contemporary conerns regarding these giant cetaceans. The book features color photographs, illustrations and range maps.

$12.95 • ISBN 10: 1-55105-342-X • ISBN 13: 978-1-55105-342-4 • 5.5" x 8.5" • 160 pages

SEASHORE OF NORTHERN AND CENTRAL CALIFORNIA
by Ian Sheldon

A full-color pocket-sized guide to the diverse and abundant life of the northern and central California coastline. Features stunning color illustrations and concise descriptions of 150 species of aquatic life found in the region. Color-coded tabs help with quick identification.

$14.95 • ISBN 10: 1-55105-144-3 • ISBN 13: 978-1-55105-144-4 • 4.25" x 8.25" • 216 pages

BUGS OF NORTHERN CALIFORNIA
by John Acorn and Ian Sheldon

Animal Planet's Nature Nut, John Acorn, teams up with nature illustrator Ian Sheldon to craft a witty and personable book about the myriad insects and arachnids found throughout the diverse habitats of northern California.

$12.95 • ISBN 10: 1-55105-320-9 • ISBN 13: 978-1-55105-320-2 • 5.5" x 8.5" • 160 pages

These and other fun and fact-filled nature books are available at your local bookseller, or order direct from Lone Pine Publishing at 1-800-518-3541.